SURVIVING THE HOME FRONT

SURVIVING THE HOME FRONT

PEOPLE AND THE MEDIA IN THE SECOND WORLD WAR

STUART HYLTON

The History Press

Front cover illustration: London in the Blitz of the Second World War. (NARA)

First published 2012
This edition first published 2023

The History Press
97 St George's Place, Cheltenham,
Gloucestershire, GL50 3QB
www.thehistorypress.co.uk

British Library Cataloguing in Publication Data.
A catalogue record for this book is available from the British Library.

ISBN 978 1 80399 356 0

Typesetting and origination by The History Press
Printed and bound in Great Britain by TJ Books Limited, Padstow, Cornwall.

MIX
Paper from responsible sources
FSC® C013056
www.fsc.org

Trees for Life

Contents

Acknowledgements

This book would not have been possible without the wealth of material provided by our local newspapers. I have acknowledged all the directly quoted material and have tried to contact the papers concerned to seek their agreement for its use. However, it would appear that a number of the papers are no longer published, at least under their wartime titles. If I have missed any, please accept my apologies. Please let me know via the publisher, and I will try to remedy matters in any future edition of the book. Quotes from the Oxford newspapers appear courtesy of Newsquest Oxfordshire. The copyright of all directly quoted material belongs to the relevant newspapers referenced in each case. My thanks also go to the librarians and archivists in libraries and records offices up and down the country, who look after this material.

ACKNOWLEDGEMENTS

Introduction

A word of explanation is needed. There is already a wealth of excellent books about what life was like in Britain during the extraordinary years of the Second World War. Why do we need another one?

The idea came up when The History Press decided to reprint my local history of *Reading at War*. This was based on local newspaper reports of the period, and through them I tried to capture a flavour of what it felt like to live in that community through these times. Many histories of the period are seen through one of two perspectives: either the historian applies his or her forensic analysis, nourished by the wisdom of hindsight, or they are the recollections of one or more individuals who lived through the war. Valuable, vivid and valid though both of these approaches may be, to my mind neither captures the full picture.

Journalism is said to be the first draft of history, and provincial newspaper reports of the period, whatever one may say about some of their journalistic shortcomings, sometimes capture the spirit of the times in a way that other chroniclers do not. Although the stories they carry are often rooted in their locality, their themes tend to have a much wider relevance. In them, we see the editorial efforts to stir the readership to greater war efforts or to seek out the bright side even in the darkest days of the war. We learn how the people looked for normality and diversion in such strange times; the mind-boggling detail of the bureaucratic control the authorities sought to exercise over wartime life (and sometimes their incompetence in doing so); the ingenuity or ineptitude of the criminal classes in trying to circumvent those rules (and the fact that a large part of the normally law-abiding population found themselves, wittingly or unwittingly, committing offences against the impenetrable jungle of wartime regulation); and the efforts of the business community to drum up new lines of custom from the war. The accounts were revealing and often (sometimes unintentionally) funny.

What I have therefore done is to start by drawing material from the three wartime histories of the Home Front that I have already written, and complemented them with similar accounts from more than twenty local newspaper reports covering other communities up and down the country. I hope in this way to present an anthology which gives some insight into what life was like for the British civilian population in those times.

The approach does not claim to be an authoritative or comprehensive overview of the period. Like all first drafts, press reports could be prone to error or misinterpretation. Some aspects of life which are of interest to us now might not have been considered newsworthy at the time, and vice versa. All other considerations aside, the censor's pen could have a marked impact on what was reported and how it was covered. Nonetheless, I hope my book nicely complements the many fine books which give the grand sweep of that period of history, a selection of which are acknowledged in my bibliography.

* *Reading at War* (Sutton 1996, The History Press 2011), *Kent and Sussex 1940: Britain's Front Line* (Pen and Sword 2004) and *Their Darkest Hour* (Sutton 2001, reprinted as *Careless Talk*, The History Press 2010).

1

War is Good Business: Early Days

> This is what is known as 'the silly season' when, apart from Hitler (who is in any case one of the silliest creatures in the world) the newspapers can't find much to write about. Slough appears to be suffering from the complaint as much as anybody … hardly a single good meaty subject in the news worth getting one's teeth into …
>
> *Slough Observer* editorial, the week before war broke out

The First Days of War

The hope that war could be avoided was shared by a large proportion of the population, right up until the end of peace. As late as 24 June 1939 the *Illustrated London News* was carrying an advertisement from German Railways, promoting tourism:

> Seeing is believing. Come and see Germany.
> Visitors from Britain are heartily welcomed at all times.
> They will find that friendliness and the desire to help are the characteristics common to every German they meet.
>
> *London Illustrated News*, 24 June 1939

The film The Great Dictator *finally got released, despite fears that it might offend the Führer.*

For its part, *Picture Post* in late July carried a piece, written in both English and German, entitled 'We want peace – Britain does not hate Germany'. Readers were urged to send a copy to their contacts in Germany. Even the Americans got involved, their State Department bringing pressure to bear on Charlie Chaplin to delay production of his Hitler satire *The Great Dictator*, for fear of offending the real dictator. A survey at the end of August suggested that only 18 per cent of the British public thought war would break out. Most thought Hitler was bluffing, and would step back from the brink. When it became clear that Hitler was not bluffing, the feeling was that he had made a massive miscalculation in assuming that he could win a lightning victory over the Poles before the Allies could mobilise support for them. There was a third, equally misplaced, hope:

> The German people themselves may revolt against the black act that is being done in their name. If they do, the people of

> this land will be the first to come to their aid to secure the re-establishment of law and order in their country.
>
> *Swindon Advertiser*, 2 September 1939

But readers of the letters page of the *Hampshire Chronicle* had more than hope to rely on:

> As an Associate of the Federation of British Astrologers I think it unlikely that war will result from the present crisis. Astrologically, the chances are no more than two in six.
>
> Letter to the *Hampshire Chronicle*, 26 August 1939

On the very same page, a spiritualist wrote in to report that several séances had revealed to him that there would be no war. In one, no less a figure than the newspaper magnate Lord Northcliffe (who died in 1922) had been in touch with the medium and had described the following scene to him:

> I see a very high mountain with a vast plain at the foot … the plain is filled with legions of armies, all armed ready for war. They rush up the mountain but at the top they are halted … The white-robed and radiant figure of Jesus stands before them. On each side are white-robed figures bearing palms … and rejoicing in the great victory of peace.
>
> Letter to the *Hampshire Chronicle*, 26 August 1939

By the end of September, the latest edition of the magazine *Psychic Review* was being advertised in the same paper; its cover story? 'False "no war" prophesies exposed: Enquiry demanded.'

Some of the impacts of war were felt immediately. The black-out was imposed and the mass evacuation of major towns and cities swung into action. Petrol rationing was introduced and sports venues and places of entertainment were closed down. It was soon recognised that these latter distractions would become

The closure of places of entertainment at the outbreak of war prompted widespread criticism and was soon rescinded.

more, not less, important in wartime and this last measure was rapidly reversed.

Every community had its own local reaction to the war. Maidenhead and Bray Watermen's Regatta blamed the decline in the number of both competitors and spectators on a mixture of bad weather and the outbreak of hostilities. The declaration of war also came right in the middle of Oldham Wakes Week, forcing many of the revellers at Blackpool to return home early. In St John's parish hall, Hollington, the usual round of domestic talks about cake-making and embroidery was interrupted by one on how to protect your baby from poison gas. Hitler already had a lot to answer for. Looking on the bright side, the Twilfit Corset-fitting Week at Paulden's department store in Manchester was able to proceed without interruption – the shortage of spring steel and elastic would not become an issue until much later in the war.

On the day that war was declared and Mr Chamberlain made his momentous speech on the radio, something else was preoccupying the ladies' page of the *Oxford Mail*:

> How to behave beautifully – a mannequin tells our readers how to exercise graceful control of our bodies. Among its most timely advice:
>
> Women destroy their charm by some of the ugly and fussy acts they frequently commit. Avoid running in the street. You have no idea how running detracts from your poise and personality. Don't trip either – frankly it looks just silly. A very bad habit is continually putting your hand up to your mouth. While sitting down, avoid arranging your clothes too punctiliously. It looks so fussy. Keep control of your face. Don't jerk your nose, forehead and lips about. Your eyes should express enough without obvious facial contortions. Don't blow your nose as if you're wreaking vengeance on it and don't clear your throat too often.
>
> *Oxford Mail*, 3 September 1939

By the following May, their ladies' page would be reconnected with reality. Recognising that huge numbers of women had by then been mobilised into the armed forces or other war work, their focus had moved from how to behave like a debutante to care of the feet, in acknowledgement of those many readers who were now on them all day.

This is not to say that every ladies' page was oblivious to international events. In the *Henley Standard* they were looking at different diets and their effects on personality, and they offered readers this unusual insight into the origins of the war:

> Little Hitlers, it seems, are filled to the brim with sodium and the cause may be too much celery, spinach and cucumber.

'Figure perfection' would not be an option once shortages of rubber and spring steel hit the corset industry.

> 'Tis a pity we cannot put the dictators on a diet – a diet say of prunes. This would be a pleasant little act demonstrating the natural law of compensation. We would retaliate on these eaters of celery, spinach and cucumber who are striving to drive iron into our souls by driving iron into their bodies … the biochemical effect of an undue proportion of iron is to produce a love of the arts!
>
> *Henley Standard*, 25 August 1939

War work needed to be done. In the week before hostilities broke out, Manchester Corporation announced plans to recruit some 6,000 Air Raid Precautions (ARP) staff – 2,000 wardens, 2,000 first-aiders and 2,000 volunteer firemen – who would be needed to deal with the estimated 300,000 people who would be trapped in the city centre in the event of a daytime air raid. Over 250 private basements were identified as being suitable for conversion into public air raid shelters. Against this bonanza of new employment, around 2,000 Mancunians were put out of work by the closure of places of entertainment that September. For others, war was good business:

> With their usual enterprise the shopkeepers have 'jumped to it' and are showing all kinds of articles which war conditions call for … A roaring trade is being done in identity discs.
>
> *Liverpool Echo*, 11 September 1939

This company recognised at the outset that food production would become a major preoccupation for the duration:

> War! Rear more poultry! The nation depends on YOU for MORE EGGS! Keep birds fighting fit – produce MORE EGGS with JOHNSON'S TONICS. 7½*d*, 1s 2*d*, and 5*s*. Corn stores everywhere.
>
> *Berkshire Chronicle*, 6 October 1939

The most surprising retail opportunities were thrown up by the war. Ironmongers offered incendiary bomb scoops and rakes, or paraffin stoves for your air raid shelter. Car dealers had headlamp shields to comply with the bewildering new Motor Car Lighting Regulations. Opticians offered gas mask sides for your spectacles and there were builders who would gas-proof any room in your house. All sorts of ploys were tried to get people to shop. Some retailers warned of the return of the inflation and shortages that were a feature of the First World War and urged their customers to buy before it was too late. Even the threat of invasion could be good business for some. By 1940, the advertisements for Jeyes Fluid dwelt upon the outbreak of typhoid that had occurred in Holland after it had been invaded, due to the disruption of public health and sanitary services. Householders were advised to have copious supplies of a reliable disinfectant around as part of their ARP precautions. But for some retailers, patriotism (sometimes misguided) overcame profit, like the Portsmouth jeweller who refused to carry out repairs on a watch because it was of German manufacture.

But the war was far from being a golden age for retailing, and some shopkeepers would go on to feel that they were particularly hard done by: accused of profiteering on the one hand, and faced with bewilderingly complex price limiting and rationing regulations on the other; forced out of parts of their business by the non-availability of luxury goods to sell, and by competition from cheapjack street traders who disregarded all the rules; their trading areas reduced by requirements to remove anything flammable from their top two floors against the threat of incendiary bombs, and by the loss of their basements as air raid shelters. There was also the fact that there was virtually nobody about during the blackout hours to come and shop. Last but not least, there was the fact that a lack of coupons encouraged shoplifting, even by those who could readily afford the monetary cost of the item.

Identity discs – another new line of business thrown up by the war.

For the true patriot wishing to do his bit for the war effort, there was only one possible course of action:

It brings us together

The Chancellor of the Exchequer demands of all of us 'moderation in all things'. We must 'pull in our belts'. And we are doing so.

But in one way we can still enjoy ourselves with a clear conscience. And that is – in the pub – over a round of beer.

Beer is good for your health. Its barley malt gives you strength – its hops give you good appetite. And it is the most

A record retailer promotes sales of a German composer.

economical of all drinks and yet, with every glass you drink – Britain's revenue benefits.

Beer, too, is the drink of moderation. In days like these, when the nerve and stamina of each one of us are of importance to the country, stick to beer. It comes from our own soil, that is why it suits us best. It heartens without harming. It brings us together in that cheerful democratic freedom of the pub – the freedom for which we are fighting. Beer is best!

Maidenhead Advertiser, 24 January 1940

However, not everyone agreed with the sentiments of the brewing industry, which paid for that advertisement. The Friends Temperance Union wanted to ration beer, in order to turn the land released over to the production of foodstuffs. They also called for all pubs in areas likely to be bombed to be closed during blackout hours. They challenged Quentin Hogg MP on the matter and he replied:

> The Temperance Council must understand that the national emergency is not a moment to introduce temperance propaganda under the cloak of national security ... Beer is the innocent pleasure of many millions, especially among those who bear the brunt today. Chocolate and confectionery are other people's pleasures and may have to be limited, but I am not going to be a party to discriminate against any one of them.
>
> *Oxford Times*, 11 October 1940

For some communities, the impact on the local economy was swift and dramatic:

> WHAT THE WAR MEANS TO SOUTHSEA
> Everything is closed down
> As a seaside resort it is now stagnant
>
> Headline in *Portsmouth Evening News*, 5 September 1939

With the declaration of war, holidaymakers had left Southsea in droves. Everything closed down – within days, dancing around the bandstand, the miniature railway, the children's paddling pool and motorboat trips became mere memories. They would not reappear until peace returned. A number of those Britons taking

A number of brewers emphasised their products' health-giving qualities.

continental motoring holidays in the last days of peace faced the loss of their cars – hundreds had to be abandoned at the French Channel ports in the rush to get home. The main ferry operator, Southern Railways, undertook to do all they could to repatriate them, but the main fear was not of them falling into the hands of the enemy, but rather the French authorities commandeering them.

Petrol rationing led to some changes in people's shopping habits. Before the war, middle-class shoppers had got used to having everything delivered to their homes, but individual retailers did not get an individual petrol ration. Such arrangements were replaced by a communal delivery system, used by all retailers, that might only deliver to your area once a week. Some shoppers were furious at such privations and threatened to take their custom elsewhere (a futile threat when all retailers were tied to the scheme and not even separate deliveries by horse, bicycle or handcart were permitted in order to free up as many delivery staff as possible for the war economy. One Hastings woman insisted (fruitlessly) upon the instant home delivery of a single small cake of soap that would have easily fitted inside her handbag. After 1942, as petrol shortages got worse, some shoppers living within half a mile of the retailer were deprived of any delivery service at all.

The disappearance of petrol meant that bicycle sales were booming. Sales of holidays to the continent were less healthy, though excursion trips to Germany were still being offered in the week preceding the outbreak of war and residents of both nations inconveniently found themselves in the territory of the other. An International Youth Camp was being held in Marple, and the contingent from the Free German Youth League declared themselves to have no more love for the fascist cause than their English hosts, which may not have boded well for their reception back in Germany. At the same time, a party of Manchester schoolgirls were on an exchange visit to Germany. Frantic calls went out for them to return home but some were uncontactable, having gone on holiday with their host families.

Oh no it isn't, but it caught the reader's attention!

Eventually they were all rounded up and returned home, most of them oblivious to any world crisis in the making and some even sporting swastika badges.

> Wanted: strong girl as general
>
> *Berkshire Chronicle*, 1 September 1939

This small ad was placed not by the War Office promising fast-track promotion but by a Kent householder looking for a general domestic servant. Before the war, it was still quite common for middle-class households to have live-in domestic servants. But the mobilisation of women to contribute to the war effort would do much to end the practice. The war industries not only generally paid better, but also gave their employees greater freedom and the sense of doing their bit towards the war effort. Views about domestic servants were to change rapidly, until it became positively unpatriotic to employ them. By the time the following advertisement appeared in a newspaper in 1944

Bicycle sales boomed, partly on the rationing of petrol and the overloading of public transport.

(presumably not their own) it prompted editorial comment from the *Manchester City News*:

> Man and wife wanted: Man to assist in house: wife as cook: wages £5: family of two.
>
> Reported in the *Manchester City News*, 21 April 1944

The paper responded sarcastically:

> It just shows you what hardships people will suffer in the cause of the war effort. Here is a family of two, content to muddle along with only two people to look after them … What more magnificent inspiration could our men fighting in Italy want than the self-sacrifice evident in that advertisement?
>
> *Manchester City News*, 21 April 1944

The outbreak of war seemed to provide everyone with a bee in their bonnets to redouble their efforts. As we saw, teetotallers lobbied for restrictions on alcohol for the duration of hostilities. In a disturbing parallel to Hitler's anti-Semitism, a Mr Walter Mayo tried to persuade the Protestant Reformation Society that the war had been started in defence of a Catholic nation (Poland) and that there was biblical evidence to show that the Roman Catholic Church was anti-Christian. Others were simply openly anti-Semitic. Posters appeared at Capel-le-Ferne, just outside Dover, calling for all Jews to be conscripted: 'It's their war! Let them fight it, not finance it!' A self-styled 'lover of animals' called for all pet owners to have them put down now, rather than subject them to homelessness and starvation when the inevitable apocalypse came.

The Women's League of Unity announced that it was forming a worldwide organisation that would bring the war to a speedy and honourable end (by means of which their advertisement did not specify). The *Hants and Berks Gazette* tried to clarify their policy in their editorial coverage, but the reader was left little the wiser. Apparently their primary object was:

> To recruit and maintain a peace army of women that will be sufficiently powerful to override any issues that might threaten the future peace of the world.
>
> *Hants and Berks Gazette*, 12 January 1940

In the *Bucks Herald*, a long-standing campaigner against fox-hunting saw the outbreak of hostilities as a new argument to add to his case:

> ... to follow the hounds at a time like the present would be extremely bad taste, an act entirely opposed to the spirit of sacrifice that is expected of all.
>
> *Bucks Herald*, 22 September 1939

Leaving aside the quantities of food consumed unnecessarily by horses and hounds in wartime, there was the damage to farmers'

The Women's League of Unity announces an early end to hostilities.

property and production caused by the hunt and the claim that hunts actually encouraged the breeding of foxes to provide them with their winter entertainment. Without the hunts, our campaigner alleged, foxes would by now be extinct. But the hunts were undoubtedly feeling the pinch: in Hampshire, the Vine Hunt announced that it was reducing down to a skeleton staff and pack to keep the costs down, and that they would no longer be paying the handouts and compensation they were accustomed to giving to the local landowners over whose property they hunted. Even with all of these cutbacks, the Garth Hunt decided that they could not hunt over their patch twice a week with a budget of less than £2,500.

In some quarters it seemed to be felt that the fox was the wrong target, and that they ought instead to be declaring war on rabbits. The government was busily issuing instructions and paying incentives for thousands of acres of grassland to be ploughed up and sown with cereals. Countrymen warned that if something was not done about the rabbits first, then the only crop this was likely to produce would be a lot of very well-fed rabbits.

Wartime farmers were told to plough up huge areas of grassland for crop production.

The outbreak of hostilities led to a flurry of hurried weddings. The Ramsgate Register Office reported a three-fold increase, and in Portsmouth the register office staff were working until 10.30 p.m. to keep the backlog down. Some of the arrangements were very hurried indeed; one member of the armed forces was given just one hour's leave to get married, which must have seriously interfered with any honeymoon plans he might have had. But once the initial panic had subsided, members of the armed forces were generally allowed four days' leave to tie the knot, which came to be known as 'passionate leave'.

As the war proceeded there would be increasing criticism of the rash of wartime brides, often very young women. They were advised to wait until after the war and some saw the bridegrooms as having dubious motives:

> Many war marriages are simply a commercial transaction and there is not that sincere feeling which ought to exist between couples. Many marry simply to obtain the marriage allowance for the wife. If the man were in a civil occupation, they would wait until he had established a position for himself. Fear of unemployment and low wages would keep them from marrying.
>
> *Swindon Advertiser*, 19 February 1941

The humourists picked up on this. One newspaper cartoon had a serviceman embracing a young girl. She asks: 'You'll never stop loving me, will yer?' He replies: 'Course not. What's yer name?'

Britain's early efforts to prosecute the war effort combined incompetence with an almost comical gentlemanliness. A bombing raid on the German fleet descended into farce, with a third of the attackers missing the target entirely; some missed it by as much as 110 miles, bombing neutral Denmark. Three bombs that were dropped on the *Admiral Scheer* failed to explode and the *Emden* was only damaged when one of the bombers accidentally crashed into it.

However, most of the early bombing raids did not even involve the use of bombs – instead they dropped leaflets, over 6 million of them on the day war broke out alone. Squads of Hitler Youth were apparently employed to collect them up before they fell into impressionable hands. This policy attracted much ridicule; Noel Coward put it about that the government's policy was to bore the Germans to death and Aneurin Bevin suggested they might do the same thing to our side. When an American news reporter asked for a copy of one of the leaflets he was refused, on the grounds that it contained 'information that might be of value to the enemy'. Given that millions of copies of it had already been dropped on Germany, it is hard to see what state secrets it would have given away.

By the end of September, the air force had dropped more than 18 million leaflets on the enemy; the Ministry of Information spoke very highly of them:

> The value of these paper raids has proved to be considerable. Pamphlets have given millions of people in Germany the opportunity to receive authoritative presentations of the allies' case. Flights have also been most useful reconnaissance.
>
> *Portsmouth Evening News*, 26 September 1939

A real bombing raid had been proposed to Minister Kingsley Wood as early as September 1938; it involved setting light to the Black Forest (which, being full of arms dumps, was a legitimate military target). His response had been: 'Oh we can't do that, that's private property. Next you will be suggesting we bomb the Ruhr!' Such was the resolve with which the war effort would be pursued under Chamberlain.

However, both sides would bring the leaflet offensive on to home territory. On Christmas Eve 1941, shoppers in central Manchester were terrified by the sound of three bombers, flying low over the city centre. Everybody ran for cover but it later transpired that they were ours, being used by the chief constable of Manchester to drop 10,000 road safety leaflets. The initiative was not widely appreciated. For their part, the Germans came over in August 1940, dropping copies of Hitler's final attempt to get Britain to sign a negotiated peace. One bundle failed to open and landed on the head of a policeman guarding the entrance to the civil defence control and report centre in Salford.

As far as the original war aim, aiding Poland, was concerned, the initial Allied offensive did no good whatsoever. It took five weeks simply to get the 158,000 men of the Expeditionary Force over to France, by which time Poland was virtually conquered. The French briefly occupied some 21 square miles of German soil, but this was relinquished by 4 October without the Germans needing to divert a single soldier or tank from the Polish front. The British public began to steel itself for what could be a long and hard war, and the local press faced up to the challenges of reporting it.

2

'Better wear a little white': The Blackout

Two rules the walker must obey
If he would reach his home today;
On roadway always keep the right,
On footpath, just the oppo-site;
And, if by chance, he walk at night
He'd better wear a little white.

A Surrey coroner waxes poetical, after hearing the case of a pedestrian killed in the blackout, *Swindon Advertiser*, 13 September 1939

The blackout was introduced two days before the outbreak of war, and people were given one day to comply with its daunting requirements. As one historian of the war put it, the blackout transformed conditions of life more thoroughly than any other single feature of the war. It also gave rise to some of the most formidable regulation of the war. The Lighting Restrictions Order ran to thirty-three articles and innumerable sub-clauses that even Lord Chief Justice Caldecote described as 'incomprehensible'.

Not everyone initially saw the need for a blackout. In the week war was declared:

> A good deal of indignation was expressed to the *Observer* over the extinguishing of the Front Line illuminations and those at Alexandra Park, as well as the general reduction of lighting in the streets. Correspondents declared that this was creating an unnecessary atmosphere of war panic, particularly in the minds of elderly people, and this was doing as much to harm the holiday season by scaring people as the crisis itself. They argue that the lights could surely be switched off in an instant if the need arises, and it was reprehensible to aggravate an already grave situation by carrying precautions to such an apparently absurd length.
>
> *Hastings and St Leonards Observer*, 2 September 1939

The Blackout Death

The blackout was responsible for many of the first casualties of the war. In December 1939 alone there were 1,155 deaths on the nation's roads, compared with 683 the previous December. Of these fatalities, 895 occurred in the blackout. The king's surgeon, Wilfred Trotter, was highly critical of this aspect of the blackout, claiming that by:

> ... frightening the nation into blackout regulations, the Luftwaffe was able to kill six hundred British citizens a month without ever taking to the air, at a cost to itself of exactly nothing.
>
> *British Medical Journal*, 1940

His opposition would have had the support of the Medical Officer of Health for Swindon, who was reported as saying in January 1940 that the blackout was bad, and a cause of depression. In his judgement, the chances of being bombed were remote in the extreme. On the streets, white lines were painted down the centres of the roads, on lampposts and car running boards. One motorist was fined for failing to apply white paint to his car, despite the fact that the entire vehicle was cream coloured. Even pillar boxes were part-painted yellow (though this doubled as a gas detection measure, as the yellow paint changed colour in the presence of poison gas). One disgruntled Aylesbury resident described his newly decorated town centre as looking like 'a blessed milk bar'. Manchester tried painting its bus stops with luminous paint, for the benefit of staff and passengers alike. Sartorial elegance became one of the first victims of the war, as men were advised to leave their shirt tails hanging out when they went walking in the blackout, in order to be more visible to motorists with dimmed lights. For those not prepared to commit this crime against fashion, the Portsea, Southsea and District Drapers' Association (who knew a new market when they saw one) suggested white cloth armbands. Carrying a rolled-up newspaper was also suggested (not by the newspaper industry, but by a coroner, while adjudicating on the fate of someone who had failed to do so). Those who favoured wearing something white were advised by the marketing men to ensure that whatever they wore had the maximum visibility, by being whiter than white – that is, Persil-white. Luminous armbands were also introduced for pedestrians to wear.

Pedestrians who failed to make themselves visible and then got knocked down were deemed to be partly responsible for their misfortune. Leading Aircraftsman Geoffrey Allport tried to claim damages from the motorist who ran him over but the judge, hearing that he had been in military uniform at the time, told him that this made him into 'a camouflaged object' and dismissed the case. Pedestrians were officially warned by magistrates that it was dangerous to drink and walk in the blackout. In support they could quote the case of Marcus Woods, a soldier from Withington, who was first seen in the evening drinking in a pub, then seen falling over in the road outside – and finally found dead, covered in tyre marks. Two women in Reading were run down and killed by a bus one Sunday night.

The baby they were pushing was hurled out of its pram but, by some miracle, caught by its grandfather (despite the blackout) before it hit the ground. The coroner recorded a verdict of accidental death and cleared the bus driver of all blame.

Pedestrians in Slough faced another equally lethal threat:

> In the pitch blackness of the darkened streets pedestrians in Wellington Street have learned to be careful of the sentries standing on the narrow pavements outside the Drill Hall. The bayonet slopes forward just at the right height to cut the throat of any person clumsy enough to stumble into them.
>
> *Slough Observer*, 8 September 1939

The very operation of bus services in the blackout was problematic. Buses could not show an illuminated display of their destination, which made it difficult at stops serving several routes to see which the right bus was. Conductors could not see to give change and there was an increase in the number of foreign coins passed to the conductors in the dark. Added to that, the passengers could not tell when to get off. The local press encouraged conductors to shout out the name of each stop as they reached it (though how they were better able than the passengers to see where they were was not explained). One additional challenge the crews were fortunately spared was having to drive a bus in the pitch darkness while wearing a gas mask, given their tendency to mist up. Silent-running electric trams had the additional problem that passengers could not always tell whether they had come to a halt, and so stepped off moving vehicles with dire results. Even worse were the fates of those passengers whose trains stopped outside the station, and who mistook a bridge parapet for the platform. Thomas Gillings of Blaydon did so and fell 20ft into the icy waters of the River Tyne. He at least managed to swim to the bank. Another man in Denham, Buckinghamshire, thought his train had stopped at Ruislip station. He was at least half right – the train had stopped. He stepped from the carriage and disappeared over the side of an 80ft viaduct, with no water to break his fall.

Motorists were equally disoriented. A common mistake was to confuse the kerb with the newly painted white lines in the middle of the road. One Wokingham motorist who made this error was surprised to find first a lamppost and then a tree in the middle of what he thought was the highway. He demolished the first and came to a shuddering halt, embedded in the second. This motorist may have been relatively unscathed, but disorientation could have far more serious consequences. The driver of an army lorry in Reading thought he was going along the main Oxford road, which ran uninterrupted through the town. In fact, he was on the road running parallel to it, which suddenly came to an unexpected halt in the form of a brick wall. In the crash which followed, two of his passengers were killed and another thirteen injured.

Passengers are asked to stop their fellow travellers falling from the train.

As petrol rationing began to bite, a new blackout problem arose in the form of increased horse traffic. The blackout regulations were silent on how to illuminate a horse (painting them white presumably was not an option – though one pet owner in Herne Bay painted white stripes on their black cat and an Essex farmer did the same with luminous paint on his cattle). But lack of regulation did not prevent a court in Basingstoke fining a gypsy who failed to provide suitable (if unspecified) lights for his horse and cart, while a court in Slough dismissed a charge against a cowman for herding unlit cattle across a road. A related issue concerned what you did with your horse if the air raid warning sounded while you were travelling. Official guidance was issued on this, but at least one householder disregarded it and shared their air raid shelter with not just the milkman but also his horse.

Nobody was safe in the blackout; the Regional Commissioner, Sir Auckland Geddes, was run down by a lady cyclist whilst inspecting ARP measures in Hastings. In coastal areas there was the added hazard of falling into the docks, making drowning a further blackout problem. This was not entirely restricted to harbours; in Pencester Gardens, Dover, they dug an air raid trench on the site of an underground spring and it spent most of its time full of water. A similar problem arose with one in London, and a 22-month-old child drowned in it. There was even a case where an elderly lady was knocked down and killed by a hurrying fellow pedestrian, prompting a campaign in the local press for pedestrians to keep strictly to the left of the pavement (assuming they could see which side was left). Doncaster was one area that actually introduced such a scheme, complete with pavement white lines.

As ever, helpful official guidance was on hand. This included closing your eyes before leaving a lighted room, in order to enable them to adapt to the darkness. (How many people, following this advice, injured themselves by tripping over the furniture on the way out?) In fact, a Gallup Poll in January 1940 found that one in five of those surveyed had already suffered some kind of major or minor blackout-related injury.

Blackout: The Mother of Invention

The initial reaction to the blackout regulations for vehicles by the maintenance crews of the Hampshire and Dorset Motor Services was to take a crowbar to the headlamp brackets of their buses and bend them to point downwards. This was entirely successful, except that the drivers could not see where they were going, while German bombers probably could. They were forced to revert to the approved methods. Even the government had to concede that this part of the blackout regulations was a particular problem and allowed a relaxation of the rules for headlamp dimming. These regulations are a good example of the minute rules to which the wartime population were subjected:

> Headlamp dimming
> A suitable type of mask for motor car lamps has been devised by the Ministry of Home Security, and will be placed on the market as soon as possible.
>
> Until the new mask is available, the following simple method of screening headlamps will be allowed under the Lighting Order. The bulb must be removed from the offside headlamp. An opaque cardboard disc must be fitted immediately behind the glass of the nearside lamp and must cover the

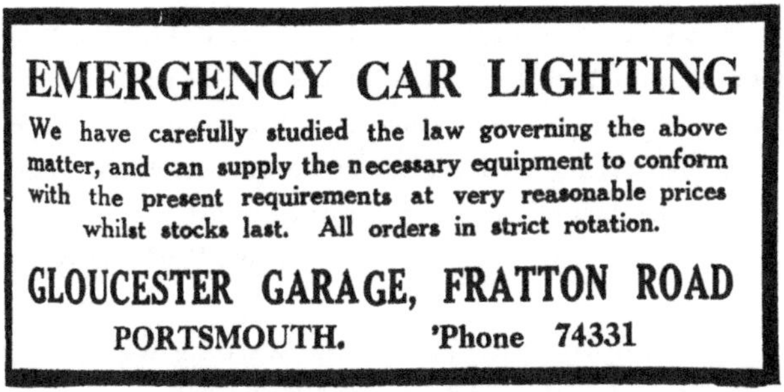

One garage bravely claims to have understood the emergency car-lighting regulations.

> whole area of the glass except for an aperture of a semi-circular shape 2 inches in diameter with the circle uppermost. The centre of the base must coincide with the centre of the lamp. The lower part of the reflector must be completely blacked out to a distance of half an inch above the centre line of the reflector. If these regulations are observed, no hood will be needed.
>
> *Berkshire Chronicle*, 15 September 1939

That was just for the headlamps. There were equally minutely detailed regulations governing each of the car's other lights – how much (if any) of the light could be visible at all, how far it needed to be dimmed with layers of newspaper, and so on. Rear number plates were not to be illuminated at all, and direction indicators (the old semaphore arm versions) were not allowed to display an illuminated strip more than 1/8in wide. This latter regulation became the cause of a number of accidents, as it rendered a car's indicators all but invisible in the daylight; the Royal Society for the Prevention of Accidents was forced to issue an appeal for motorists to paint the blacked-out part of their indicators white, to make them more visible by day.

However, even with minute regulation there could be unintended consequences. It was reported that Oxfordshire police were running spot checks on motorists because:

> In some cases, the angle of the headlamp has been altered, with the result that the beam is lifted above the regulation distance from the road. The result is a blinding glare infinitely worse than the light which came from the unscreened headlamps in the days before the new mask was introduced.
>
> *Oxford Mail*, 2 May 1940

Things got simpler when the air raid warning went, at which time all the car's lights had to be turned off – or so people thought. In October 1940, the Minister of Home Security found it necessary to issue a clarification to the effect that only the headlamps needed to be extinguished in an air raid – and if the car was engaged on official business, even these could be kept on. In addition, a 20mph speed limit during the blackout was introduced from 1940. Quite how motorists were meant to observe it in the pitch darkness is not immediately clear, but the police enforced it by cruising the streets at what they hoped was 20mph (insofar as they could see their speedometer) and waiting for someone to overtake them. The first person to do so was the driver of a hearse.

Not only car lights, but also traffic lights were dimmed, so that they only displayed a small cross of light, which was barely visible either by night or day. There was a dispute about whether this measure was legal, and a Rochdale bus driver got off a charge of disregarding a masked traffic light on this basis. The Ministry of Transport then issued a ruling that, even if they were not legal, they should still be obeyed. They were supported in this by the motoring organisations. As always, ingenious inventors were on hand to offer solutions to the problem. Enter Mr Sidney Gare from Mere, the inventor of the 'Hy-vis Nil-beam ARP sign'. He claimed in the local paper that it would make street signs visible from 350 yards for a motorist but invisible from an aircraft flying at over 300ft. Little more seems to have been heard of it, so presumably it was not quite as 'Hy-vis' or 'Nil-beam' as he made out (or possibly rather too 'hy-cost'?). Another member of the public, Reginald Wingfield, decided that some hazard lights, warning motorists of some deep excavations in the highway, were too bright. He took matters into his own hands, stuffing the offending lights with grass – until he was arrested.

Those pedestrians who used torches to find their way about were also deemed to be a potential hazard, in that they tended to dazzle motorists whose eyes had adjusted to the darkness, and who could even be dazzled by the rising moon. The blackout regulations were therefore extended to cover torches, which had to have their apertures reduced to 1in in diameter and be dimmed by having a single thickness of newspaper (or its equivalent) over the lens. One commuter made the mistake of using a sheet of green paper to dim his torch, with the result that he caused a train to leave the station prematurely. Measures for dimming torches were in any event somewhat academic for a large part of the population, in that torch batteries were one of the commodities in permanently short supply throughout the war.

Blacking out buildings was no less problematic. Some householders reported that two or three layers of blackout curtaining were required to achieve a satisfactory result and that it took up to a month to make the curtains for all the rooms in the house. Despite government claims that blackout material was cheap enough for all to afford, many poorer households, who could not afford decent clothing or food for their children, thought otherwise, and they were reduced to the tiresome process of pinning sheets of black paper over their windows each night. Retailers not only had to black out their windows but also had to deal with the problem of lights showing as customers came in and out of their shop. Generally this meant installing a second, blacked-out door with a lobby between the two and preferably at least one right-angled turn in it, to minimise the leakage of light. Farmers had problems blacking out their cowsheds, where lighting was required for the early morning milking, and factory owners often had premises lit by roof lights. These had to be painted over and the building permanently lit by artificial light. This was both expensive for the company and bad for the morale of the workforce.

Blackout Breaches

Observation of the blackout could be less than perfect. People on the top of Portsdown Hill used to refer to Portsmouth's efforts at concealment as 'The Illuminations'. In Buckinghamshire and elsewhere, some householders were under the mistaken impression that only the windows fronting on to the road needed to be blacked out, thinking the ones at the back did not matter.

Public opinion on the blackout was somewhat ambivalent. On the one hand, people could get very angry with those who were seen to be flouting the regulations and abetting the enemy. Mr Arthur Nash of Ramsgate was fined £15 for a breach of the blackout regulations, after a mob gathered outside his property, threatening to put stones through the offending windows. Similarly, in Slough, Brighton, and even Tunbridge Wells, angry crowds gathered around shops whose owners had failed to turn the lights off, and had to be restrained from doing damage to both the premises and the proprietors.

Given that any enemy bombers would be several miles up, the blackout regulations were sometimes enforced to a ridiculous degree. One woman was fined £1 for a breach of the blackout regulations by allowing a red light to keep flashing on and off in her house. It turned out to be the pilot light of her electric iron as she ironed in the dark. A man who accidentally coughed out his false teeth in the street was fined 10*s* for striking a match to look for them and another was fined for smoking his cigarette too vigorously and thereby causing it to glow too brightly. The Mayor of Reading called upon his citizens not to leave washing out on the lines on moonlit nights, lest it gave the game away to German bombers that they were above inhabited areas.

Public phone boxes were effectively rendered unusable at night, since it was an offence to use matches or torches to illuminate the dial. This made something of a nonsense of asking people to telephone the authorities in the blackout to report incoming parachutists. A reporter from the *Slough Observer* decided to test the system. After much struggle in the darkness, he managed to dial 0 for operator. The operator asked what number he wanted, which the reporter neither knew nor had any means of looking up, so he asked to be connected to the emergency services. This the operator refused to do, unless the caller told her the number he was calling from – which he also could not see. After further unproductive exchanges, the reporter hung up, leaving the paratroopers (in this case, fortunately hypothetical) to do their worst.

In the circumstances, it was perhaps not surprising that the ARP wardens who enforced the blackout so zealously were not the most universally popular of officials. How many quiet smiles were prompted by the newspaper report of the ARP warden in Reading who went shinning up a drainpipe in pursuit of an errant chink of light, but was now 'as well as could be expected' in hospital after falling off the roof? One official in Swindon, failing to gain access to a property to deal with two errant lights, smashed the windows and shot the lights out with an air gun, leaving the owner with a repair bill, as well as a fine.

However, in some cases, the cooperation of the public was equally disproportionate:

> A milkman on bringing the morning milk was surprised to see that the empty bottle he had to collect was shrouded in black, carefully fastened with a safety pin. As he stared in amazement an old lady's voice called through the window: 'It's all right, you can remove the wrapping. I put it on so that the moon should not shine on the bottle and give the show away if the air raiders happened to come'.
>
> Quoted in Hylton (1996, 2011), p. 17

In Slough, a factory charged with showing a light claimed it was not even a result of human error. They said their Alsatian guard dog had switched it on. Scratch marks around the switch suggested that this might indeed have been the case, but it did not save the company from a £5 fine. But for some, the bother of making blackout curtains was all too much. When a woman from Chiltern Foliat was prosecuted for allowing a light to show, it turned out that she had used her supply of blackout material to make a coat.

Curiously, what was possibly the most spectacular breach of the blackout regulations occurred in the yard of Hastings police station. Under the Defence of the Realm Regulations, the police had confiscated all local retailers' supplies of fireworks. These were kept in the yard of the police station, awaiting destruction. In the early hours of one night in July 1940, nearby residents leapt from their beds, thinking that an unannounced air raid was taking place. The fireworks had caught fire and provided the town with the largest display of pyrotechnics they would see this side of peacetime.

The Bright Side of the Blackout

There is a curious link between the blackout and the wartime Dig for Victory campaign to grow more of our own food. One of the big successes of the latter campaign was the carrot; so much so that, by January 1942, the government found itself with a surplus of 100,000 tons on its hands. Various measures were taken to remedy this: Walt Disney was called upon to create the cartoon character Dr Carrot to popularise them with children. Sometimes bizarre recipes using carrots were publicised (including curried carrots, carrot buns, mock apricot tarts made with carrots, carrot jam and carrot fudge). Last but not least, it was claimed that the carotene in carrots was the secret ingredient that enabled RAF pilots to improve their performance in spotting and shooting down German bombers. It was a falsehood, designed to conceal the development of airborne radar, but the suggestion was nonetheless made that a carrot-rich diet would make civilians better able to see (and therefore survive) in the blackout.

There were a few who took advantage of the blackout. The money councils saved on street lighting helped them to keep the rates down, though they had battles with the gas and electricity companies over contracts entered into before the war, which assumed they would supply enough energy to keep the streets fully lit. There were also some activities for which

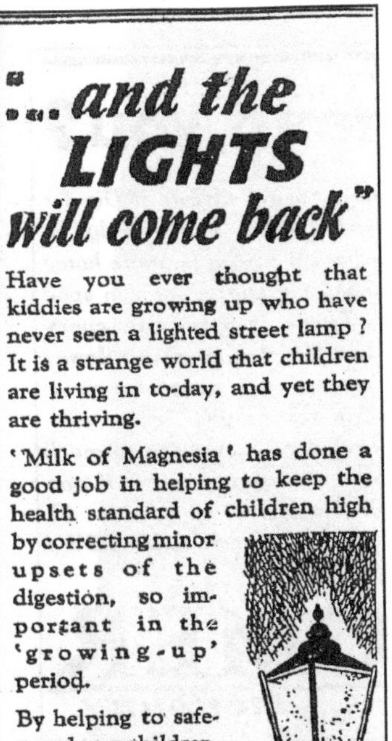

The excitement of street lights – one of the post-war treats to which children could look forward.

allow the streets to be bathed in the equivalent of moonlight. Children who had grown up with night times of pitch blackness were taken out into the streets to witness the marvel of street lighting for the first time. Many communities welcomed their return joyously:

> Scenes of rejoicing took place in many parts of the town when the lights were switched on promptly as the Town Clock struck the quarter after nine. In the Broadway quite a reasonable crowd had gathered and raised a hearty cheer, which was re-echoed by knots of people up and down the streets. Quite the most interesting place to stand was on the steps of the Regal cinema in Bartholomew Street and take note of the reaction of people as they came out. 'Look! Look! The lights'. It was surprising the number of small children about, and quite

Not even infants could evade the great drive for the nation to eat its way through the mountain of surplus carrots.

darkness was a positive advantage. The Piccadilly commandos, the ladies of the night who frequented the streets around that part of London, found it helpful in serving the needs of their customers in what might otherwise have been relatively public places, like doorways. The more energetic among them did not even let air raids interrupt business. In Dover, a man was fined 5*s* for what the court intriguingly described as 'committing a nuisance' in Market Lane, and the police told the court of the 'considerable difficulty' they had in catching such miscreants since the introduction of the blackout. One who was caught was a 17-year-old Cirencester youth, who attacked several women in the blackout to frighten them, because 'a funny feeling' had encouraged him to do so. Quentin Crisp,

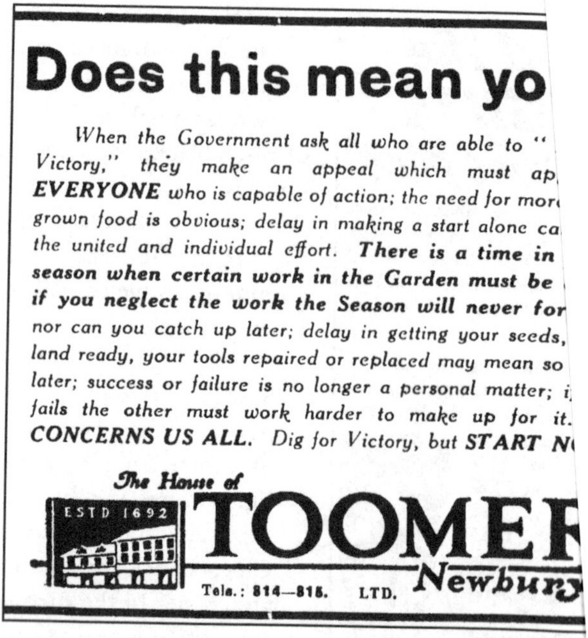

Dig for Victory – and it just so happened that this company stocked eve the gardener might need.

the self-styled 'stately homo of England', described the l out as 'heaven' for the (then illegal) activities of wh would today call the gay community – and there was one group that welcomed the darkness. What with the absen street (or indeed any other form of) lighting and the red pollution caused by limiting car mileage and reducing supplies, the British Astronomical Association reported research conditions were the best they had had in twenty- years. Meanwhile, the Methodist churches in Newbury w ahead with a plan – arranged before the war – to organi moonlight ramble, illuminated only by Mother Nature.

Come the final days of the war and the blackout regulati were relaxed generally – from September 1944 the blac out became known as the dim-out and local authorities co a number did not seem to remember what lighted streets were like.

Newbury Weekly News, 21 September 1944

And what was this festival of light that so captured the community's imaginations? On that first night, Newbury's street lighting consisted of just twenty-four 100-watt bulbs, spaced about 90 yards apart and scattered over a number of town-centre streets, but they were enough to read a newspaper by, if you stood directly beneath them. Naturally, the new arrangements were not without bureaucratic regulation: the lights could only be used where they were all controlled from a central switch and could be turned off instantly, if necessary. This effectively meant electric lights only; gas lamps were subject to additional limits to the amount of light they were able to give out. Meanwhile, the small town of Hungerford found itself propelled to fame by being possibly the best-lit town of its size in the country. Its council had had the foresight to install concrete lampposts and buy in a supply of fittings for them before the regulations were relaxed.

3

'So happy and contented': The Evacuation

> All of us are so happy and contented that we nearly forgot those we left behind in Barking.
>
> Quoted in the *Swindon Advertiser*, 8 September 1939

> One small girl, evacuated from Portsmouth … said that she hoped the war would last a long time, as she liked Basingstoke.
>
> *Hants and Berks Gazette*, 8 September 1939

Plans for the evacuation of children and vulnerable adults from our major towns and cities began to be prepared as early as 1934, shortly after Hitler came to power. When the nation came close to war with Germany during the Munich crisis of 1938 there was a small-scale rehearsal of the evacuation, after which the plans were worked up in more detail. Even so, there remained some elements of confusion in the evacuation policy. For example, Reading was seen as a 'reception area' – a place to which Londoners might safely be evacuated – and plans were made for the town to take 25,000 of them. At the same time the town, with its concentration of industrial and government activity, was also liable to receive the unwelcome attentions of the Luftwaffe in its own right. Towns along the south coast were also designated as reception areas for evacuees. It was only in 1940, as Hitler assembled an invasion fleet along the facing coast, that the authorities spotted a possible flaw in that policy.

Before the war even began, the mass movement of schoolchildren, their teachers, mothers with children under 5, pregnant women and some people with disabilities got under way. In just three days in September 1939, 1.5 million people were relocated, including 600,000 from London. The *Oxford Mail* called it 'an exodus on a scale without precedent in human history. The Exodus of the Bible – the flight of the Israelites from Egypt – was insignificant by comparison.' Massive though this achievement was, it only represented half the government's target; the rest refused to go.

As the children arrived at their destinations, labelled like suitcases and clutching a few treasured belongings, they were issued with initial rations – a wholesome diet of a tin of meat, two tins of milk (sweetened and unsweetened), 1lb of biscuits and 4oz of chocolate. They were also given a postcard to send back to their anxious parents. At Slough station (and no doubt elsewhere) they were also greeted by 'stentorian voices booming out loud orders' over specially installed 'huge loudspeakers' (*Slough Observer*, 1 September 1939). Anything more calculated to disconcert already bewildered small children is difficult to imagine (though if they were anything like Henley's contingent – 'all plucky as little Britons and never showing the trace of a tear' (*Henley Standard*, 8 September 1939) – they would doubtless have been undaunted).

Happiness Everywhere

The authorities everywhere were at pains to convey the message to anxious parents that everything was going smoothly, and the newspapers played their part in this:

> The manner in which the Government evacuation scheme is operated in the Borough of Aylesbury is a revelation of high competency, faultless organisation and loyal, tireless service. Few, if any towns, of whatever size can have surpassed it.
>
> *Bucks Herald*, 8 September 1939

The headline in the *Portsmouth Evening News*' account of events was:

> HAPPINESS EVERYWHERE:
> Everywhere the children have been given a very warm welcome and they are being cared for by their temporary guardians with every consideration for their comfort.
>
> *Portsmouth Evening News*, 6 September 1939

The papers even reproduced testimonials to the idyllic lives the evacuees were leading. As the weeks went on, these grew almost poetic:

> This week has been, for them, a holiday full of sunshine, fresh air and new experiences. They have picked bunches of wild flowers, seen the village blacksmith at work, watched trout darting in the river, fed chickens and played games in the meadows. Their remarks are very quaint. One little boy said that he did not know the sky was so big – he had never seen so much before.
>
> *Portsmouth Evening News*, 13 September 1939

Henley's evacuees were:

> ... so happy that they are asking their mothers and teachers if they can stay there always.
>
> *Henley Standard*, 29 September 1939

While in Newbury:

> Newbury people have given the little Londoners and their mothers a hospitable welcome, and the evacuees, for their part, have taken immediately to their warm-hearted hosts … Already these pale-faced Londoners are showing the benefits of walks on the common, bathing in the river and cricket and football in the parks.
>
> *Newbury Weekly News*, 7 September 1939

Not everyone was as deliriously happy as the newspapers would have had us believe, as this evacuated teacher told them, with rather more honesty than diplomacy:

> We were expecting – and rather hoping – we should end the journey in Truro, but I have been to Newbury before, and I know there could be many worse places.
>
> *Newbury Weekly News*, 7 September 1939

A few commentators, like this one on the *Swindon Advertiser*, foresaw problems ahead in terms of the gulf between the evacuees and many of their new hosts. Even as the evacuation was still under way, they sounded this warning:

> Remember that the children you have in your care have been brought up according to somebody else's plan. Their standards of conduct, cleanliness and character may not be the same as those on which you have based the education of your own kiddies. Your job is to continue the work of upbringing which these children's parents have already begun …
>
> Secondly, it would be wise to make quite certain from the start that you are, for the time being, in authority. Children can be very troublesome when this fact is in doubt. And whilst we naturally want them to be happy during their stay with us, to regard it, if possible, as something in the nature of an adventure, we do not want to have

> crowds of unruly youngsters in our midst. So be kind, but at the same time be firm.
>
> *Swindon Advertiser*, 2 September 1939

The Problem with Evacuees

Inevitably, the reality was that such a mass migration would not be without numerous problems. Swindon set up a Tribunal of Appeal within a week of the evacuation taking place. In Winchester they were considered serious enough for the Diocesan Moral Welfare Council to provide experienced social workers to try to resolve some of the problems of the evacuees and their hosts, and many areas set up welfare committees to deal with the difficulties.

Many of the evacuees were homesick and wanted to be back in the city. Some of their hosts wished equally fervently for the same thing. Back in the cities, husbands who had been 'abandoned' by their evacuated wives demonstrated how utterly helpless they were without their domestic ministrations. Many of them reported running out of clean shirts and washed dishes from which to eat their next meal, and the *Kent Messenger* coined the term 'washupees' for these tragic early victims of the war. But some of the mothers who had been evacuated with their children seemed scarcely more competent, according to the North-west Regional Commissioner Sir Warren Fisher:

> It is a big strain on a housewife already burdened with heavy family duties to undertake the care of a number of strangers suddenly billeted on her. There have been cases where mothers with children have been under the impression that their responsibility finished as soon as they have taken up their new quarters. The ideas of parental responsibility exhibited by some adults who have been evacuated are limited, to put it mildly … The need is for evacuated mothers to give all the

help they can to promote their own comfort and to reduce the inconvenience to their hosts.

Liverpool Echo, 8 September 1939

Hosts tried to exercise control over who got placed with them. Some looked for children who were big enough and strong enough to work their passage on the farm or in their business, whilst a lady in Wolverhampton specified that she wanted two little girls with fair hair and blue eyes. Her wish was granted, but the little blonde-haired, blue-eyed girls arrived dressed in rags, smelling foul and crawling with lice. They wet their beds and did not understand how to use cutlery. Other hosts found that their new guests urinated or defecated on the living room floor, being unfamiliar with the normal facilities for these functions. The billeting officer at Hungerford reported that 40 of the 170 children he had been given to rehouse were verminous, and shops in the reception areas experienced unprecedented demand for Keating's insect powder, soap and disinfectant.

Evacuation highlighted living conditions in our cities that some found distinctly disturbing. Within a week or so of the evacuation, the papers were saying:

Evacuation has given Manchester the biggest shaking it has had in a century, and it is as if suddenly the whole city had been turned inside-out and daylight had been allowed to penetrate corners it had never reached before and the revelation has not been pleasant.

We have seen depths of poverty, filth, ignorance and degradation such as few could have imagined. We have seen evidence of children being brought up in conditions and in ways which most of us thought no longer existed.

We have seen and heard things which should make us ashamed of Manchester, ashamed of ourselves that we have permitted such conditions to exist.

Manchester City News, 9 September 1939

> A lot of them have not been used to much fresh air or sun and, judging by the work they have provided at the town hall cleansing station, some of them had not much to do with soap and water before.
>
> *Swindon Advertiser*, 9 September 1939

A number of the evacuees arrived with little more than the clothes they stood up in, and wearing shoes that consisted mainly of holes. Babies and toddlers arrived without prams or pushchairs – there were between fifty and sixty infants in Swindon alone who were without these essentials. Appeals went out around the country for gifts of children's clothing and baby carriages.

One writer thought the solution was to construct big camps along the lines of holiday camps, where children could stay indefinitely under the proper supervision of teachers, doctors, welfare workers, ministers, and so on – in effect, a whole generation of children taken into care. The Education Committee in Reading were also asked to consider some sort of hostel arrangement for their more difficult evacuees. A man of the cloth, Father F.J. Kernan, addressed the meeting with the view that:

> … there were certain recalcitrant boys who were hard to place and it would be very much better to have these in a hostel with a man in charge of them.
>
> *Berkshire Chronicle*, 21 June 1940

It did not take long for the first cracks to show in the evacuation arrangements – to be precise, the first weekend after the evacuation, which prompted this letter to the *Oxford Mail*:

> I am sure that a wave of indignation must have swept over the hospitable Oxford people upon the arrival yesterday of coach-loads of mothers (and sisters) from London to see their children.

> The already heavy burden of the hostesses was unwarrantably increased by these unwanted guests, and the children were unsettled by the renewed contact with the life they had happily abandoned.
>
> In many cases, I understand, the visiting mothers raised complaints.
>
> Oxfordshire has stood up nobly to the demands upon her hospitality, but it is hoped this new menace will be firmly dealt with by those in authority.
>
> *Oxford Mail*, 11 September 1939

Even some of those who tried to make the evacuees welcome found their enthusiasm cooling, as their new guests turned out to be variously wild and unruly (the local papers optimistically called it 'high-spirited') or, as previously mentioned, verminous and totally unschooled in the use of toilets and washing facilities. The people of Wolvercote were urged by one correspondent to the local paper to return their evacuees to the town hall from whence they came, and to take them back 'only when they are in a fit condition'. One Kent family left their own children playing with the 'nice quiet boy from Limehouse' who had been settled on them, and returned to find that he had stolen all their toys and was beating them over the head with a coal shovel.

The 'high spirits' of some of the evacuees were not helped by the fact that schools were closed for an extended holiday whilst the new teaching arrangements were worked out, leaving the children with a lot of time on their hands. Even when the schools re-opened in the reception areas they tended to be unable to cope with the increased numbers. A shift system was introduced, whereby the evacuee children had the classroom from 8.30 a.m. to 12.30 p.m. and the local children from 1.30 p.m. to 4 p.m., swapping between morning and afternoon shifts on a weekly or monthly basis. In Blackpool, the scale of the influx of evacuees necessitated a three-shift system. For teaching purposes the evacuees and the locals tended to be kept separate; however justified this may have been in terms of differing educational needs, it cannot have helped with their social integration. A further complication with the schooling arrangements in some cases was that pupils from the same school might be scattered across eight or nine villages, making it very difficult logistically to bring them all back together for educational purposes.

> One of them little trees bit me!
>
> One evacuee's first encounter with a thistle, *Liverpool Echo*, 4 September 1939

One source of revenge came for some of the hosts in the form of laughing at their guests' ignorance of anything outside their impoverished urban backgrounds. The Ministry of Information encouraged this by running a competition for the funniest howlers. From this we learned that potatoes were a kind of fruit, picked from trees, that a cow was 'an 'orse wiv 'orns' and that gas masks were useful to counteract the smell of pigs (which they mistook for enemy gas attacks). One child, seeing a chicken being plucked, enquired whether the poultry had to be undressed for bed every night and another wondered whether he had to remove his shoes before taking a bath. They marvelled at the sight of matching crockery and found the quiet unnerving because 'Mum and Dad always 'ave a row on Saturdays'. Given a sixpence for the collection plate when he was sent off to church, one child returned with the coin, explaining that 'the vicar let me in free, so I didn't trouble'. Another complained about being sent to bed too early. Asked when he normally went to bed he replied, 'not until the old man comes home from the boozer'.

Proper food was a mystery to some of them; one party of evacuees, presented with a meal of roast lamb, garden peas and potatoes, rejected it, explaining: 'We don't eat meat; we never have it at home. Can I go for a penn'orth of chips?'

Many of the evacuees were bewildered by the absence of fish and chip shops in their new rural surroundings; so much so that in the villages around Bury St Edmunds a mobile fish-and-chip shop was laid on. The unlikely provider of this amenity was the Duchess of Grafton, assisted by the ladies of the Women's Voluntary Service (WVS).

Beneath the humour often lay a patronising view of their guests' capabilities. One host family gave a broadly affectionate account of their experience of hosting 10-year-old Mary, but which included this assessment:

> Mental work is naturally much harder for her than physical endeavour. Coming from a family stock which has lived for several generations in Docklands, she has an innate propensity to use her hands. Nothing pleases her more than to scrub a step or polish a floor.
>
> *Liverpool Echo*, 20 December 1940

Some of the evacuees were frightened of going to bed, being afraid of falling out of them (never having slept in one before). Some even refused to stay with the 'too posh' family with which they had been billeted. Jewish evacuees, often lodged with Gentile families, could find it hard to follow the dietary and other requirements of their religion. Some committed members of Christian churches found themselves equally mismatched.

The Drift Back

However, the bombers did not come immediately and many of the evacuees very quickly drifted back to the cities. For them, the whole exercise had to be repeated when the Blitz began in earnest, in the autumn of 1940, and again in 1944 when Hitler's vengeance weapons led to a new, if short-lived, reign of terror. The drift back to the cities began within a week or two of the initial evacuation. In Slough, it was reported that one evacuee in ten left during the first week and almost a quarter by the end of September 1939 (apparently Slough had the particular problem of being too close to London – many evacuees had hoped for somewhere more distant from London and hence safer). Nationwide, by January 1940, some 60 per cent of all evacuees had returned home. Some simply vanished without telling their hosts and there were suggestions that cynical evacuees had seen it as a way of getting a country holiday on the cheap. Three small children were picked up, exhausted, in Slough, 14 miles into a 50-mile hike from their evacuee home in Twyford, on their way back to see their mother in the East End of London. Another, equally determined to return to London, set out from Reading and was found some miles away, striding out in completely the wrong direction.

By contrast, there were a few evacuees who were particularly picky. One refused to be billeted in a house that had no piano, and another objected to dining with a host family whose table manners did not meet their standards. But happiest of all were those who were able to glory in their new-found comfort. There was one report of a smart chauffeur-driven shooting brake (luxury estate car, for younger readers) seen gliding through the leafy lanes of Cheshire. In the back were three scruffy evacuee youths, marvelling in the unaccustomed luxury. However, few can have experienced a life-changing experience to match that of the thirty-one children from the Curzon Crescent nursery school, Willesden. They, their teachers and some of the mothers found themselves decanted to Highclere Castle (better known to modern television viewers as Downton Abbey), where they became the guests of the Earl and Countess of Carnarvon. The grand libraries of the castle became their playroom (though their dining was strictly limited to the servants' quarters).

One case, sufficiently unusual to be regarded as newsworthy, illustrated how little impact ethnic differences had on the national psyche at this time. The unconscious racism in its reporting is almost pre-racist:

> Among the schoolchildren who were evacuated to Weymouth was a little black boy and the billeting officer had to find a home for him.
>
> He was presented at one house with a school chum, but the lady of the house indignantly refused to take the little black boy.
>
> So the little darkie had to be escorted to another place where he was welcomed by the housewife – colour did not count. Once he had been accepted the black boy took from his pocket an envelope, which he handed to his new 'mother'.
>
> It contained a cheque for £40 and a note saying it was for the person who looked after the boy.
>
> *Portsmouth Evening News*, 13 September 1939

Unwilling Hosts

Some people went to great lengths to avoid having evacuees billeted on them, and a number of them ended up before the courts. A Reading woman said that she could not take evacuees because she had rehoused friends who had been bombed out. On investigation, it turned out that all that she was rehousing was some of their spare furniture; she was fined and required to take her unwelcome guests. A Wargrave vicar tried to refuse to accept evacuees on the grounds that he 'conscientiously objected' to them (an unintended extension of the concept of conscientious objection). Another unwilling host tried to rid herself of her guests by making their lives unbearable. She laid down the following rules:

- No access to the kitchen or bathroom;
- Loan of crockery refused;

- No laundry to be carried out on the premises;
- A charge of 1*s* a week for electric light;
- All residents to be home by 10.30 p.m.;
- Residents to be out of the house between 10 a.m. and 8.30 p.m. on a Sunday;
- No smoking;
- Absolute quiet at all times;
- Residents to leave the house whenever the genial host is visiting her invalid mother (though they were allowed the concession of awaiting her return in the porch or the summerhouse in the garden).

This novel idea of hospitality earned her a £15 fine, plus costs.

In Swindon, one Richard Leighfield tried to refuse taking an evacuee on the grounds that his wife had threatened to leave him if he did so. His arguments won him the sympathy of the tribunal, but nothing more:

> Leighfield may say that he is willing to accept the child and that his wife is unwilling and has brought domestic pressure to bear on him to take up this attitude. That arouses my sympathy, and may arouse yours, but the sole responsibility is on the occupier. It does not matter at all for what reasons he refuses to take a child, the refusal itself is the offence.
>
> *Swindon Advertiser*, 24 June 1940

He was fined £25, with £2 costs. But one man whose refusal brooked no opposition was former Brighton schoolmaster John Drummond. He was recovering from a nervous breakdown and, when he learned that he was to have five evacuees billeted on him, stuck his head (terminally) in the gas oven.

The allowances paid to those hosting evacuees also became a bone of contention. One Blackpool landlady took to varying the diets of her six evacuees, according to whether their parents would pay extra towards their keep (and how much).

This practice was firmly stamped out by a tribunal. The disciplinary role of the hosts was also an issue. One lady went to a tribunal complaining that the eldest child lodged with her was a hooligan.

'What would you do if he were your own boy?' the tribunal asked.

'I would wallop him.'

The tribunal thought this was a splendid idea and advised her to do just that.

In some cases, though, there were extenuating circumstances when hosts objected. A Caversham man, who ran a dental practice from his home, had some particularly 'high-spirited' children visited on him. They leapt about on his furniture, played with his dental equipment and climbed out of upper-floor windows, leaving their host in fear for their lives. He applied to have them removed.

The problems with evacuation were sufficient to warrant a government inquiry. As their report admitted:

> A wide gulf is fixed between the sentiments, habits and outlook of town and country. The London woman is gregarious. The busy multitudes, the crowded streets and shops, the cinemas and other diversions form the background of her life. The life of her sister in the country parish or provincial town is more often centred in her home. She is more house-proud and a better cook. Outside her home, the social activities of the churches or the Women's Institute occupy her leisure hours. The outlook of the London mother is hard for her to understand.
>
> *Berkshire Chronicle*,
> 31 January 1941

However, there were success stories, like the two Reading sisters who happily took care of no less than nineteen evacuee babies, and still found time to manufacture a small mountain of handicrafts. Another woman took on as many as sixteen London youngsters, in addition to her own four children, and found full-time employment simply in repairing their clothes. Particularly touching was the story of Mrs Robert Erskine Beall from Manchester, who had married late in life and had a childless marriage. She and her husband decided to take in a couple of evacuees to give them the benefit of a normal country life. But instead of doing as so many did and going for the most aesthetically appealing ones, or those who could earn their keep, they decided to opt for the most hopeless cases. They sought out the cross-eyed, the bow-legged, sufferers from rickets, hare lips and other infirmities, many of which they were able to get cured. They ended up taking in – and finally adopting – at least six children.

Some evacuees' stays were tragically short. The day after arriving at their new billet in Hallaton, Leicestershire, 6-year-old Michael Moscow and his brother went out exploring the surroundings. In an outhouse they found an old gun and, while playing with it, Michael was shot dead. Down in Seaford, Sussex, 11-year-old evacuee Kenneth Holden discovered a new hobby – collecting birds' eggs – which culminated in him falling 80ft down a cliff to his death. Supplementing one's diet from the hedgerows was also fraught with danger when you did not know the difference between blackberries and deadly nightshade, and warnings had to be broadcast to the evacuees and their hosts.

The Other Evacuees

Children, mothers and the vulnerable were not the only ones likely to be looking for accommodation. Within a week of war breaking out, the Army Council announced their standard rates for paying those who had soldiers billeted with them in the event of an emergency. Once again, it highlighted the dual standards for officers and other ranks. For ordinary soldiers, their host could expect to receive 10*d* per night for the first soldier and 8*d* for each additional one, for lodging and attendance in premises where meals were provided (and paid for separately). Breakfast, 'as specified in Part 1 of the Second Schedule in the Army Act', was payable at a rate of 8*d* a time, with an equally closely specified dinner coming in at 11*d*. Officers clearly expected better, and their lodging was to be paid at the rate of 3*s* for the first officer and 2*s* for each subsequent one. Officers were to make their own arrangements for meals (and pay for them).

There were also some groups of evacuees who received relatively little publicity. There were plans in the event of war to move long-term prisoners out of London gaols like Pentonville to provincial prisons, and many short-term prisoners were to be released entirely. Approved schools were also evacuated. One, from South Norwood in London, found itself in the Nutbourne Holiday Camp. Security there was obviously less challenging than in their previous accommodation, since three of its inmates absconded within days of arriving and, on their recapture, got sent to borstal for two years.

In addition to urban evacuees and military lodgers, there was soon another army, of war workers, looking for accommodation, as witnessed in this advertisement:

> BILLETING WORKERS IS WAR WORK
> They've done their day's National Service, making the war weapons that help our forces to win. Now it's up to you to do YOURS! Give them lodgings to come back to, a square meal, a comfortable bed – and send them back tomorrow refreshed and ready for another hard day beating Hitler.
>
> Thousands of war workers are coming into this district. They have left their own homes behind them, everything they hold dear, because they want to do their duty. The … Ministry of Labour and National Service appeals for your help in housing them.
>
> *Swindon Advertiser*, 1 July 1941

In addition to evacuee children, the public were called upon to billet a small army of war workers.

In some cases, the evacuee's lot could be communal living in the extreme. In Oxford, the Majestic cinema became home to some 550 evacuees, a purpose for which it had not been adapted and was hopelessly ill suited. It became a national scandal and its amenities were further undermined by the presence of one Alice Smith, a 60-year-old charwoman, who appeared before the court on charges of drunkenness and insulting behaviour. The prosecution told the court:

> She had proved herself a considerable nuisance at the cinema, being drunk practically every night. Her language was most offensive to the other evacuees. The officials at the cinema are anxious to get rid of her.
>
> *Oxford Mail*, 22 November 1940

For her part, Alice pleaded shrapnel injuries in mitigation. It would be 1941 before these evacuees could be rehoused in more suitable accommodation.

In addition to the evacuation of a resident population, some areas found themselves on the end of a more welcome migration, of businesses fleeing the perils of London or what was expected to become the front line of the south coast towns. Oxford was one such destination. By the end of 1940, the city had done well enough out of it for the *Oxford Times* to run a special advertisement feature for them all, with up-market house furnishers, ladies' outfitters and antique dealers prominent among them.

Come the end of the war and evacuees were once again seen through rose-tinted spectacles. This is how one mayor bade farewell to the last of his town's evacuees on the station platform:

> It can safely be said that the people of this area played their part magnificently in welcoming into their own homes, in what was considered a safe area, children from parts which were expected to be the target for enemy bombing. They

> looked after them in nearly every case as if these children were their own, welcomed the parents into their homes during weekends when they came to see how their youngsters were faring under wartime conditions and generally cooperated to a loyal degree.
>
> In fact it was the beginning of a wonderful spirit of camaraderie which permeated this country.
>
> *Berkshire Chronicle*, 22 June 1945

He may have got nearer the truth when he added, on behalf of the town: 'This is indeed as happy a moment for me as it is for you.'

4

'Angels are watching overhead': The Blitz

> We've got Hitler rattled, I do believe, or he wouldn't do such silly ass things.
>
> Bath resident, with an optimistic interpretation of the Baedeker raid on his city

> We keep open during alerts. In the event of a direct hit, we close immediately.
>
> Notice displayed in a public house

First Line of Defence

In planning air raid precautions in the pre-war years, the authorities were inclined to the view of former Prime Minister Stanley Baldwin, that the bombers would always get through. According to one estimate, the first week of serious air raids on the capital would leave some 66,000 Londoners dead and another 134,000 seriously injured. (In fact, the national total of civilian deaths from bombing in the entire war barely reached 60,000.)

The authorities' pessimism was based on the unimpeded success of pre-war bombing raids in overseas conflicts, the difficulty the RAF had in even finding nocturnal raiders before the development of airborne radar and on the almost total inability of the defenders in pre-war exercises to hit anything with anti-aircraft fire. In one such exercise, in 1926, the defences were presented with a target flying at a known speed and a fixed course, and at an ideal altitude for the gunners. They still managed only two hits from 2,935 shots. Under real-life conditions, one hit in every 2,000 shots was considered good shooting. This track record is perhaps understandable when one considers, for example, that most of the Manchester Anti-Aircraft Regiment's training consisted of so-called silent practice inside a drill hall. When they were finally allowed outside with real ammunition, the chosen location was Fort William, where the weather was so bad that for three days they were unable to fire a single round.

By 1942 there were more women than men operating the anti-aircraft defences. But women were still not considered suitable for combat roles. So, while they could operate the range finders and predictors that aimed the guns towards the target, firing the gun was strictly a man's job. More to the point, the women got different medals and a third less pay than the men, despite bearing an equal share of the dangers and discomforts. Nor did it stop the *Portsmouth Evening News* waxing lyrical about 'the men' who operated the anti-aircraft guns having to undergo rigorous psychological and physical tests to establish their suitability to operate this equipment (in particular, those parts of it with which women were more often entrusted).

Give me Shelter

So, if they did not expect to shoot them down, how did the authorities prepare for the inevitable arrival of the bombers? The default form of shelter for the resident population was the cellar of their house, assuming they had one. Failing that, every home was supposed (according to Air Raid Precautions advice, issued by the Home Office in 1938) to equip itself with a refuge room. This would need to be protected against gas, blacked out, have blast-proof barriers, be equipped for emergencies and contain basic fire appliances. A 10ft by 10ft gas-proofed room, households were informed, would house five people for twelve hours without needing external ventilation, provided the occupants did not engage in any strenuous activity and did not smoke. They were advised to choose a room looking on to a garden, since there was a better chance that a bomb falling on to soft soil or the lawn would embed itself into the ground, making its blast less damaging than would be the case on a hard surface. Among the more unrealistic proposals was that households should fill the bath with water to refuel fire buckets in the five- to seven-minute warning they were theoretically supposed to receive before an air raid.

Those without a cellar, but who had a garden, were offered the Anderson shelter. It was named after the Home Secretary, Sir John Anderson, and consisted of curved sides of corrugated iron that bolted together to form an enclosed space. Much of its protective strength came from the fact that it was to be sunk into a deep pit in the garden and then covered with earth to a depth of at least 15in.

Some who received them (and they were free to people earning less than £250 a year) were too idle, clueless or infirm to do the necessary digging and simply erected them (if at all) on top of the garden, where they offered virtually no protection. Others were victims of the design flaws inherent in an insubstantial subterranean building. It was by no means unknown for people to rush to their shelter as the warning sounded, only to find themselves up to their knees in water. They were, however, remarkably strong once erected properly. One was tested by having 75 tons of pig iron balanced on it, and a London family survived having a Messerschmitt Bf 109 fighter plane crash into theirs.

Another problem with the Anderson was that it was designed for the wrong kind of air raid. Pre-war planners had tended to

A rather more sophisticated (if intrusive) indoor ARP refuge than the government's Morrison shelter.

assume that air raids would be short and sharp daytime affairs, during which the discomforts of the Anderson shelter could be endured. It was not anticipated that there would be raids that lasted most of the night, and the Anderson was by no means designed for sleeping in (notwithstanding the efforts of some to make them so). Indeed, some of the first ones were made too short to take full-sized bunks, as a cost-saving measure. Some households were lulled into a false sense of security by the Phoney War, and decided to wait before providing any kind of

Concrete – the only material for building an air raid shelter – or so the concrete manufacturers would have you believe.

shelter. One householder was reported as saying that they would wait to see what the Germans dropped on them first. If it was only leaflets, they would get some wastepaper baskets rather than digging trenches. Only the invasion of the Low Countries in 1940 led to a belated surge in their installation.

About 27 per cent of the population relied on an Anderson shelter and there were plenty of owners who went to town in turning them into something approximating a home from home. The best had waterproof flooring, bunk beds, rudimentary heating and lighting, and anti-gas curtains at the door, not to mention marrows growing on the roof, though the presence of all this equipment, along with piles of bedding, only added to the cramped sensation of the shelter. The press had some fanciful notions about how comfortable they could be. The *Daily Sketch* offered these thoughts about 'making the best of a sheltered life':

> Some people find it most restful to lie down, and it's a grand idea to put a nice warm rug on the floor if you haven't got a Lilo and there's no room for a small mattress ... Then with two pillows on which to rest your head, you can doze away to your heart's content until the all-clear sounds.
>
> *Daily Sketch*, August 1940

One danger was that any doze you had in your shelter could be your last. A Mr Henry Higgans of Southsea fell asleep in his, and was asphyxiated by the lamp which doubled as a heater. He had reckoned without the fact that the shelter had been constructed to be gas-proof and was therefore very poorly ventilated. By July 1940, word was issued that the future supply of Anderson shelters would be severely restricted, due to the lack of steel with which to make them, and the emphasis shifted back on to making your home into an air raid shelter.

For those with neither a cellar nor a garden, one option was a Morrison shelter. These consisted of a steel-mesh cage about 6ft 6in long and 4ft wide, by 2ft 6in high, with a ½in steel top that could double as a table. This was kept in the house itself and the whole family would climb into it in the event of an air raid. These were again self-assembly and the Boy Scout movement made it one of their wartime services to assemble them for more challenged residents (which may have been all but the most muscular, as the shelters weighed about 5 hundredweight (around 250kg) and the top alone was a hundredweight (50kg). What they would not protect people from was the dense cloud of dust generated by a falling building, and there were cases of people in Morrison shelters surviving the falling masonry but choking to death on the dust. The authorities later issued a larger two-tier Morrison shelter. This held more people but was much less useful as a substitute dining table unless you ate standing up, being 4ft high.

For many, public shelters were the only choice. These were supposed to be primarily for people caught out in the street when an air raid began, and official guidance was that priority in a raid should be given to them, rather than those with homes nearby. In London, the Underground rail network could (once official opposition to it was ignored by the public) provide shelter for vast numbers. Twelve thousand shelterers could be accommodated at Finsbury Park station alone, with Borough High Street and King's Cross each taking 8,000 or 9,000. At the height of the Blitz, some 177,000 Londoners were sheltering in tube stations, though even this represented only 4 per cent of the residents of central London.

The big department stores offered basement shelters; John Lewis was one that saw the retail potential of a captive audience, and offered a range of foodstuffs, books and handicraft items for sale in the basement, to help pass the time while the bombs fell. One problem was that these shelters tended to be closed out of shopping hours. For the rich, the deep shelter beneath the Savoy offered a very safe and comfortable refuge. East End Communist Party members objected to this bastion of privilege and tried to occupy the shelter, on the grounds that 'what was good enough for the Savoy Hotel parasites was reasonably good enough for the Stepney workers and their families'. Class war was only avoided when the all-clear sounded.

Then there were the brick and concrete shelters that stood in the middle of terraced streets. Some of these had flaws, in that they used the wrong cement mix, and/or were poorly constructed, with the reinforced concrete roof not properly bonded into the brick walls. The air pressure from a bomb dropping near the entrance to one could lift the roof off the walls, whilst pushing the walls outwards, leaving the roof to drop on to the hapless occupants. 'Morrison sandwiches' was the dark nickname given to these facilities. One hundred and twenty communal shelters in Hammersmith had to be torn down and rebuilt after one of theirs collapsed. The council's clerk of works and the building contractor were arrested on corruption charges and only narrowly escaped a murder charge. Even leaving aside concerns about faulty design and construction, public air raid shelters were not always as secure as the authorities might have hoped. It was belatedly discovered that one of Maidenhead's had been erected right beside an underground storage tank containing several thousand gallons of highly flammable fuel oil.

Communal shelters offered their users another potential hazard. It was found that there was a greatly increased risk of infectious diseases associated with them. Cases of pneumonia went up 70 per cent between December 1940 and January 1941, while whooping cough increased by almost 40 per cent over the same period. There was even a new form of nasty cough, which acquired the name 'shelter throat'. The problem was serious enough to prompt the king's own physician, Lord Halder, to undertake a tour of the nation's communal shelters early in 1941. He criticised the poor standards of construction in many of them, along with other health hazards such as the chemical toilets that tended to get knocked over, spreading germs. All things considered, he thought it was touch and go whether people were in more danger staying at home when the bombers came or making for a communal shelter. Lord Halder may have seen that choice of shelter as being class-based. He spoke of 'a group of shelterers, generally poor who, by birth, status, race or type were unable to stand up to the terror of the blitz and the noises accompanying it'. Such people in his view went to big communal centres and many of them were enjoying happier conditions than those they knew before night bombing began. He went on to say that:

> These modern troglodytes are building a communal life in their own way, which breeds a spirit of good temper and dignity. These urban people are very gregarious and their motto is the more we are together the happier we shall be.
>
> *Liverpool Echo*, 3 April 1941

Diphtheria was another public health worry of the day, and a mass immunisation campaign was launched. But there were some who would not be helped:

> Anyone who has the children's welfare at heart can, like myself, obtain irrefutable unbiased medical evidence that immunisation does not prevent diphtheria and that not only have children been made seriously ill, but that not a few deaths have resulted.
>
> Inoculation and its evil twin vaccination are filthy superstitions, handed down to us from the dark ages. Unfortunately not all the evils are made in Germany, and evil forces call for strong weapons to combat them.
>
> Letter to the *Swindon Advertiser*, 7 January 1941

Other factors led people to resist using public shelters. They were subject to various forms of abuse, with fly-tippers leaving all sorts of rubbish in them (one at the rear of Ashworth Street, Bury, had a consignment of sheep heads dumped in it), drunks using them as latrines, children as playgrounds, adult couples for coupling and thieves as a source of anything saleable in them. Uxbridge Juvenile Court had to deal with the case of a 12-year-old boy who had gone into the public shelters, chopped up the benches in them and sold them for firewood. One shelter user rather optimistically wrote to the local paper, suggesting the problem could be solved by erecting signs saying that it was forbidden to use the shelter for anything other than sheltering.

Some people felt embarrassed at being seen there in their night attire. In one case an elderly woman refused to leave her bedroom because she could not find her teeth. 'Get down in the shelter!' her exasperated son cried. 'They're dropping bombs, not bloody pork pies!' Communal shelters could also modify behaviour. In Belfast, rival Catholic and Protestant communities found themselves forced to share the same communal shelters. They expressed their mutual hostility by taking it in turns to sing the rallying songs of their respective communities. Then, as the bombs got closer, the singing was gradually silenced until, at the height of the raid, they joined in a single chorus of *Nearer my God to Thee*. Singing – as loudly as possible – was official policy in Manchester, where the city corporation issued instructions about what to do in an air raid, which included the following:

> During the raid sing community songs, play a musical instrument, or do anything that will help to keep your spirits up and drown any noises outside.
>
> *Manchester City News*, 2 September 1939

Communal shelters often took their tone from the character of the marshal who was responsible for running them. They might be classified as quiet, drunken, courting or fighting. The best of them (depending on one's definition of 'best') might be the super-organised ones that had their own entertainments committees and programme of events. One such read as follows:

> *Monday:* keep fit, darts
> *Tuesday*: concert, religious service
> *Wednesday*: musical evening
> *Thursday*: religious service, concert
> *Friday:* whist drive
> *Saturday*: keep fit, religious service followed by dancing
>
> Shelter entertainments programme

One downside of this was that whatever small chance you had of sleeping through a raid would be lost, if the rest of the shelterers were having a lusty singsong around you. But there were some who not only could sleep under any circumstances, but could also drown out the noises outside at the same time. Manchester shelterer George Hall found himself sentenced to fourteen days behind bars for snoring loudly during an air raid. The charge read that he 'did wilfully disturb other persons in the proper use of an air raid shelter'. George's defence, that if he had been asleep at the time his actions could hardly have been wilful, cut no ice with the magistrate. George was not alone, if this account of shelter life from a non-sleeper is anything to go by. She advanced the view that the bad posture in which shelterers were forced to sit or lie promoted a rich variety of sound effects:

> Occasionally, a pair of snorers, synchronising badly, would answer each other. Deep called unto deep, bass was echoed by tenor. Some sawed wood, while others drew water. One fellow entered upon an unintelligible discourse, while a further one punctuated his regular snore with what sounded like 'Yah-hey-yah' 'Bon-bon-phe-a-ew'. I had no idea people could snore in so many languages ... I sighed for the day when those who go down to earth to snore shall have deep shelters of their own – and the deeper the better.
>
> *Liverpool Echo*, 3 October 1940

Whilst on the subject of sound sleepers, a bomb blew out the windows of a house in Widdecombe. One of those windows was the bedroom of an elderly matron, who was both stone deaf and bedridden. Awaking next morning to find her windows gone and her bedspread covered in glass, she commented, 'We must have had a very bad storm in the night'. Another woman in Broadway awoke to find that her bedroom ceiling had been replaced by the sky; she had slept through her roof being blown off by high explosives.

Ramsgate was one community that really went to town with its communal shelters. From March 1939, it built some 2 miles of tunnel, 60ft underground and with twenty-three public entrances. It started to become known as the holiday destination you could go to in wartime free of fear from bombing raids, but the authorities decided that this did not quite chime with the slogan by which local tourism was promoted before the war – 'health and sunshine'. In Newcastle-upon-Tyne the basement rooms of the medieval castle were pressed into use as a shelter – its 16ft-thick walls, built to resist medieval siege weapons, were deemed to be robust enough to resist those of the twentieth century.

The Cement and Concrete Association naturally thought the likes of Anderson and Morrison shelters a most inadequate solution. They called for every household to be given its own concrete pillbox, offering 'in every home a miniature Gibraltar which would serve to protect the families of the nation and also maintain the morale of the people'. This proposal was not taken up by government, but some of those wishing to be one-up on their neighbours commissioned a bespoke concrete air raid shelter. For an added status symbol, the Bruce air raid shelter came with a roof that could be removed, come the end of hostilities, leaving you with an instant swimming pool. Some builders reported quite a boom in business from people wanting either purpose-built shelters or measures to make their homes more bomb-proof.

Torbay millionaire Mrs Ella Rowcroft commissioned what was regarded as possibly the finest private air raid shelter in the country, 30ft deep with a whole suite of rooms off a central corridor. A bronze plaque above the head of the bed in the master bedroom read: 'Angels are watching overhead. Sleep sweetly then, goodnight.' Unfortunately, Mrs Rowcroft died of causes entirely unrelated to the Luftwaffe, before she had a chance to make use of her investment.

However, the prize for eccentricity in shelter design must surely go to a Glasgow 'character', Mr A.E. Pickard. The shelter he built in the grounds of one of his mansions was conical in shape, with the outside festooned with neon lighting. As horrified air raid wardens contemplated this nightmare breach of the blackout regulations, he airily explained to them that the Nazis would never dare to bomb A.E. Pickard.

The public nationally saw Londoners in large numbers disregard the instructions of the authorities and take to the relative security of the Underground stations. Nor, as we have seen, did it pass unnoticed that the rich could buy safety in the deep basements of the Savoy and other bastions of privilege. The demand for deep shelters for the masses steadily grew as the war progressed, promoted, among others, by the Communist Party of Great Britain. It was left to Home Secretary Herbert Morrison, through the medium of the local press, to explain the unreality of such a policy:

> Anything like a universal policy of deep shelter for the whole population, or the greater part of it, is beyond the bounds of practical possibility … To attempt to build more than a limited amount in suitable places would mean providing deep shelter for a given number at the cost of leaving a much larger number with no good shelter at all.
>
> *Berkshire Chronicle*, 8 November 1940

For its part, the paper saw the 'deep shelter cry' as a form of defeatist agitation, and suggested that campaigners for better shelters were undermining the confidence of women. But the communists were not the only ones campaigning for the provision of better shelters:

> A pressing problem, now that winter is approaching, is the provision of properly-equipped air raid shelters for the civilian population. The majority of shelters have no light, no heat and do not offer adequate protection. They were never intended for all-night occupation and the Government lacked both foresight and imagination when planning them. As usual, the authorities are being pushed by public opinion.
>
> *Liverpool Echo*, 2 October 1940

For some communities which received regular visits from the Luftwaffe, a further option for large numbers of the population was 'trekking' – fleeing their town or city each evening for somewhere safer, sleeping in caves, barns, tents, hedgerows or whatever other facilities came to hand. In Southampton, the local bus company made some of its vehicles available, which doubled as both transport out of the city and somewhere to sleep. Officials were on hand to enforce strict rules of propriety, with the ladies sleeping downstairs and the men (regardless of whether their wives were below) upstairs.

The First Raids

At the start of July 1940, well before most of Britain had had any experience at all of bombing, and certainly before the full fury of the Blitz had been unleashed upon the nation, at least one local paper could claim that they had civil defence mastered:

> Three facts emerge from the South of England's first experience of air raiding. They are: the civil defence services in all their branches have proved their efficiency; the once-criticised Anderson shelter, the public shelter and the simple home refuge have proved their effectiveness; and the public has proved its ability to come through its baptism of fire calm and unshaken …
>
> there is every reason to believe that when more intensive raids are attempted by the enemy, the plans which have been so well prepared and so long rehearsed for the protection of people and property, will not fail …
>
> *Berkshire Chronicle*, 5 July 1940

> The casualties from air raids in the present war will tend to become proportionately fewer as the public acquires the soldier's instinct to take cover whenever sirens or anti-aircraft fire give warning of a raid.
>
> *Berkshire Chronicle*, 26 July 1940

However, at the same time there was public disquiet at the fact that the early small-scale nuisance raids were provoking little in the way of a defensive response; no anti-aircraft guns were being fired, no sirens sounded and there was little or no evidence of defence by the RAF. The authorities felt obliged to respond through the local papers and said (in so many words): that the risk from lone raiders passing overhead was very small, and that to sound the sirens or fire the guns every time would be a disproportionate response. This was particularly true, since one of the objects of these raids was to interrupt people's sleep patterns and disrupt industrial production. To wake people and have them scurry to the shelters each time was only playing into the enemy's hands. The authorities quoted the misleading statistic that people were more likely to die from a road accident than from bombing (bearing in mind that the additional traffic risk from the blackout applied to the entire nation, whereas the dangers from bombing were much more localised).

As for the lack of response from the RAF, all they could say in their defence was that it was awfully difficult to find the bombers. Our fighters were likely to be closing on their bombers at a combined speed of over 500mph in the dark and it was, as one pilot put it, 'like looking for a gnat in the dome of St Pauls'.

ARP Wardens

The other main defence against the bombing was the appointment of a small army of Air Raid Precautions staff. During the Phoney War, or *Sitzkrieg*, that preceded the real outbreak of hostilities, they were not popular. As well as the sometimes bureaucratic vigour with which they enforced the blackout in the face of non-existent bombing raids, there was the cost of them. It emerged that Manchester Corporation were paying £21,500 a week for their ARP staff, in addition to their food and transport costs, and this for a staffing establishment which was well below the 20 per cent of full-time employees recommended by the government. Similar complaints were surfacing in communities (and their local newspapers) up and down the country:

> Thousands of men, many in good jobs, are drawing £3 a week as Air Raid wardens; hundreds of girls and youths are getting good pay for doing nothing; fantastic sums are being paid to motorists for merely putting their vehicles at the disposal of the ARP or ambulance work; demolition squads are standing in the streets twenty-four hours a day twiddling their thumbs; auxiliary firemen are also on the job; 'log-rolling' and intrigue are rampant.
>
> *Manchester City News*, 23 September 1939

According to some reports, willing volunteers were having unwanted money forced into their hands:

> We are constantly hearing stories of patriotic citizens volunteering for full-time service as wardens, neither wanting nor expecting payment, and finding themselves placed on the ARP Committee's payroll. There seems to be little room to doubt that many posts have been filled by paid wardens when there were volunteers available ... It will be an abrogation of the great voluntary spirit of the movement ... to turn public-spirited volunteers into hirelings.
>
> *Slough Observer*, 22 September 1939

ARP wardens were not best pleased at the suggestion that they were all being paid lavish sums for doing nothing; 'three quid a week army dodgers' was the unflattering nickname given to them. The head of ARP in Tring felt obliged to write to his local newspaper, scotching rumours that his staff were all paid:

> The powers that be state that Tring is not a danger area and therefore does not come under the whole-time personnel, and our wardens ... have worked, and are working, absolutely voluntarily.
>
> *Bucks Herald*, 10 May 1940

However, come the real offensive, if the ARP officials did not have a difficult enough job coping with air raids and their aftermath, they faced another obstacle:

> After the raid is over the curiosity of sightseers is having serious effects which are probably quite unforeseen by the sightseers themselves. From near and far they hasten, on foot, on bicycle, in cars, in their hundreds or even thousands. The roads leading to damaged streets or burning buildings are soon blocked by the throng … many of my fellow ARP workers were … prevented from reaching the scene of the bombing.
>
> *Berkshire Chronicle*, 30 August 1940

Bureaucracy and the Blitz

The Blitz was as subject to regulation as every other aspect of wartime life. For example, 'the sounding of any siren, hooter, whistle, bell, horn, gong or similar instrument' was banned unless it was being done under the instruction of an ARP warden or other responsible party. Pensioner Arthur Smith fell foul of this within days of the war starting. He got into some sort of trouble in central Winchester and blew a whistle he carried to summon police help. He did not appreciate that this was now an air raid signal, and everyone within earshot scuttled into the nearest shelter. Some stayed there for several hours, awaiting an all-clear which, naturally, did not come. Smith was fined £5 for the offence of 'sounding without authority a whistle within the hearing of the general public'.

There was generally a good deal of confusion, among the public and officials alike, as to the signals used for gas attacks, bombing raids and the all-clears from each. Different authorities seemed to use different combinations of sirens, handbells, rattles and whistles. Home Office guidance did not resolve the

Smelling salts for harassed ARP workers.

matter, since it appeared to be capable of more than one interpretation, and there was much to-ing and fro-ing between the authorities to try to establish a common code. In Merseyside they eventually reached some sort of consensus, although (a) it was probably too complicated for many members of the public to remember and, (b) Birkenhead went its own way with something slightly different. Humourists in the local press picked up on the confusion. The *Liverpool Echo* carried an imagined conversation in which someone became increasingly bewildered as the arrangements were explained to him. His final question was:

> 'What if it's an all clear but the guns are still firing?'
> 'Perhaps it's the King's birthday.'
>
> *Liverpool Echo*, 18 October 1940

For its part, the Noise Abatement League was campaigning against unnecessary noise of any kind during the day, arguing that it was helping Hitler in his war of nerves by depriving night-shift workers of their sleep. The police told them they did not have the manpower to enforce against noisy people. One group to whom this would have been immaterial would have been the deaf who, more to the point, would miss any audible warning of an air raid. As part of their war service, the Boy

Some practical advice for those who get into trouble dealing with incendiary bombs.

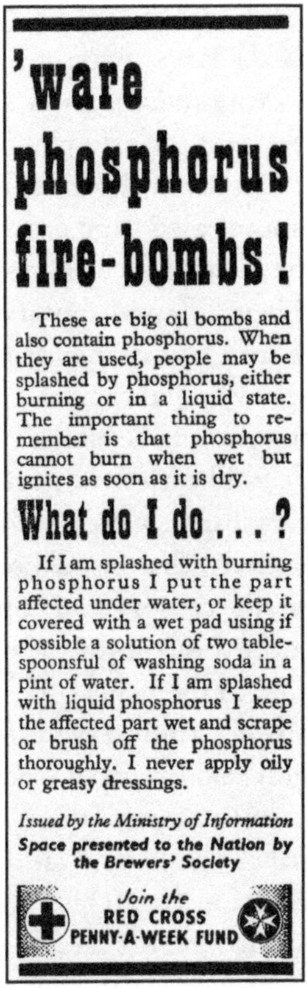

Scouts volunteered to deliver air raid warnings to the deaf in person.

The authorities also found it necessary to issue the following instruction to the public: 'If you find a bomb, take the official to the bomb, not the bomb to an official.' This may have been prompted by one individual, who turned up at the police station with an unexploded incendiary bomb in a bucket, then complained when the police kept the bucket. Elsewhere, there were reports of children finding, playing with and ultimately being killed by unexploded bombs. Their youthful foolishness may be understood; less so that of a man from Caversham, who bought a Messerschmitt cannon shell from a man in Brighton, clamped it in a vice and set about trying to dismantle it with a hand chisel. It shot him through the forehead.

There were strict rules (the Control of Photography Order (No. 1) 1939) against photographing bomb damage, or indeed anything remotely war-related, lest the pictures were used to assist the enemy in some way or to demoralise the British public. A photographic record of Reading's worst air raid only exists because the council commissioned an 'official' photographer to take pictures.

Quite how strictly these rules could be enforced is illustrated by the experience of a father and son, walking along the banks of the River Avon at Bath. They found themselves opposite the picturesque Pulteney Bridge and weir, the subject of a million peacetime tourist photographs, and were just taking one of their own when they were arrested by the Military Police. They were not released from detention until they had satisfied the authorities that they were not spies, and their film was confiscated. Their 'offence' appears to have resulted from the fact that there were a few strands of barbed wire forming a barricade next to the weir and they had therefore unwittingly been photographing part of the nation's defences.

Publication was even more fraught with difficulty. If the newspapers were not forbidden to publish bomb damage details entirely, there would often be a long delay before they could do so (the censors could operate a twenty-eight-day rule to make it more difficult for the enemy to link a particular event to a picture in the paper). The editor would also be required to make any description vague for the same reason; hence Reading's biggest raid occurred – according to the local paper – in 'a home counties town' (though it is unlikely that most readers of that paper would have failed to notice that large parts of their town centre had been blown to pieces).

However, there does not always appear to have been consistency in the way the newspaper censorship rules were applied. Following Portsmouth's worst air raid, in January 1941, the Air Ministry's official statement on the matter simply refers to 'a town in southern England' having been attacked. A second report in the same edition of the *Evening News* refers to a 'south coast town' having been the victim, tying it down a little more closely. But, immediately opposite that report, another one names Portsmouth as the recipient and goes into great detail as to which civic buildings had been damaged. It even pointed out the irony that, while many government offices had been destroyed, the Inland Revenue office and its sign, 'open for the payment of income tax', survived unscathed.

You could still take photographs, but be careful what you shoot.

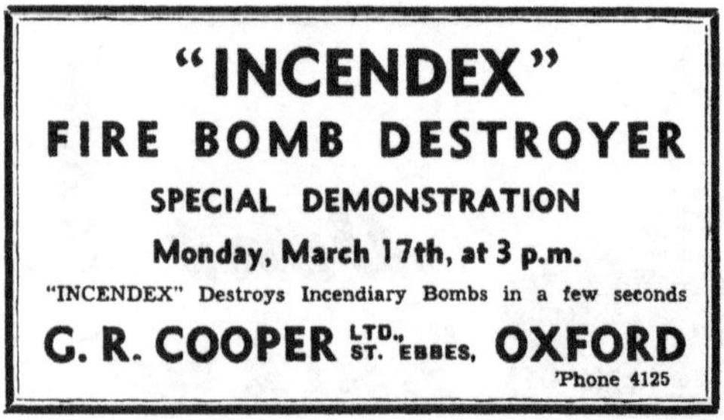

Many thousands of incendiary bombs fell on our towns and cities.

Moreover, the censors' pen was not restricted to domestic matters. In the early days of the war they refused to allow morale-boosting pictures of an RAF raid on the German fleet. The press was indignant:

> One picture shows the bursting of a shell on one of the battleships – 'the confirmation of a gallant exploit'. What information can this be giving the enemy about his own mishap?
>
> *Liverpool Echo*, 7 September 1939

The Manchester Blitz

Many of our cities suffered major damage in bombing raids. The following is an account of just one of these, the raids on Manchester in December 1940, drawn largely from what its citizens could learn about it at the time from their local newspapers. Christmas 1940 was approaching and the press was in a festive mood, insofar as wartime conditions permitted. The editorial in the *Manchester City News* was typical:

> For the second time during the war we welcome this festive season with increased cordiality – remembering at the same time, with a tinge of regret and resentment that we might have had great fun, had it not been for the war. But even the

> barking of guns and the wailing of air raid sirens will never spoil the true British Christmas spirit.
>
> *Manchester City News*, 21 December 1940

The paper listed the various attractions on offer for a family Christmas: the circus at Belle Vue, pantomime – with Tommy Trinder in *Cinderella* at the Opera House and Stanley Holloway in *Robinson Crusoe* at the Palace – and the various films showing at the city's cinemas. It ended with the cheery (but, in retrospect, ominous) words 'forget the blitz in Manchester this Christmas!'

However, at the same time, preparation for the worst continued. Readers were advised to make plans now to go and stay with friends or relations, in case their house was destroyed – 'it's comforting to feel that everything is fixed up, just in case'. The state of the evacuation measures, with the drift back to the cities, was also causing a lot of concern. The town clerk described the public's response to his appeal to evacuate the children – and to keep them evacuated – as 'appalling'. It was estimated that only 5,700 of the city's children were still evacuated by this time. One problem was that, should parents change their minds, the corporation had no immediate plans to carry out a second large-scale evacuation. The paper campaigned for something to be done about it:

> The time to get your children out of the city is now … No child should remain in a vulnerable area for one day longer than is unavoidable once the parents have consented to have him or her sent away.
>
> *Manchester City News*, 21 December 1940

The war was creeping towards Manchester. On the night of 21 December, Liverpool and Merseyside were attacked, and the authorities learned from intercepted radio traffic that an attack on Manchester was imminent. The night-fighters, anti-aircraft and ARP services were alerted, but to no avail.

The following night, the sirens wailed and within minutes the bombers, guided in by the fires still raging on Merseyside, were overhead. Incendiary bombs began falling around Albert Square. Almost 10,000 fell within thirty-eight minutes. The first wave was followed by Heinkels dropping a mixture of target-illuminating flares, high explosives and incendiaries. This first phase alone lasted over three hours, and was followed by a further phase that lasted into the early hours of the morning. A total of 272 tonnes of high explosive and over 37,000 incendiaries were dropped on the city centre.

The Princess Street/Clarence Street area was ablaze and, in the Deansgate area, the Royal Exchange, the Victoria building and the gas main at St Mary's Gate were all burning. Warehouses were alight in Portland Street, Sackville Street and Watson Street, and buildings in Grey Street, Stafford Street, Cooke Street and Erskine Street were demolished by high explosives. A total of 400 fires were raging, and much of Manchester's firefighting capacity was still in Liverpool, helping to put out the previous night's fires. Even if it had been on the spot, access to the fires was in many cases blocked by buildings that had collapsed across the road. Manchester put out a call for help, which was answered by fire brigades from as far away as Teeside and (by Christmas Eve) London. They were still fighting the fires when, next evening, the Luftwaffe returned. This time their payloads included some of their biggest bombs, the LM1000 parachute mine, and a series of huge explosions shook the city.

By 3 a.m. on Christmas Eve the fires were at least contained, if not totally under control, until a strong wind sprung up. This carried sparks and embers over a wide area, re-igniting a lot of old fires and starting new ones. Very soon, large sections of the city centre, from Moseley Street, across Piccadilly to Portland Street and beyond, were ablaze. The authorities could see no option, other than the demolition of sound buildings to create a firebreak. Large parts of the square mile around Albert Square had been devastated. In total, 165 warehouses, 150 offices, five banks and 250 other business premises were either destroyed or unusable; 30,000 houses had been damaged, some extensively, and 5,049 had been made homeless. In Manchester itself, 363 people were dead and the death toll over the wider urban area exceeded a thousand.

In the midst of one of the worst affected areas of the bombing, Manchester's most historic building, the cathedral, took its share of punishment. The Dean of Manchester, Dr Garfield Williams, recorded his account of events, in which he found a strange and terrible beauty:

> I have always thought of Manchester Cathedral … as a lovely jewel set in the midst of the most appalling and disgracefully unworthy surroundings. There must have been a period in its history when many of the citizens of Manchester had ceased to care what happened to the old church so long as they made a lot of money.
>
> But that night the cathedral in its setting was a thing of entrancing, shocking, devastating beauty … All around, instead of hideous ugliness, there were flames shooting, apparently hundreds of feet into the sky. Remember that the old Shambles was one vast bonfire, and the wind was driving in the direction of the cathedral – wind so filled with sparks as to give the effect of golden rain. There was much more flame than smoke, so it seemed to me, and the roar of the flames was terrific.
>
> The stained glass windows of the cathedral were all lit up so as to produce a colour effect which was sublime. And there was 't'owd church', a fairy-like scintillating thing in the midst of a blaze of fire.
>
> Quoted in Hylton (2010), p. 258

Right up to the end, it looked as if the cathedral might escape damage, but at 6 a.m. virtually the last bomb of the raid hit its north-eastern corner:

> The blast had lifted the whole lead roof of the cathedral up and then dropped it back, miraculously, in place. Every window and door had gone; chairs, ornaments, carpets, furnishings, had just been swept up into the air and dropped in heaps anywhere. The High Altar was just a heap of rubbish ten feet high. The two organs were scattered about in little bits ... The Lady Chapel, the Ely Chapel and much of the regimental chapel had simply disappeared.
>
> Quoted in Hylton (2010), pp. 256–8

The reporter from the *Manchester City News* struggled to find his way into the city the following day and evidently struggled with his emotions, as he saw the carnage:

> ... I wormed my way through rubble and dust and glass. Here and there a pathetic heap of tortured brick and bricks and plaster told of a home destroyed. That day I saw many a tragic and dramatic sight, but nothing touched at my heart and made me quiver so much as the sight of poor, patient folk bending over the ruins trying to retrieve some little bit of home, or tidily sweeping up glass ...
>
> At the hospital I found glass everywhere, as ubiquitous and penetrating as dust. The matron and superintendent (who had been blown downstairs twice) were discussing plans in low voices. Silent, efficient sisters were swiftly going to appointed tasks. These young nurses of eighteen years of age or so had refused to take shelter, but had sat on the beds of the patients comforting them while hell roared around, and not one patient whimpered.
>
> When I penetrated to where the rivers of water ran through shattered glass and snuffed the tang of smoke and saw little flames flicker onto the skeletons of buildings, and a holy place desecrated, and the offices of my friends gutted by fire, and grimy and weary firemen and ruddy-cheeked soldiers with fixed bayonets ... aye, as I

gazed at the destruction wrought by the filthy hands of precocious murderers, I realised something I had not consciously realised before ... I knew that I loved Manchester. Its dear smoky streets against which I had so often railed, its kindly, comradely folk, the very nooks and alleys of it – I loved it ...

Then something or somebody within my heart said: this is not Manchester; this is but a transient outer shell. Manchester is not a congerie of buildings – it is built in the lines of its citizens – and that is unquenched, its courage and resolve inextinguishable, high in aloof pride above Hitler's hatred. And so through the acrid smoke and above the ruins and shambles I saw the real Manchester arising, even as St John saw the new Jerusalem over the sea from the isle of Patmos. I saw noble thoroughfares, I saw lovely white buildings standing clear in a smokeless air, and I saw no slums there and no shoddy, weary buildings, and I saw a nobler church arising aflame with the message of the Christ, a church that will set its bells ringing at a coming Christmastide. Hitler, I saw had done much of what we should have done long ago and in sacrifice and suffering and flame had laid the foundations of a fairer city. The all-conquering energies of this virile folk and their inextinguishable courage will create where Germans destroy.

If this be the Battle of Manchester then Hitler has lost it. The gates of hell shall not prevail in this city.

Manchester City News, 28 December 1940

Despite being hard hit itself by the bombing raids on the city, Manchester was later in the war to 'adopt' the London borough of Camberwell, one of the most heavily bombed areas in the entire country, and collections of furniture and other essentials for them were organised around the city.

Bombed Out: Help for the Survivors

Despite the extensive damage wrought by the bombers, there was nothing like the forecast level of fatalities. One consequence of this was that the authorities seriously underestimated the numbers of bombed-out survivors who would need rehousing. The responsibility for this was given to the Poor Law authorities, the public assistance committees who had administered the hated means-tested benefits during the 1930s. But the immediate impact was felt by the rest centres, set up for those who had lost their homes and their possessions. These were often hopelessly inadequate for the purpose, being able to offer little more than a cup of tea, a snack and a hard chair, on the assumption that anyone passing through their doors would move on again within twenty-four hours. They generally had no bathing facilities, insufficient sanitation and catering, and were themselves unprotected against bombing. But the scale of need was such that there was nowhere else for the bombed-out to go; by the end of May 1941, about one person in six in London was without a home.

Moreover, the arrangements were dogged by disagreements between local and national government (and its various agencies): about who was responsible for which homeless families; by red tape and paperwork; and by the kind of Poor Law mentality that prevented the London County Council from supplying blankets in case they encouraged people to stay in the rest centres for longer than was strictly necessary. The homeless would find their various needs being dealt with by a host of different bodies scattered around their town or city, few of which seemed to know where the homeless person should go to get his next need met. After one of the early raids on Liverpool, an inquiry was launched into the feeding arrangements for bomb victims:

> It is a remarkable thing that a week after the big raid it was still possible to find people who did not know that an elaborate

> organisation was there to help when they were bombed out of house and harbour, that could give them free food and financial assistance and could help in salvaging and removing their furniture.
>
> The suggestion is now made that, immediately after a raid, a bureau should be set up in each affected district, to which people could go for information and advice, and that loud-speaker vans might go around broadcasting the location of the bureau.
>
> *Liverpool Echo*, 6 December 1940

Their concerns were later echoed by Lord Woolton, who said that feeding centres in bombed areas were as necessary as the fire brigade. He had been able to find only ten towns that had made preparations against the possibility of bombing; the remainder would have to improvise in that eventuality. He went on: 'it is a meal people want; snacks are no use to bombed people.' He called on authorities to find alternative premises with coal and oil heating, given that gas and electricity supplies could not be guaranteed after a raid. Liverpool, at least, learned from bitter experience. They soon had one well-patronised feeding centre and were planning two more.

By early 1941, the Ministry of Food had organised eighteen food 'flying squads', available to go to anywhere that needed help in feeding the population. They were completely self-contained convoys, with their own food, water supply, solid fuel and utensils, and could turn out 12,000 meals of tea, bread, margarine and vegetable stew. The queen donated the first eight of these and most of the rest were funded by public donation (including fundraising in the United States and the Empire).

A reporter visited the scene of one early raid on Liverpool and met some of the victims. Many of them may not have had a roof over their heads, and the help from the authorities may at that time have been chaotic, but were these Liverpudlians downhearted?

> When I made a tour of one of the worst-hit areas of Liverpool today, writes an *Echo* reporter, what impressed me most was not the evidence of the Germans' inhumanity, though that was bad enough, but the inspiring spirit of the people.
>
> Many of them stood outside their ruined dwellings – some of them had been extricated from debris only a few hours before – but there was not one who wanted to cry quits. They were even cheerful. This attitude was common to the old and to the young. A schoolboy of ten, Tommy Boyd, put the matter philosophically when, between bites of an apple as rosy as his own cheeks, he said 'Well, anyway, we won't have to go to school today'.
>
> *Liverpool Echo*, 29 November 1940

Pets and the Blitz

The British were greatly exercised about the fate of their pets in the event of war. Many people panicked in September 1939 and had them put down. According to the RSPCA, some 200,000 pets met this fate. In Manchester, city councillor Edwards proposed that the government should be lobbied to have all dogs, except working dogs, put down. He cited the danger of them attacking humans under wartime stress, the food they would consume and their ability to spread disease. His proposal was greeted with hilarity from start to finish by his fellow councillors and he could not even find anyone to second his motion. Also in Manchester, a conman purporting to be from the ARP was going around taking delivery of dogs which, he said, would have to be put down in the event of war, and which he subsequently sold on to new owners. The Canine Defence League produced advice on how to feed your dogs without depleting the national food supplies and the Animal Defence Society launched its own evacuation scheme for dogs and cats in vulnerable areas.

The Home Office issued ARP Handbook No. 12 on how to deal with animals in an air raid. The People's Dispensary for Sick Animals felt this was so important that they bought 100,000 copies of the document, to give away to pet owners who could not afford to buy it. The RSPCA and other bodies also provided advice about the care of pets in wartime. They did not go to the extreme of proposing gas-proof kennels or – worse still – gas masks for pets. (Experiments were carried out in zoos involving monkeys wearing masks, but apparently they got quite agitated. They were even upset by seeing their keepers put them on.) If the family had a gas-proof room, the public were advised to leave the animal there. Dogs were not allowed in public shelters at all. The Canine Defence League offered postcards for pet lovers to display in their windows, offering a temporary shelter for any dog caught away from home during an air raid. Some recommended dosing dogs with bromide to tranquillise them in the event of a raid.

As for horse owners, they were advised in the event of a raid to take them to the nearest archway or to tie them firmly to the wheel of the vehicle they were towing. They should also keep a supply of empty sacks in their stables, for placing over the head of the horse if they had to be led out of the stable in the event of fire. But at least one horse had need of no such aids. When an incendiary bomb fell into his stable and set fire to his tail, he apparently not only managed unaided to extinguish that fire, and the one that started in his straw, but also managed to kick the burning bomb out of the stable door, saving both the stable and his seven fellow occupants.

Zoos in particular had a hard time of it, what with maintaining food supplies for their exhibits and putting in place contingency plans for all sorts of wartime eventualities – how, for example, would they deal with a group of terrified lions being let loose if the zoo suffered direct hits from a bomber? Chester Zoo took in evacuees from other zoos deemed to be in more front-line locations. Manchester's traditional pet shop area – Tib Street – was predictably doing little business. The one bright spot was the growing market in house dogs or guard dogs, which people were buying to protect their property in the blackout, or while the husband was away on military service.

A call went out in 1941 for intelligent dogs to be signed up for army service. Full training would be given for their (unspecified) duties. One incentive to recruitment might have been the increasing difficulty for owners in feeding their pets. By this time, the Canine Defence League was advising that:

> Many people have been forced to get rid of their large dogs because it is too difficult to obtain sufficient meat for them, and large dogs don't thrive unless they are given a big meat ration … so there is a very great demand for small dogs of every type.
>
> *Swindon Advertiser*, 1 January 1941

Dog biscuit production had been cut to a third of its pre-war level and horse meat, supposed to be reserved for animal consumption only, was finding its way on to the black market. Under the regulations it was supposed to be dyed green to prevent human use (apparently dogs were not bothered about the colouring, which could not be removed by boiling) and sold at a controlled price of 8*d* a pound. However, some traders were failing to dye it and were selling it for human use at 1*s* 2*d* a pound. The Food Committee in Slough closed down one such stall selling horse meat for (unrationed) human consumption, prompting a petition from disappointed customers, some of whom waxed quite lyrical about their fondness for 'a bit of gee-gee'. The reason for their action, the committee explained, was health and safety. Horses were slaughtered at knackers' yards, rather than at licensed abattoirs, where there were food inspectors to ensure satisfactory standards of hygiene were being observed.

However, it was not only intelligent dogs that could contribute to the war effort – hairy ones could also do so. The Canine

Defence League called for the owners of long-haired dogs to send them the combings they got from grooming. They had a team of volunteers poised to spin them into yarn and make them into army comforts.

There were calls for domestic racehorses to be transferred to the dominions, to save on their foodstuffs. Someone with time on their hands calculated that the 5,000–6,000 tons of oats that racehorses ate each year could, if fed to chickens, produce millions of eggs. The Minister for Agriculture, questioned about this in Parliament, put the matter in context by explaining that this amounted to about a quarter of an egg per year per person, and suggested that this was not sufficient grounds for destroying the racing industry. In any event many racehorses, some of them well loved by the punters, went to the knacker's yard because of the difficulty of obtaining food for them. Things looked doubly difficult for racehorses in the Marlborough area, where it was announced in July 1941 that tanks would in future be galloping across the areas of the downs where racehorses previously exercised.

5

Ho! Ho! and Haw-Haw: Wartime Fun

In this chapter we look at some of the ways the population tried briefly to forget about the privations of the war and have a little fun.

Radio Fun

With television broadcasts suspended for the duration (for the few who had a set), radio was the nation's sole form of broadcast entertainment. The BBC was a cause of widespread despair in the early days of the war. Under Lord Reith it had always been somewhat lukewarm about the 'entertain' part of its charter, and the start of war saw it slip even further into the role of information provider, just when what the country most needed was cheering up. The constantly repeated news bulletins contained very little news and what they did provide was variously upbeat to the point where the public began to distrust it, sometimes contradictory and – worst of all – desperately dull. One correspondent to the *Oxford Mail* suggested that the best way to listen to the BBC's output was by turning your set off, and this editorial summed up listener dissatisfaction with the early wartime radio offer:

> Censorship in war is unavoidable and the proper control over the spread of news is an enormously important factor in the maintenance of public confidence. It is idle to deny that all is not well at the moment in this part of our organisation. The BBC and the Ministry of Information between them have been far from successful in these first days of war, either in the efficient use of the medium at their disposal or in supplying the public demand for reliable guidance. Dull repetition of dull regulations is unnecessary and demoralising. There is no reason why the whole country should be required to hear, even once, the detail of a regulation controlling railway wagons and to repeat the statement in successive bulletins showed a lack of understanding of the function which the BBC could usefully perform.
>
> *Swindon Advertiser*,
> 8 September 1939

The following editorial started out criticising rumourmongers, but soon deviated into an attack on the BBC:

> News services are being organised on a wartime basis and the Ministry of Information must issue official bulletins about the war as promptly as possible. It will be understood that as regards air raids some details will not be given because they would provide information for the enemy. But apart from that important consideration, which affects the civilian population and the troops, the nation will get frank information, for it has entered the struggle under no illusions and is prepared to stand shocks. The BBC has announced that it will curtail its news service. Its frequent repetition of stale and unimportant news was exasperating and its choice of gramophone records was poor, though one admits that any emergency brings difficulties in its train. Many of those facing the BBC might have been foreseen.
>
> *Liverpool Echo*, 7 September 1939

For many listeners, it seemed not to matter too much whether their set was on or off. Radio dealers were plagued with complaints that the BBC transmissions were fading badly. This turned out not to be due to faulty sets, but to the BBC transmitting programmes from stations in the north of England and Scotland, rather than those nearer their main audience (and the enemy – possibly to stop them being used as direction-finding beacons by the Germans). It meant, however, that in parts of England reception of the German broadcasts was clearer than the home-grown article. There were also complaints that the BBC, by limiting itself to two broadcast wavelengths, encouraged propaganda, by leaving the rest of the bandwidth open to the enemy.

The Germans even had the temerity to broadcast some of their propaganda programmes on the BBC North frequency. Some German stations purported to be the voice of disaffected British opinion, prompting this warning from the BBC:

> The Nazis are still attempting to deceive British listeners by the use of a station calling itself 'The New British Broadcasting Station', and a warning that the station is in Germany and that it issues only enemy broadcasts was given in a BBC announcement in the news bulletin today.
>
> 'We believe that the percentage of people who listen in to these broadcasts is comparatively small' an official of the BBC told the *Echo*. 'The majority of people know that they come from Germany and listen into them more out of curiosity than for any other reason. Others may not know the truth and are thus warned'.
>
> *Liverpool Echo*,
> 26 June 1940

While the Germans made it a criminal offence to listen to foreign broadcasts, Britain relied on appeals to our better nature. This came from the Ministry of Information:

> WHAT DO I DO … if I come across German or Italian broadcasts while tuning my wireless? I say to myself 'Now this blighter wants me to listen to him. Am I going to do what he wants?' I remember that German lies over the air are like parachute troops dropping on Britain – they are all part of the plan to get us down – which they won't. I remember no one can trust a word the Haw-Haws say. So, just to make them waste their time, I switch 'em off or tune 'em out!
>
> Quoted in the *Oxford Times*, 9 August 1940

Notwithstanding the complaints about the corporation's dullness, the headline in the *Oxford Mail* in the first week of war was 'BBC GOING GAY'. It was announced that on Sunday evenings, at 11.30 p.m. they would present dance music on gramophone records. This would be the first time in the history of the BBC that dance music as such had been broadcast on a Sunday. Under Lord Reith's rule as Director General (which only ended shortly before the outbreak of war), control of all

B.B.C. HOME SERVICE

Owing to the B.B.C. change of wavelengths, many people are unable to receive the programmes satisfactory—some not at all.

In the first case this may only be a slight deterioration in the performance of your receiver caused by continual usage and can be easily rectified. K. H. Bushell has had considerable experience with radio defects of all kinds—let him attend to your set—charges are very reasonable.

To receive the revised programmes perfectly, we cannot do more than recommend an up-to-date **1940** model.

The present News Bulletins and Announcements are very important—you should not miss hearing them.

Consult K. H. Busnell about your present receiver, or ask his advice regarding a new one without delay.

K. H. BUSHELL

THE RADIO SHOP, 33, DUKE STREET, HENLEY

No mention of the BBC changing transmitters, just a sales pitch for the public to buy new radios.

Sunday programming had been the responsibility of the corporation's Director of Religion. But the new Director General, F.W. Ogilvie, had brought in a progressive lightening of Sunday programming, with parlour games and popular drama. But few listeners had expected dance music to make its appearance in this way.

From March 1939, the German station *Reichssender* began broadcasting the news in English every evening. Its aim, the Germans said, was 'to give the listener in foreign lands something quite new – the truth'. German radio also gave us one of the most famous names in wartime broadcasting – Lord Haw-Haw.

Some found him sinister, others comical, but many thought there was some truth in what he said. He became in a strange way something of a celebrity: there was a comedy review named after him; the Western Brothers had a hit with 'Lord Haw-Haw the humbug of Hamburg'; and Smiths Clocks advertised 'Don't risk missing Haw-Haw. Get a clock that shows the right time always, unquestionably' (reference to an alleged wartime propaganda coup in which Haw-Haw purported to know that a British town hall clock was running a few minutes slow).

The name Haw-Haw was coined by Jonah Barrington, radio critic of the *Daily Express*, who:

> A gent I'd like to meet is moaning periodically from Zeesen [A German radio station]. He speaks English of the haw-haw damit-get-out-of-my-way variety, and his strong suit is gentlemanly indignation.
>
> *Daily Express*, 14 September 1939

The voice Barrington first heard was probably a German named Wolff Mittler, but it was an American-born son of Irish emigrant parents, William Joyce, who came to be associated with the name Lord Haw-Haw. He was a former deputy leader of the British Union of Fascists, who left them to form his even more extreme National Socialist League and who fled to Germany as war was breaking out.

Whilst the British Government did not make it illegal to listen in to enemy broadcasts, repeating them so as to spread alarm and despondency was another matter – and misrepresenting them so as to make the alarm and despondency greater was even worse. This was the charge facing Sidney House, an employee of the Mansfield Labour Exchange, when he appeared before the court in June 1940. He was heard to tell people that Lord Haw-Haw's latest broadcast had contained certain details of the occupation of Mansfield schools. Given that the decision to which the alleged broadcast referred had been made in Mansfield only just over an hour before the broadcast, not even the omnipresent Haw-Haw could be expected to have laid his hands on the information so quickly. House was forced to concede that he had not even heard the broadcast referred to, and was simply repeating what he had overheard other people say. He was fined £10 with 5 guineas costs, and was told he was lucky to have avoided a prison sentence.

Whether one hated, feared or mocked him, Haw-Haw became quite an institution in the early period of the war in particular, such that the Bishop of Bristol felt it necessary to pronounce on the subject:

> It is my firm belief that these rumours (about what Haw-Haw was alleged to have said) are put about by Fifth Columnists in an attempt to disturb and upset us. I do not believe that any such things have even been broadcast at all. I make it a practice to listen to Haw-Haw's broadcasts from time to time, because I want to find out the kind of stuff which the German propaganda machine is putting across for English folk to listen to.
>
> Never once have I heard him say anything remotely resembling the kind of things which people constantly tell one

> another that their uncle or aunt or a friend of theirs heard him say last night.
>
> *Swindon Advertiser*, 2 January 1941

Joyce's British connections led to a good deal of misinformation circulating about his supposed contacts and relatives in this country. The *Hants and Berks Gazette* was by no means the only paper to pick up on such stories. In July 1940, they were happy to quash the rumour that was circulating, that a pillar of Basingstoke society, a Mr Arnold Joice, had been unmasked as Lord Haw-Haw's brother and arrested. As they pointed out, the name was not even spelt the same way. There is more about Haw-Haw and the supposed British Fifth Column in a later chapter.

Against Haw-Haw was posed possibly the BBC's most iconic wartime comedy show, *ITMA* (short for *It's That Man Again*). 'That Man' was a Liverpool variety comedian, Tommy Handley, who in the first wartime series of the programme played the Minister of Aggravation and Mysteries at the Office of the Twerps (a thinly disguised version of the hapless Ministry of Information, which had the unenviable task of communicating much of the welter of wartime regulation to the public). Handley's version attracted a huge listening public:

> Good evening, Great Britain. As Minister of Aggravation it is my duty tonight on the umpteenth day of the war against depression to explain to you that I have 700 further restrictions to impose on you. Here in the heart of the country I have been able to think out some of the most irritating regulations you've ever heard of.
>
> *ITMA*

Other wartime series were set in the rundown seaside resort of Foaming-at-the-Mouth. It was a show that feasted on catchphrases, with charlady Mrs Mopp asking 'Can I do yer now, sir?'

No new radio sets for the general public – business users only.

and Colonel Chinstrap slurring drunkenly 'I don't mind if I do'. It even had its own German spy, Funf ('this is Funf speaking'). Other catchphrases from the show filtered down into daily language – 'ta-ta for now' (abbreviated to TTFN), 'it's only being so cheerful as keeps me going' (spoken by a character called Mona Lott) and 'after you Claude; no after you, Cecil'. The humour may not have weathered well but, in its day, volunteer organisations found it extremely difficult to get people to turn out on Thursdays – *ITMA* night.

However, by 1942, some were predicting a crisis on the broadcasting front. It was reported that no new wireless sets had been made for domestic consumption since 1941 and spare parts for existing sets were in equally short supply. Moreover, anyone with expertise in repairing radios tended to be in great demand by the armed forces. It was forecast that, if something was not done, by 1943, 2 million of the nation's sets (on which the government relied heavily for communicating with the public) could be out of order. The electrical company Murphy produced a leaflet telling listeners how to carry out do-it-yourself repairs (if the spare parts could be obtained). At the same time, the local press up and down the country carried requests for spare radios to be donated to hospitals, far-flung military outposts and other deserving causes.

Many in the entertainment business wondered what future there was for them in wartime Britain, particularly when the outbreak of hostilities saw all places of entertainment temporarily closed down. The young singer with Ambrose and his orchestra lamented that 'just as I am beginning to get well-known, bang goes my career'. But Vera Lynn would find that the war years did no harm at all to her prospects.

Football and Other Sports

> Football enthusiasts will be pleased to hear that this year arrangements are being made by the LMS Railway to provide cheap travel for the increasing number of supporters who want to follow away matches as well as home games.
>
> *Bucks Herald*, 25 August 1939

Like so many leisure activities, professional football was one of the victims of the government's blanket ban on mass entertainments, introduced as war broke out. However, the authorities very quickly realised that leisure activities were going to be important for the maintenance of morale. The ban was relaxed, but the version of football that emerged during the war years was very different to its peacetime counterpart.

For a start, many of the players disappeared. Fit young men, like professional footballers, were just what the armed forces were looking for, and there was a rush from the football stadium to the recruiting office. The entire Bolton Wanderers side was one that signed up en bloc (all but one of them surviving the war). In all, some 783 professional footballers joined the forces during the war years. Others, finding themselves unemployed, returned to their places of origin. As we will see, this had some interesting consequences for team selection. The lifting of the initial ban left teams scrabbling around, frantically trying to contact their scattered players by telegram, or revealing their preferred team selection to the press in the hope that their missing players would read of their selection and make their way to the ground on the appointed day. Reading's first wartime fixture was a 4-0 defeat by First Division Chelsea. The reports said some of the Reading side looked a little fatigued, a fact which became less surprising when we learned that six of the Reading team had been working in factories until 1 a.m. that morning.

As with every other aspect of wartime life, football was subject to minute regulation. In relation to crowds:

> In neutral and reception areas the proposed arrangements must first be reported to the local police headquarters. No general limit on the number of spectators to be admitted

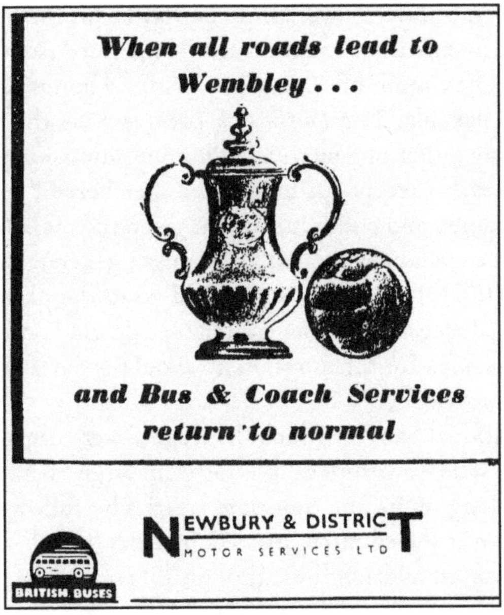

The FA Cup, one of the victims of the war.

> has been fixed, but the Chief Constable may for special reasons impose a limit on any one ground. In evacuation areas the spectators at any one match must not exceed 8,000 in number; or half the capacity of the ground, whichever is less (though, where the ground had a capacity of 60,000 or more, the Chief Constable had the discretion to increase capacity to 15,000). But in every case: Spectators must be evenly distributed in the stands and terraces available.
>
> *Portsmouth Evening News*, 21 September 1939

The professional status of the wartime game also became a subject of debate. Were the clubs to donate any profits to charity and the players to be asked to play for nothing? This would be a reversion back to the wholly amateur days before 1888 and the setting up of the Football League. Or was it to be conducted on a commercial basis, with the players being paid (in which case, some felt, the players would in some way be profiteering from the war)? Eventually it was decided that players' pay would be fixed at a maximum of 30*s* a week, with no bonuses or other expenses payable. The *Portsmouth Evening News* thought this level of pay rather ungenerous. Minimum admission fees were to be set at 1*s* (except for uniformed members of the armed forces, women and children) which, given the maximum permitted gate even in evacuated areas, might generate takings of £300–£400. Of this, only £33 could go to the players. One commercial aspect of the game was closed down. Football pools were suspended for the duration, to avoid the extra burden on the postal service.

The national basis on which the leagues were organised was scrapped. The government did not want large bodies of supporters clogging up the transport arteries by following their teams all over the country. Instead, matches (which were officially counted as friendlies, though there were varieties of league and cup competitions) were organised on a regional basis. The theory was that no club should ideally have to travel more than 50 miles to an away fixture. One consequence of this was that some of the biggest names in football – Arsenal or Manchester United – could find themselves facing some very unfamiliar teams, such as Clapton Orient or New Brighton, to take two examples. In fact, one of these unfamiliar sides – Lovells Athletic, a works team from a Newport sweet factory – ended up winning the League West for three years in a row. This meant that a team like Portsmouth, who fell outside the catchment area for London, would have been limited to matches with teams within a radius defined by Brighton, Bournemouth and Guildford. The 50-mile rule was later relaxed, provided the team could make the round trip to their away match in a single day. But outlying clubs still found themselves in difficulty in finding suitable opposition that could still be reached. The chairman of Norwich City was particularly critical of the London clubs in deciding to organise a cup competition among themselves, leaving his team without any opposition and forcing them to close down. He told them: 'We have the players. We have the supporters. All we want is the games.'

Similarly the FA Cup was suspended, which meant that the 1939 holders, Portsmouth, held it until 1946. It was replaced by the Football League War Cup, for which the winning team was rewarded with War Savings Certificates, rather than medals. These new competitions did not always fire the imagination of the spectators; when Millwall played Tottenham Hotspur in a London cup tie in January 1941 (one of only two matches to be played in the south of England that day) they drew a crowd of just 600.

The blackout naturally meant that floodlit evening matches were ruled out, and initially the authorities only allowed matches to be played on Saturdays and Bank Holidays. This restriction lasted until September 1940, when the authorities realised that this was denying hard-pressed war workers on a six-day week any opportunities for leisure. Thereafter, Sunday matches were permitted. Where games did attract big crowds, the limits on the numbers of spectators that could legally be admitted could often result in thousands being locked out on match day (or, at least, having to climb over the walls of the ground when no one was looking). The attendance limits were gradually relaxed, as the fear of bombing receded. Thus Everton could declare an official attendance of 35,226 for their derby match with Liverpool on Boxing Day 1944, and the England *v*. Scotland internationals at Hampden Park in 1944 and 1945 each drew crowds of 133,000.

Nevertheless, the combination of the limited opportunities to play matches and the initial restrictions on the capacity of the ground could have serious consequences for a club's finances. By the end of 1940, many of the clubs – particularly in the south of England – were in dire straits and a conference was called to try to address their problems. The *Liverpool Echo* set out what it saw as the prevailing ethic of football in those days:

> It has always been football's proud boast that it isn't out for profit. What it makes one year it usually lost the next, but when it isn't, it all goes back into the game.
>
> Most of the supposedly wealthy clubs are rich only in their assets, which unfortunately are neither realisable nor revenue-bearing in wartime. Quite a lot of those that are looked upon as 'well to do' have big overdrafts … in many cases … the directors themselves have had to dig deep into their private pockets to keep their sides going … Now the position in the south has come to the point where many are considering the wisdom of carrying on … I hope some scheme can be evolved, such as sharing grounds and expenses, and maybe with assistance from the Football Association … which will enable the Londoners to weather the storm.
>
> *Liverpool Echo*, 11 December 1940

In that same month, *Sporting Life* announced that the authorities had come up with a new idea to help clubs with their financial problems:

> Another new feature, so far as League football is concerned, is that on Christmas Day fourteen clubs will play home and away fixtures, one game in the morning and another in the afternoon. The clubs to introduce this novelty were Watford and Luton – towns less than twenty miles apart – who decided to meet at Watford in the morning, and then, after a suitable meal, take the road for a second game at Luton … The decision to play two games on Christmas Day when the geographical position of the clubs makes it possible is inspired by the necessity to make up for the serious financial loss on the season to date.
>
> *Sporting Life*, December 1940

To add to the confusion, some players opted to turn out for different clubs in the morning and the afternoon matches. Thus, Tommy Lawton turned out for both Everton and Tranmere, while Len Shackleton tested local loyalties even further, by playing for both Bradford City and Bradford Park Avenue on the same day.

Despite such money-making schemes, many clubs still faced severe financial problems. Reading took gate receipts of just £44 for one game and were so strapped for cash that they only had one match ball to last them the entire 1940/41 season, until a benefactor stepped in. (Shortage of rubber, following the loss of our far-eastern rubber-producing dependencies, would later make it difficult to get the inners for footballs, when their manufacture was restricted.) The club's goal nets were so holed that there were fears of disputed goals and, in the close season, the club was reduced to launching an unusual appeal for bags of leaf mould, for use in rejuvenating the pitch. Even the biggest clubs, like Manchester City and Manchester United, were leading a hand-to-mouth existence. They were sharing City's ground, following the bombing of Old Trafford, and were having difficulty assembling the coupons needed for their team kits at the start of 1945, until a group of servicemen with the Far Eastern

Command presented them both with a complete set of kit. (They were able to obtain it coupon-free.)

For some, sharing a ground was the only option. A number were lost – to varying degrees and in different ways – to the war effort. Manchester United's got bombed in March 1941 and they thereafter became lodgers at Manchester City's Maine Road ground (an arrangement that continued until 1949). In Arsenal's case, their Highbury ground was requisitioned as an ARP centre and they were forced to share with London rivals Tottenham Hotspur. Everton, Leeds and Bradford City were among the other clubs whose grounds were requisitioned. Reading had at least temporarily to give up control of their ground when it was taken over by American airmen based nearby for a demonstration game of the American variety of football. The local paper tried to outline the rules for the benefit of bewildered natives, but one of the American spectators explained them more succinctly: 'A player is allowed to do almost anything but bite his opponent.' The paper solemnly advised its readers that ambulances would be in attendance.

The fact that wartime matches were officially described as friendlies, and therefore did not count against a player's record, was to cause controversy later on. It meant, for example that Stanley Matthews did not receive the twenty-nine caps for his wartime internationals. More recently, it meant that Newcastle United legend Jackie Milburn, who was denied 38 of the 238 goals he scored for the club, had Alan Shearer overtaking him as the club's leading goal-scorer.

At every level, the volunteering or conscription of the nation's footballing talent made team selection a hand-to-mouth process. Which players were billeted in a camp near you? Could they get leave to play, and was that leave just for a home game, or could they play away? Who else was after their services? Sometimes it could work to a team's advantage: Reading, being near the huge army camp at Aldershot, did not do too badly out of the arrangement – one week they held out

"WINGS FOR VICTORY"
On Saturday, 29th May, 1943,
AT
YORK ROAD FOOTBALL GROUND
at 3 p.m.
Baseball Match
BETWEEN
TWO AMERICAN ARMY TEAMS
Admission - - 1/-

Britain's wartime guests brought their own quaint customs with them.

the promise of fielding no less than six internationals in their side. (The Aldershot team no doubt did even better from the arrangement.) But for many clubs it created far more problems than opportunities.

Sometimes a sandwich board would go round the crowd, asking any professional players among them to report to the dressing room – a few fantasists also took advantage of this request, though it generally did not take long for the imposters to be revealed for what they were. Even when a full team was assembled, getting them on to the pitch could be a problem. Bristol City set out with a full line-up for their away match with Southampton. Due to the vagaries of wartime transport they were travelling not in a team coach but in three cars. For some reason, only one of these arrived in Southampton, containing a centre forward, a fullback and a complete set of team kit. The team had to be augmented by five Southampton reserves, the Southampton trainer and three unsuspecting members of the crowd. The surprise was not so much that Southampton won, but that Bristol managed to keep the score to a respectable 5-2. The same could not be said of Brighton, who turned up at Norwich with a five-man team. Their team, similarly brought up to strength from the opposition benches and the terraces, went down 18-0.

This ad hoc team selection could happen at any level. In December 1939, Tommy Pearson turned up at the St James' Park ground, where he was a member of the Newcastle United squad, expecting to watch the England *v*. Scotland international. He then discovered that one of the England players had been injured

Greyhound racing – one of the sports whose operations were seriously curtailed by the war.

during the warm-up, and this Scotsman found himself being drafted into the England side, playing against his home nation for the old enemy. After the war, he was awarded international honours by his home country, making him one of a small band of players to have represented more than one country. Not even soccer legends like Stan Mortensen were immune. He was picked as England substitute against Wales in 1943, but found himself drafted in to replace an injured member of the Welsh squad. Despite his help, the Welsh went down 8-3. Last, and quite possibly least, the England *v.* Wales match in 1941 featured the last amateur player to put on an England shirt, when Lester Finch of Athenian League Barnet played for his country.

Not only was the initial ban on sporting fixtures reversed but, in view of the extended working week for many people, the use of the parks was liberalised to allow local sporting fixtures to be played on a Sunday. The proposal to allow this in one park in Hampshire prompted stiff opposition from a Mr Charles J. Jeffries, who described himself as 'a long-term Scoutmaster and Sunday School teacher'. He reminded readers that the park had been created as a memorial to the dead of a previous war and that the best way to honour their memory was to go to church, not to play football. He asked:

> How can we expect any response from God when we ourselves are preparing to break his commandments? The seventh day belongs to the Lord thy God.
>
> *Hants and Berks Gazette*, 31 May 1940

Quite apart from which, he wanted to be able to enjoy the amenities of the park in peace of a Sunday. Possibly he should have prayed in aid of the 1677 Sunday Observance Act, which (the *Swindon Advertiser* reminded us) was still in force at the outbreak of war. This made it unlawful to assemble outside your parish for any game or sport on the Sabbath.

As for other sports, most were affected in one way or another. Horse racing was eventually allowed to continue on a restricted number of courses, limited partly because some of the other courses were taken over for war-related purposes such as anti-aircraft batteries, and partly to minimise the cost of transporting animals about the country. Newbury, Newmarket and Thirsk were allowed to continue to run race meetings, on account of the large number of horses that were stabled conveniently near to them. Cricket also went on, though, among others, the Oval's hallowed turf was taken over by the army and Warwickshire's ground became an Auxiliary Fire Service station. Floodlit evening greyhound race meetings were clearly a non-starter, but they were allowed to run one weekday afternoon meeting a week. These soon came to be associated with spivs (colourfully dressed street-corner salesmen of black market goods), the black market and other nefarious dealings, and attracted a lot of attention from the police. Only bowls continued relatively as normal, given that few of its players were of an age where they were likely to be called up for military service or war work.

Theatre and Pantomime

> The dancing is well-disciplined and the 'fifty beautiful girls' live tolerably well up to their labels.
>
> Part of a review of the 1942 production of *Jack and Jill* at His Majesty's Theatre

In the theatre, London's big success of 1938 was now touring the provinces, and had made its way to the Prince's Theatre, Manchester. *Idiot's Delight* was set in the cocktail lounge of a hotel on a mountain peak near 'a central Europe frontier'. Prophetically, war breaks out and predictably an extremely mixed bag of guests find themselves detained there; they include a troupe of American dancing girls and their male manager, an old German scientist, an armaments manufacturer, a French communist and 'an Englishman'. The setting may seem contrived, but it won a Pulitzer Prize back in the United States and the advertisements spoke most highly of it. According to them, 'the audience see bared the folly of war and the tenderness and pathos that came with it'. Clark Gable and Norma Shearer starred in a film version of it.

Having trailed the highlights of its Boxing Day 1940 programme on its pages, the Christmas edition of the *Radio Times* felt emboldened to say, 'In view of all that, who cares for the blackout? Who cares if it snows?' But quite a few of their would-be listeners were braving the blackout, for the Christmas pantomimes were enjoying a wartime boom. Three months earlier, the theatre had seemed doomed when the authorities closed public entertainments down. But these restrictions were gradually eased until, by December 1939, even establishments in the most at-risk area – the West End – could stay open until 10 p.m.

Whilst theatre-going was generally a middle- and upper-class activity, pantomime was one form of theatrical production that drew huge audiences from all the classes during the war years. In the days before mass television viewing, its stars were drawn from variety and from popular radio programmes. Very often their stage act or radio format would be carried across into the pantomime. There were exceptions: comedian Max Miller's risqué material got him banned from the BBC and, while he became hugely popular through his appearances on Radio Luxembourg, he was never considered 'safe' to unleash on a family pantomime audience.

It was the great age of the speciality act. These became an integral part of any pantomime, though quite how the likes of Wilson, Keppel and Betty's Egyptian sand dance, the Dagenham Girl Pipers or the Magic of Kardoma ('he fills the stage with flags') fitted into any of the traditional pantomime storylines was not always immediately obvious.

This pantomime bill includes Valerie Hobson, film star and future wife of disgraced Cabinet Minister John Profumo.

Beneath the starry ranks appearing at the major theatres was a whole network of provincial pantomimes, featuring people who were hardly household names even then. Whilst most are largely forgotten today, a few went on to greater things, like the wartime production of *Red Riding Hood* at the Opera House, Leicester, which featured a couple of young comedians named Morecambe and Wise.

The productions themselves may also have had some differences. Many of the popular songs of the day that might have made their appearance in the show had a wartime theme: 'We're going to hang out the washing on the Siegfried line' and 'Kiss me goodnight sergeant major'. The butts of the humour had also changed. Whereas before the war jokes about Hitler had been banned by the Lord Chamberlain (theatre censor of the day) lest they caused the Führer offence, he was now considered fair game. Even the song *Even Hitler had a Mother*, twice previously banned, could now be performed. During the 1939 pantomime season, ARP wardens were also a ready source of humour. At this time, they were seen as draft dodgers who had settled for a cushy routine of inactivity. Attitudes were very different by 1940, when they were putting themselves in harm's way at the height of the Blitz. Nor were the traditional plots of the pantomimes immune from wartime tweaks. In one production of *Cinderella* our heroine left behind not a glass slipper but her gas mask, and Hitler made at least one appearance as the wicked fairy.

Theatregoers would have noticed some other differences from peacetime productions. The management were obliged to precede the performance with an announcement of the air raid arrangements, which they also had to publish in their programmes. The audience for *Cinderella* at the Winter Garden, Drury Lane, would have read:

> If a public air-raid warning is sounded in the course of a performance, the audience will be notified on the illuminated sign in front of the footlights. This does not necessarily mean

> that an air raid will take place and we recommend you to remain in the theatre. If, however, you wish to leave, you are at liberty to do so. All we ask is that, if you feel you must go, will you depart quietly and, as far as possible, without disturbing others. The 'raiders passed' signal will also be shown in the illuminated sign.
>
> *Cinderella* programme

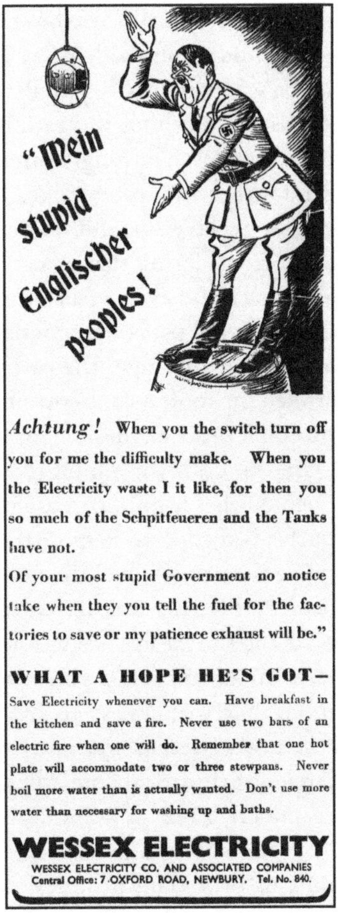

Hitler and his fellow Nazis could always provide a good negative role model for the advertisers.

Throughout the war few of the audience tended to take the opportunity to leave the theatre when a raid was announced. Even when a V2 rocket destroyed large parts of the Ilford Hippodrome in 1945 the audience responded in an exemplary manner, making for the exits in an orderly fashion under the direction of the stage manager, as what remained of the orchestra played them out. Cinemas also had similar arrangements. In Chester, if the all-clear had not been sounded by the end of the programme, the cinema would play gramophone records to keep the audience entertained; they then had a couple of horror films that were kept in reserve and (if all else failed) there were always the short films that were to be shown to the children in the Mickey Mouse Club – apparently *Flash Gordon* was particularly popular with the adult audiences.

By 1941, clothing was rationed and the government set up an Emergency Clothing Committee to allocate clothing coupons for theatrical productions. The most any production could hope to receive was 400 coupons for the entire cast's wardrobes. Considering that a coat cost sixteen coupons, a pair of shoes seven and even a pair of gloves two, 'make do and mend' became a vital part of any designer's repertoire. In addition to the coupon shortage, the cash price of everything had gone through the roof. As one costumier complained, 'Before the war you could make a crinoline for ten pounds. Now you are lucky if you can do it for a hundred and twenty pounds.' Another lamented that it once cost £35 for a principal boy's wardrobe, but that had gone up to more than £100.

The theatre also had the headache of ensuring that the cast was fed. Touring artistes were issued with traveller's ration books and the theatre had to notify a grocer and a butcher, three weeks in advance of a production, of the number of people whom they would have to supply. Catering for the cast from these raw materials was entrusted to the more or less tender mercies of theatrical landladies, whose legendary 'hospitality' became a rich vein of humour for stand-up comedians.

No such constraints affected one performance of a pantomime in 1944. This production – *Old Mother Red Riding Boots* – was performed at Windsor Castle and starred the Princesses Elizabeth and Margaret. Despite it being staged primarily for the amusement of the family, they were able to call upon the Salon Orchestra of the Royal Horse Guards, scenery designed by the Academy Award-winning art director Vincent Korda and help with the sound from the BBC.

For those in the armed forces at home and overseas, ENSA – the Entertainments National Service Association (or 'Every Night Something Awful' to their not always grateful audiences)

– was set up in 1939 to take shows to them. Outposts beyond even their reach had to rely on home-made productions, and many an improvised pantomime was assembled from whatever scrap materials came to hand, very often using the medium to subvert local authority.

Attempts to secure Sunday opening of theatres, to ensure some relaxation for hard-pressed war workers, met with predictable opposition. The Free Church Federal Council opposed it in terms that made it sound like a moral crusade or war aim. According to them, it was:

> … causing great concern to innumerable Christian people, disturbing thereby national unity and hindering what is said to be a struggle for Christian ideals.
>
> *Liverpool Daily Post*, 1 April 1941

Finally, two extracts from pantomime reviews at opposite ends of the scale of production values. First, part of the *Manchester Guardian*'s review of the London Coliseum's production of *Aladdin*:

> We looked for makeshift settings, compensated by much tuneful wit and topicality. Instead we were delightfully fobbed off with a positively pre-last-war excess of bewitching scenery and costume and blessedly granted a bare minimum of contemporary references. The Widow Twankey did, it is true, join the Chinese WAACs for a single scene that hardly interrupted the tenor of the story. Wishee-Washee for a few moments looked after Peking's balloon barrage. Some incidental monster was described as being as big as Goering and something else declared as black as the blackout. But, these half-ashamed asides apart, the pantomime's course is traditional, cheerful, and highly decorative.
>
> *Manchester Guardian*,
> 24 December 1940

Meanwhile, in Reading:

> It was very plucky of The Hospital Players to take on the production of a pantomime in wartime, with all its difficulties, but those who attended the performances of Aladdin on Friday evening and Saturday afternoon were agreed that, taking all these setbacks into consideration and the fact that many of the cast were quite new to the stage, the presentations were very creditable, while affording much diversion.
>
> *Berkshire Chronicle*, 17 January 1941

Christmas

> We're short of turkeys, short of beef and other juicy joints
> But Christmas cheer is flowing here, and you can't put that on points.
>
> *Radio Times*, Christmas 1942

War meant an end to many of the traditional high days and holidays of the British calendar. Bonfire night was an obvious candidate for cancellation, being a bit of a giveaway in the blackout and because the explosives required were more urgently needed elsewhere. Summer holidays became difficult, due to many of the traditional seaside beaches being mined and barb-wired, while the additional demands of war work had left people with little time to take them. Easter, or at least the secular part of the celebrations, had been hit by chocolate rationing. Christmas remained the one festival that united families (so far as wartime conditions permitted) and that people felt they could still celebrate, albeit in a drastically modified form.

Some signs that wartime Christmases were to be radically different began to emerge in the run-up to Christmas 1939. As the winter evenings closed in, the lights on the Christmas tree outside St Paul's did not glow more brightly, but were turned out. Shop windows that would normally have illuminated the pavements were obscured by anti-blast tape and remained unlit, until the Ministry of Home Security devised a means of lighting them that would not give the game away to any passing German bomber.

Now it is no longer the price but the points value that becomes the key sales pitch.

Should Christmas have even been celebrated in such circumstances? Could not the money that went on presents and other indulgences be better devoted to the war effort? Opinions were divided. The Chancellor of the Exchequer, Sir John Simon, said that money spent on Christmas presents was money wasted. Others begged to differ and even went so far as to argue that the spending was not only good for morale but positively patriotic. Someone even calculated that, if everyone smoked forty cigarettes a day and drank half a bottle of whisky, the taxation on those items would pay for the war effort by itself – not that, after half a bottle of whisky, most people would have been capable of conducting the war effort.

In 1939, gifts were not yet in seriously short supply in the shops. France had not yet fallen and the public was encouraged to buy the products of our gallant allies. As a result, many a serviceman based in France received food parcels from England containing French produce. There were still even some German-made goods to be had, much to the indignation of some shoppers.

The culinary excesses of Christmas carried on largely unchanged from peacetime in that first Christmas. Most

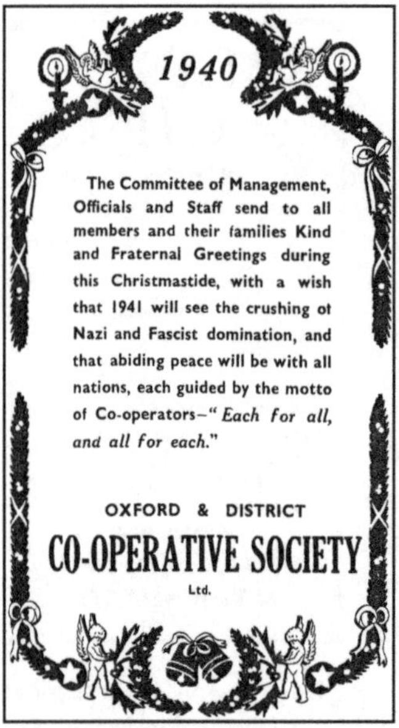

A Christmas wish for the crushing of Nazi and fascist domination.

Another example of a Christmas gift priced in coupons, not pounds.

rationing had not yet been introduced and few goods were in short supply. The mere suggestion from the Ministry of Food that households might forego their usual Christmas ham was very poorly received by the public. Sayers Croft in Ewhurst, Surrey, was one of fifty self-contained evacuee school camps, set up by the government and housing some 200 evacuees from Catford. Their Christmas lunch menu read:

Porc roti et farci a la mode de Sayers Croft
Sauce de pommes
Choux de Brusselles
Pommes roti
****

Pudding Noel a la mode de Catford
Sauce crème
****
Boissons varies

Quoted in Brown, p. 30

You would hardly have known there was a war on, but for the sentiment expressed at the bottom of the menu:

> May God guard and keep the valiant men of the Royal Navy and the Merchant marine who bring us our food.
>
> Quoted in Brown, p. 30

However, the war was already having its effect on the choice of presents. For the children, there were board games such as 'Blackout' and 'Invasion', model barrage balloons and (one that was surely less popular by Christmas 1940) replicas of a Maginot Line fort. Uniforms – a nurse or a pilot or naval officer – were also popular with the children. For their parents, there was the status symbol of a gas-mask case in 'neat morocco and calf-grained leathercloth' for 2*s*, steel or Bakelite helmets, and siren suits for the well-dressed air raid shelterer. Also on offer, though not destined to become a wartime fashion icon, was the Take Coverlet, a cross between a sleeping bag and an overcoat, designed to enable the wearer to walk (or possibly waddle or hop) to the shelter without technically getting out of bed. But already magazines from *Woman's Own* to *The Guider* were dispensing ideas for the home-made Christmas presents that would become an ever more important part of wartime Christmases as shortages bit deeper.

For many families, the biggest difference was the absence of family members. Many a husband or son was serving in the Expeditionary Force in Europe, and hundreds of thousands of children and other vulnerable groups had been evacuated as part of the state evacuation scheme (though their drift back to

National Savings gift tokens – the patriotic choice of Christmas presents.

the cities had already started in the absence of the expected air raids). Christmas parties and other entertainments were laid in the reception areas to try to persuade the evacuees not to return home. Newspapers and other donors funded these, to the tune of £15,000. Last but not least, there were the deterrents for far-flung family members to travel for Christmas reunions, as a result of petrol rationing and the difficulty of wartime rail travel.

By Christmas 1940, the reality of the war was clear. Large-scale bombing raids had begun, a wide range of foodstuffs and other commodities was rationed and the British Expeditionary Force had been roundly defeated in France. Christmas presents were getting more modest, and often more home-made. Soap was among the most popular gifts, along with such items as scribbling pads and pencils, a decorated paste pot (for the scrapbook enthusiast), lengths of ribbon and bag-fuls of thimbles (for sewers who were in the habit of losing theirs). For the children:

> Practical jokes are a great thrill to boys of all ages, who love to catch people out at Christmas with squeaking buns, plates

One home comfort for the shelterer.

which writhe mysteriously and lumps of sugar perpetually garnished with a fly … Hills Rubber Goods … [has] … a whole table filled with these jokes.

Berkshire Chronicle, 13 December 1940

For those willing and able to spend more, shelter comforts once again came high on the list – sleeping bags, thermos flasks, rugs, camp beds and warm clothing. The previous year's dalliance with siren suits was given impeccable fashion credentials when Winston Churchill gave one to the king that Christmas. With rationing, any kind of foodstuff – including home-made – was a welcome gift. Presents of artist's materials and jigsaws were much in demand, but the patriotic choice – albeit not the most exciting of presents – was the War Savings Bond; £9.5 million worth of these were sold in a week leading up to Christmas 1940.

As the war went on, real Christmas trees got harder and harder to come by – the nation needed its timber for building the infrastructure of war and for keeping the nation warm. People relied increasingly on artificial ones, which got tattier and tattier with each Christmas that they were fetched down from the loft. One person who did get a real Christmas tree was the Norwegian King Haakon VII, then exiled in London. In 1940, in what seems a disproportionately risky mission, a group of Norwegian commandos returned to their occupied homeland and came back with a tree for their monarch. From this began the tradition of the Norwegians presenting Trafalgar Square with a Christmas tree each year.

Decorations were also increasingly improvised. Home-made paper chains became the norm (if you could find the paper); Christmas trees were hung with earrings, coloured buttons and spent light bulbs, painted silver and decorated with coloured paper shapes. But sometimes the ingredients of a merry Christmas just dropped from the sky. When the Germans threw strips of aluminium foil from their bombers as a means of jamming British coastal radar, locals gathered it up and used it to decorate their Christmas trees. Mother Nature at least had not introduced rationing, and a festive snowy effect could be achieved on holly and other evergreen vegetation by dipping it in a strong solution of Epsom salts.

Children's Christmas presents by now were also minimal by modern standards, as one child of the war recalled:

> Presents were whatever mum could get: Plasticine, chalk and a slate, crayons and a colouring book, whatever came along. Also in the stocking we might get a threepenny piece and an apple and a plum. I remember paper sheets with a doll and clothes with tabs on which you could cut out so you could change her clothes. Mum knitted clothes for us – I remember she once made me a cardigan. Once she bought me a stuffed doll with a china head.
>
> Quoted in Brown, p. 30

However, for the very rich, choice was much less of a problem. Fur coats were unrationed and from just 10 guineas you could give her a mink wallaby or a squirrel coney; silver foxes were even more affordable, starting at 3 guineas.

On the food front, 1940 was again the first real wartime Christmas. In mid-December the meat ration was reduced from

Fur coats – an attractive necessity for the well-off.

2*s* 2*d* to 1*s* 10*d* per person per week (it was reduced further to 1*s* 6*d* in the first week of 1941). Against this meagre allowance, chickens (where available – they were in short supply) could cost anything up to 3*s* 3*d* a pound, geese were up to 2*s* 3*d* a pound and pheasants 15*s* to 19*s* a brace. Turkeys were so expensive that few retailers even bothered stocking them. However, there was still quite a selection of non-rationed foodstuffs available (at a price) and wines and spirits were widely available. But one essential item was rapidly running out that Christmas:

> Silk stockings ceased to be available from December 1940, causing chaos in Oxford as women rushed to buy up the last supplies. In Ellistons, the counter had to be closed for two hours to allow shop assistants to recover.
>
> *Oxford Times* heritage weekend website, December 2009

By 1941, toys had got even more scarce and expensive. The smallest teddy bear from Hamleys cost 15*s* 6*d*. As a result, outgrown second-hand toys – even some that were extremely second hand – became much in demand and refurbishment came into its own. But some families could not aspire even to this; one child's recollection of their Christmas stocking was that it comprised an apple, a tangerine and a tin whistle. Anything related to clothing – including even the humble handkerchief – was now subject to rationing, and sales plummeted compared with previous Christmases. Even Christmas cards and the paper to wrap presents were in extremely short supply. In the absence of anything much to buy, National Savings Certificates were once again both available in unlimited quantities and patriotic. Food was similarly scarce, and many households would save up either points or actual foodstuffs in the months leading up to the Christmas celebrations.

The other little indulgences of Christmas were also scarce and expensive – grapes could be anything up to 7*s* 6*d* a pound, nuts were in very short supply and you could pay as much as 3*s* 6*d* a pound for walnuts. Dried fruit was virtually unobtainable. Even the non-food trappings of Christmas were a problem. Supplies of French mistletoe were of course unobtainable and even the old-style silver three-penny pieces to go in the Christmas pudding were in short supply – since 1937 the government had been minting the twelve-sided brass variety, which were unsuitable for culinary purposes.

The media strove to make the best of a bad situation:

> Christmas this year will, for most of us perhaps have a deeper significance than ever before … The merrymaking, I hope,

> will be there; the holly and the mistletoe, the opening of little parcels, the coloured paper caps which will go amusingly well with the unusual uniforms which many of us – women as well as men – may be wearing; and although the table will not groan so heavily as at other Christmases under the burden of the good things on it, we may even get fun out of making the little less go a longer way – a sort of defiant good-humour and incorrigible happiness.
>
> *Woman and Home* magazine, quoted in Brown, p. 41

However, even defiant good humour and incorrigible happiness sounded a little too frivolous for the austere tastes of the *Sunday Dispatch*:

> The less merry our Christmas this year the more secure our chance of a victorious and merry Christmas next year.
>
> *Sunday Dispatch*

By 1944 the home-grown sources of presents were in ever shorter supply – even things like boxes of matches were being seen as appropriate presents. But there was a new source of supply. The Allied soldiers who had secured a beachhead on mainland Europe had access to a much wider choice of presents – at a price. There were small bottles of what we would now call designer perfumes for £3 and silk stockings at 12*s* to 30*s*. A typical British soldier could spend three weeks' pay on a small doll and an electric train set would cost an eye-watering £20. Alternatively, you may be lucky enough to have a relative overseas who could send you some of these items as gifts.

The food situation was summed up as follows:

> We are pretty well on our beam ends as far as Christmas fare is concerned. No chance of turkey, chicken or goose – not even the despised rabbit. If we can get a little mutton that is the best we can hope for. A few Christmas puddings are about.

There are shops with three Christmas puddings and 800 registered customers.

Mass Observation

According to the Ministry of Food there were enough turkeys and geese around to supply about one family in ten. For the rest, there was always this recipe for mock turkey:

MOCK TURKEY (FOR 6–8 PEOPLE)
2¾lb stewing steak, 12oz breadcrumbs, 2–3oz melted fat or suet, 4 tablespoons chopped parsley, ¼lb sprouts, ¼lb turnips (shredded), pepper, 2 teaspoons mixed herbs.

Mix together breadcrumbs, suet, parsley, vegetables, salt and herbs to form a stuffing. Cut the steak into two slices and beat each one with a rolling pin until flattened. Pile the stuffing on one slice on a tin and cover with the other slice, shaped to resemble a bird. Skewer in position and cover with a little dripping. Bake for 1½ to 2 hours. Serve with sausages to resemble the legs.

Berkshire Chronicle, 18 December 1942

Much of the Christmas fare might contain ersatz ingredients. The Yorkshire pudding could be made with powdered egg, and the Christmas pudding might include the ubiquitous grated carrot among its ingredients, as in this recipe:

CHRISTMAS PUDDING WITHOUT EGGS
Mix together one cupful of flour, one cupful of breadcrumbs, one cupful of sugar, half a cupful of suet, one cupful of mixed dried fruit and, if you like, one teaspoonful of mixed sweet spice. Then add one cupful of grated potato, one cupful of grated raw carrot and finally a level teaspoon of bicarbonate of soda, dissolved in two tablespoonfuls of hot milk. Mix all together (no further moisture is necessary) turn into a well-greased pudding basin. Boil or steam for four hours.

Ministry of Food, November 1942

Christmas cake, if it was to appear at all, was said to be likely to have marzipan and icing the thickness of a razor blade, and no more than two sultanas. You could even make mock marzipan:

> MOCK MARZIPAN
> 3 ounces breadcrumbs, 1 ounce of ground rice, 1 teaspoon almond essence, 2 ounces sugar, saffron to colour. Mix all ingredients into a wet dropping consistency. Cook for five minutes. Add saffron to colour. Allow to cool.
>
> *Berkshire Chronicle*, 19 December 1941

However, sometimes even mock marzipan was not available, and cakes would have to be given white cardboard sides, so as at least to look like marzipan. *Good Housekeeping* magazine gave its readers instructions for making a Christmas cake that looked like an Anderson shelter.

One thing that was not rationed was patriotic sentiment, and the Christmas editorial of the *Berkshire Chronicle* was one of those that dispensed a generous helping of it:

> If six wartime yules have robbed our larders and our bins, they have not broken our spirit, and the carols will still rise into the misty naves of Britain's shrines and a sprig of holly garnish the pudding on a Christmas day; a tiny tree will be sparsely laden with nondescript toys, but they will glow with the added refulgence of rarity. Absent ones will be toasted (by hook or by crook) and tear-dimmed eyes reflect memories of those valiant sons who made the supreme sacrifice. Silent toasts will be many; but the new year will soon be with us and new hopes and resolves will be born – the road does not wind uphill all the way.
>
> *Berkshire Chronicle*, 22 December 1944

The BBC had by Christmas 1939 moved away from the interminable diet of news broadcasts and Sandy Macpherson perpetually at the theatre organ which had frustrated the nation during the early weeks of the war. Among the Christmas highlights was 'The Empire's greeting', which brought seasonal best wishes from around the Empire and from members of the armed forces, including the British Expeditionary force, for the moment enjoying the quiet of the Phoney War in France. It also included what would perhaps become the most famous Christmas broadcast of all time by the monarch. In it, George VI ended by quoting something which found its way, framed, into the shop windows of the tailoring chain Montague Burton and on to many a sitting room wall:

> I said to the man who stood at the Gate of the Year, 'Give me a light that I may tread safely into the unknown'. And he replied 'Go out into the darkness and put your hand into the hand of God. That will be to you better than light, and safer than a known way'.
>
> Minnie Louise Haskins

At first, nobody knew the author of this piece, but it was finally tracked down to a 64-year-old retired lecturer, Minnie Louise Haskins, who had published it privately for charitable purposes in 1908. She became an overnight celebrity.

And there was only half an hour of Sandy Macpherson.

In the cinema at Christmas 1939, the first British war film had just been released. *The Lion has Wings* featured footage of the September raid on Kiel. The American war correspondent William Shirer later saw it and wrote of it in his diary:

> Even making allowances for the fact that it was turned out last fall, I thought it very bad. Supercilious. Silly.
>
> William Shirer

One of the cinema docu-dramas, produced with government cooperation, to help wartime morale.

Holidays at Home

Some seaside resorts, such as Blackpool, did quite well out of the war. In addition to the extra spending that local military establishments brought to the town, government and private sector businesses relocated there for the duration and the town could still function as a conventional seaside resort, the idea of invasion along this stretch of coast being considered highly unlikely. Most beaches, with their mines, barbed wire and anti-tank defences, were obvious no-go areas for tourists, but a much larger area ran the risk of even greater restriction. A 10-mile strip, including an area from the Humber to Penzance, was liable without notice to be banned to all visitors – you bought a ticket to these areas at your own risk.

In the most restricted areas, pleasure visits were banned entirely. Officialdom decreed that visits to close relatives did not constitute pleasure, and they were among the categories that were still allowed, along with business calls. Not that there were many close relatives left to visit in some of these areas, for the population of some of them fell catastrophically. Dover, faced with the threat of invasion and under direct shellfire from the French coast, as well as having its staple business as a commercial seaport wiped out, fell from 42,000 people to just 14,500 over the course of the war. The loss of activity crippled local business and the local councils alike.

However, more generally, going away for a holiday was considered a luxury a wartime nation could ill afford. In an effort to minimise the unnecessary use of the railways at holiday times, the authorities came up with the idea of 'Holidays at Home' – that, rather than travel, people should be encouraged to take their vacations where they lived. Local authorities were encouraged to arrange entertainments to encourage this (always assuming that people could not all be persuaded to spend their holidays on the government's favoured leisure activity, digging for victory).

Local authorities and other public bodies took to their new duties with varying degrees of enthusiasm, but a common pattern of activity emerged, tending to reflect what the councillors thought people ought to like. The parks were given over to donkey rides, sporting events (for both adults and children), brass band and other concerts, beauty contests, displays of model yachts and trains, monster whist drives, plays

Holidays at home – spent watching your dividend grow.

and open-air dances. The Home Guard displayed their prowess at marching and putting out small fires with stirrup pumps. Those towns with rivers staged regattas, dragon boat races and more esoteric events, such as a tug-of-war in punts, mop fighting in canoes and something intriguingly described as the greasy pole. In Newbury they had a novelty dog show, with categories including 'the dog in the most becoming hat or cap' and 'the dog dressed most like its owner'.

As part of its contribution to Holidays at Home in 1942, Reading University announced that it would be hosting a folk-dancing holiday. Under the tutelage of the English Folk Song and Dance Society, participants would become expert at folk dancing (both the country, morris and sword varieties), folk singing and American square dancing. Country dancing also featured in the line-up for a youth festival, staged in 1944

Looking forward to happier post-war days on the beach.

Part of Reading's Holidays at Home campaign for 1941.

in Portsmouth FC's Fratton Park stadium. The eclectic agenda for this event also included maze marching, pioneer and bridge building, tableaux, gun drill, hornpipe, squad drill, physical training and fire-fighting.

Manchester was fortunate in having its own rival to Blackpool, in the form of Belle Vue. Although some of its attractions (notably the fireworks and some of the fairground rides) were cancelled for the duration, a quarter of a million people went there over the Easter 1944 holiday, to see the zoo, the speedway, dancing and other amusements. The city's cinemas and dancehalls were also packed, and people queued for over two hours to go boating on the lake at Boggart Hole Clough.

However, perhaps the biggest activity generated by Holidays at Home was bureaucracy; in Reading alone, the initiative

No seaside for most of the population, but holidays at home might still need a new swimsuit.

gave rise to no less than four main committees and what they described as 'numerous' sub-committees, all dedicated to the 'gigantic' task of coordinating it all. The initiative was not judged a conspicuous success; Home Intelligence described it in July 1942 as having 'developed into a broad farce'. Others complained that it was poorly promoted and lacking in conviction, and that the events reflected the councillors' largely middle-aged, middle-class interests.

Among the most ill-conceived of schemes must have been the Holidays at School initiative, in which school children were invited to attend school voluntarily during the summer holiday. 'It's been a farce,' one teacher told his local paper. At one not untypical school three teachers had been on duty to receive the influx and only three pupils turned up. 'I am not prepared to say the scheme was a failure,' said the Chief Education Officer. 'The teachers did not lack the goodwill or organisational ability but the children did not want to be at school.' His criteria for failure were not reported by the local newspaper.

In similar vein, and with similar lack of success, the education authority in Middlesex operated a scheme of holiday supervision and activities for its pupils in the 1942 summer holidays. Its main aim was to allow parents engaged in essential war work to continue with it during their children's school holidays, but they were disappointed to see that only 536 out of almost 20,000 secondary-school pupils took up the offer. In many cases, the parents concerned were not even engaged in war work, but just wanted more time free of child care, to go to the cinema and other indulgences.

For that small proportion of the population who took foreign holidays before the war, an unexpected opportunity to support the war effort presented itself in 1942. The government put out a request through the local press for their pre-war holiday photographs of Europe, as an aid to planning a future invasion. Particularly welcome would be contributions from anyone who had spent their holiday photographing roads, bridges and installations of a strategic military nature.

6

Woolton Pie: Food, Rationing and Salvage

> Your butter is to be rationed next month. It would be scarcely possible – even if Dr Goebbels were asked to help – to devise a more harmful piece of propaganda for Great Britain.
>
> *Daily Mail* editorial comment

Before the war, Britain had got used to living off cheap foreign food. Much of the agricultural land was given over to pasture and some 55 million tons of food was imported each year, including 50 per cent of their meat, 70 per cent of cheese and sugar, 80 per cent of fruit and 90 per cent of cereals and fats. At the outbreak of war, the Emergency Powers Act gave the Ministry of Agriculture sweeping powers to bring land into more productive use, growing vegetables or cereals. Farmers had been offered financial incentives to plough up grassland since the spring of 1939 but, with the onset of war, the need became much more imperative. Farmers who failed to cooperate could find themselves dispossessed of their land and livelihood at a few days' notice. In urban areas, parks, gardens, railway embankments, roadside verges and even the earth-covered roofs of Anderson shelters were pressed into cultivation.

The Squander Bug – part of the government's campaign to promote saving.

Along with this came rationing, to ensure equal shares of such food as was available, at an affordable price. The weather, as well as Hitler, conspired against the government's efforts to feed the nation. The winter of 1939–40 was the coldest in forty-five years; root crops could not be prised out of the frozen ground and green vegetables wilted in the frost.

The *Daily Express* conducted a vigorous campaign against the whole idea of rationing, which it referred to as a form of 'folly which is difficult and almost impossible to explain', and called in a November 1939 editorial for the public to revolt against it. The general public were less hostile to the idea if it could provide an alternative to the practice of some shopkeepers, of rationing by price. In a public opinion survey, 60 per cent of those asked thought rationing was necessary, with only 28 per cent being opposed to it. Initially, from January 1940, butter, sugar, bacon and ham were rationed. Other foodstuffs were to follow, including cheese and preserves in 1941, then tea, margarine and cooking fats.

The rationing of foods such as bacon and butter tended to impact rather less than might have been the case, since some of the poorest in society could not afford (despite price control) to take up even their ration allocations, allowing the authorities to increase the allocations to the rest.

One way around rationing, for those who could afford it, was to obtain food from overseas, and there was concern that the rich might simply have their wants supplied by mail order from a neutral country. Firms based in Éire and elsewhere started advertising in the British media that they would supply commodities like butter and bacon in this way. It was made illegal to solicit food 'gifts' or to pay for them. Only genuine one-off gifts could be received, and any sausages in them even had to have their own identity card, declaring them to be either pork, beef or kosher. In one case that found its way to court, a Princes Risborough housewife, Mrs Annie Cooper, had an invalid husband who required a diet high in dairy products, which the rationing authorities were not willing to provide. She wrote to a friend in Éire to see whether she would send her additional supplies of butter. The letter got intercepted by the censors and she found herself appearing before the magistrates.

The initial bacon ration was 4oz per adult per week, which sounded like a meagre portion. (Churchill was shown the ration and pronounced it perfectly adequate, but it transpired that he thought he was being shown a day's, rather than a week's, ration.)

This retailer encourages his customers to buy less.

Nevertheless, the cookery correspondent of the *Swindon Advertiser* tried to present it in a positive light. Four ounces equated to five rashers, and she offered a series of recipes that would eke these out to provide a full working week of delicious breakfasts. However, one thing she overlooked was that her recipes required nine eggs per person per week, a quantity that would soon only exist in a cook's wildest dreams.

Nevertheless, the rationing of sugar or butter was relatively simple compared to a much more heterogeneous product like meat, for which rationing was introduced from March 1940. The government decided to stick with the approach adopted during the First World War, and ration it by price rather than quantity. Each adult was initially allowed 1*s* 10*d* worth of meat a week. Offal, game and products like sausages and pies containing less than 50 per cent of meat were initially unrationed, except by availability, and housewives were encouraged to sample the unfamiliar delights of cow heel with parsley sauce, braised ox tongue and curried tripe. But the rationing process itself was a masterpiece of complexity, as this attempt by the local press to unravel it demonstrates:

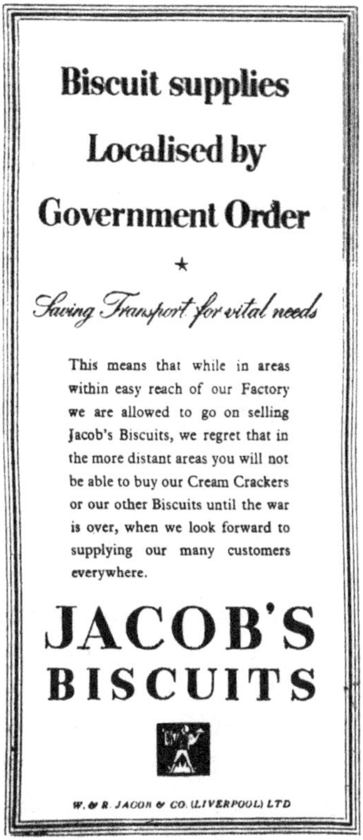

Biscuits – one of the many products zoned to minimise transport costs.

> The first nine coupons will not be used at all, so you may as well cut them out and destroy them. Housewives are asking 'What if the price of meat I choose comes to, say, 1s 6*d*? Can I get the other four pennyworth another day?' If you look at your book you will see that each week's ration for an adult is divided into four. As the present ration is 1s 10d worth of meat for each adult that means that each quarter is for 5½d worth. Now, the butchers can cut meat to the value you require – whether 5½*d*, 11*d*, 1s 4½*d* or 1s 10*d*. Or, of course, multiples of these amounts if there are several in your family and you are putting your coupons together. So the question of carrying odd pennyworths over need not arise. In just the same way, a child's weekly ration of 11d worth of meat can be divided into two 5½*d* worths.
>
> *Hants and Berks Gazette*, 15 March 1940

As a further complication, the article went on to explain that sometimes meat would have to be boned to enable the butcher to cut small enough portions and that, while meat off the bone was more expensive, at least you would be getting all meat for your money.

In an effort to rationalise transport and ensure equal shares of foodstuffs, zoning schemes were introduced, whereby food producers were limited in the areas in which they could sell their products. In this way, a manufacturer of, say, biscuits would not be allowed to sell their products in a distant part of the country which had its own local manufacturer. The scheme for fish seemed particularly restrictive and arbitrary, described by one retailer as an accountant's dream and a fishmonger's nightmare. Under this, a town like Maidenhead was limited to getting its fish supplies from Fleetwood, a port over 200 miles away.

When supplies virtually dried up in Maidenhead in 1943, it led to bad feeling between the classes, with accusations that favoured customers were being given under-the-counter supplies. Fishmongers were told to provide the authorities with detailed records of the quantities of fish they received, to help dispel the accusations of favouritism. By contrast Windsor, just down the road, was far better (and more locally) served by being 'attached' to the fish market in London's Billingsgate.

There were other reasons why, even with rationing, housewives might not always be guaranteed to get their full allowance. In January 1941, a severe shortage of meat arose in Portsmouth. Butchers were hardly able to meet more than half the demand, and were closed for sales of fresh meat by midday Saturday. Those still left in the queue were reduced to accepting supplies of sausages, tinned meat and rabbit. A number of possible explanations were offered; one was that housewives had been hoarding their coupons against an expected change in the allowance, and that too many of them had tried to cash in their hoards at once. A second was that there were too many servicemen at home on leave. They were entitled to a more generous meat ration, which depleted local supplies more rapidly.

The merest hint that rationing, or food policy generally, was going to enshrine any kind of inequality of sacrifice was liable to attract the wrath of the public:

> We are given to understand that the Food Minister is planning to provide a standard loaf at a standard price for the multitude and a superior loaf at a higher price for those who can and are willing to pay more ... under such an arrangement the minority would be better fed than the majority as regards bread. We trust Lord Woolton will not proceed with any such plan. We are all in this war and as far as possible we are all called upon to make equal sacrifices.
>
> *Liverpool Echo*, 3 December 1940

Given the paucity of the food rations, it was surprising that there was any food waste left, but there was – enough of it (someone worked out) to feed enough pigs to provide 1.5 million bacon rations a year. That same statistician calculated that every 1½lb of kitchen waste was sufficient to provide an extra rasher of bacon. Households or groups of households were issued with bins for the collection of food waste as pig feed. Farmers, initially dubious about this new source of food, were quite enthusiastic by the end of 1940, and would pay as much as 25*s* per ton for it. By September 1940, Watford Council was running a pilot scheme in which they collected 10 tons of waste food per week, with which they fed a herd of 260 pigs and sold the surplus to other farmers. Thefts of pig bins even began to be reported and the government had to issue warnings that the feeding of unsterilised swill to pigs could spread serious diseases like foot and mouth. In Fleetwood, one of the communal pig bins was always found to be empty. Eventually, it reached the stage where they put the bin under surveillance, and it was found that the local coalman's horse had developed the art of removing the bin lid, devouring the contents and carefully replacing the lid.

Cocoa – one treat seemingly unaffected by wartime shortages.

In 1944, much to the disgust of some newspaper editors, thrushes started to appear on the menus of some London restaurants. They sought a comment from one chef, who said:

> We don't go in for these small birds. To make a decent dish of them we need more fat than we can afford. Stuffed with truffles … they can be very good but skimped of fats they tend to be dry and rather tasteless.
>
> *Manchester City News*, 31 March 1944

Weetabix has to compete with other foodstuffs for the public's limited supply of points.

The editor preferred them in the hedgerows, singing.

Jam came under the spotlight in the spring of 1944, with complaints that the Ministry of Food's reduced fruit standard was leading to a dramatic decline in its popularity. Surplus supplies built up; one Manchester dealer had a ton of it that he was unable to shift, and not even the government's offer of a double ration seemed to interest most housewives. The newspaper sought the opinion of a typical housewife:

> Jam! You should hear what my husband calls it. It won't stick two pieces of bread together and even the children don't like

it. When I see a bit of plum in the so-called plum jam they are selling, I'll buy it. It's all liquid.

Manchester City News, 19 May 1944

One possible alternative offered by the government was a recipe for marmalade, made from that ubiquitous wartime ingredient, the carrot. An unexpected call for rationing related to the supply of beer; unexpected because it came not from the temperance lobby but from beer drinkers. By 1944, the fact that a large part of beer production was going to slake the thirsts of British forces in mainland Europe meant that there was a serious shortage at

Branded names on soft drinks were banned as part of the zoning policy, which meant that Cydrax disappeared.

Right: The soft drinks industry looks forward to better times after the war.

Below: Housewives begin to dream of their post-war ideal kitchen.

home. Many landlords got into the habit of opening whenever they received a supply, selling it as quickly as they could and then closing for days on end until a further delivery was forthcoming. This left many regulars temporarily homeless, and some of them called for landlords to ration sales, so that they could open on a more regular basis.

Whilst on the subject of innocent pleasures (or vices, depending on your point of view), cigarettes were in almost continuous short supply, but a Mrs J.L. Turley wrote to her local paper with the solution:

> As the cigarette shortage is being felt in most districts, it would be a good thing if the women who smoke refrain from

Bisto – making your rationed meat go further.

> doing so (at least for the duration) and so leave the few cigarettes that are available for the men.
>
> *Liverpool Daily Post*, 1 April 1941

For good measure, Mrs Turley also pointed out that it was unladylike to be seen smoking in the streets.

Elsewhere in the book we look at the problems associated with bus queues, but queuing for foodstuffs and other essentials also got out of hand:

> The main source of the trouble seems to be members of a certain section of the community who habitually spend a great part of each day attaching themselves to any queue they might chance to come across, without even troubling to ascertain the nature of the goods for which they are queuing.
>
> *Swindon Advertiser*, 5 July 1941

National wheatmeal bread was never liked by a large part of the population.

Having got to the front of the queue, they then tried to browbeat the shopkeeper into selling them whatever goods he had which were in short supply, when he might have wanted to reserve them for his regular customers. This led to the heated exchanges in which the police sometimes had to get involved.

Given all the difficulties of applying a system of strict food rationing that was nonetheless generally regarded as fair, one might be forgiven for expecting the minister responsible to be a pariah. In fact, Lord Woolton was one of the great successes of the wartime administration, as this editorial testifies:

> At the time of the last war, the most severely criticised men this country had were those who held the office of Minister of Food. It is to the credit of Lord Woolton that he has so organised his Department and so well preserved the standard of supplies that he has not been subjected to anything like the campaign of criticisms which was the lot of his predecessors a quarter of a century ago … it is a reasonable interpretation of the general attitude to say that our food distribution has been so good that no one in Britain has had to go hungry.
>
> *Swindon Advertiser*, 2 January 1941

SLOUGH BOROUGH COUNCIL.

SALVAGE OF WASTE SCRAP FOOD

THE APPEAL OF THE PIG

PLEASE HELP TO "FEED" ME AND MY FAMILY
AND
WE WILL HELP TO "FEED" YOU.

Housrholders are requested to save all scrap waste food and place it in the bin which the Council will provide in various streets throughout the Borough. These bins will be maintained and emptied regularly by the Council. The necessity of salvaging every scrap of waste food is most essential. Make this one of your contributions to the War Effort. Unusable scraps of **Bread, Biscuit, Cake, Apple and Potato Peelings, Vegetable Pods and Leaves, Scraps of Carrots and Turnips,** should be placed in the bin and kept dry. The Council aims at collecting at least 17 tons per week—it can be done if you will help. It is now a case of " no waste food for the Pig, no Bacon for the breakfast table." Volunteers are urgently required to accept the responsibility of looking after one or more bins in their particular street. Will persons willing to help please submit their names and addresses to the undersigned.

JOHN DEMPSEY,
Chief Sanitary Inspector,
Town Hall, Slough.

The public are asked to augment bacon supplies by collecting their waste food scraps.

He lent his name most famously to the Woolton pie (not one of his more conspicuous successes, despite being concocted for him by a chef at the Savoy) and there was also a Woolton pudding and the so-called 'Woolton waistcoat': 'a warm, cosy internal "waistcoat" of fuel food – or, to put it another way, a good lining of potatoes.'

Woolton had first-hand experience of malnutrition from his time as a social worker in Liverpool and had a genuine commitment to providing a fair and healthy distribution of the food available. Whilst rationing provided a relatively healthy and balanced (if unappetising) diet, and even improved nutrition for the poorest, it was recognised by the latter years of the war that it did not meet every need. In particular, children were not getting enough vitamins A, C and D, and there were fears of increased numbers of cases of childhood rickets. To address this shortage, the Ministry of Food provided free supplies of cod liver oil and orange juice, and a pint of milk a day to all children under 5.

Another suggestion that all may not be well with the health of the nation was the proliferation of advertisements for patent medicines. A glance through the newspapers would tell you that:

> Valderma was blitzing spots, eczema, pimples, barber's rash and boils. Gargling with Aspro warded off sore throats, colds and flu and a variety of other ailments. Dr Cassell's famous nerve tonic and body-building tablets were reputed to have taken thousands of nerve sufferers across the 'barrier of nerves' to robust good health and Thermogene medicated wadding guaranteed relief from congestion and breathlessness.
>
> Hylton (1996, 2011), p. 85

In addition, there were cure-all tonics and medicines whose purpose was not even revealed to the reader by the advertisements. They were exhorted to 'make life brighter by taking Vironita', but without being told anything else about it (other than that it was non-alcoholic). Some remedies, such as 'Dr Thompson's

Products that claimed to soothe one's nerves found a ready market during the hostilities.

pastilles – a time-tried safeguard' (for something or other) actually preyed on the frayed nerves of the reader by announcing that they were in short supply and that you could not have any. Some medicines seemed to be designed specifically for wartime conditions:

> On air raid nights avoid headache caused by gunfire noise and chill from cold night air. Cephos – does not affect the heart.
>
> Advertisement in the *Liverpool Echo*, 10 October 1940

There was even a cure for unpopularity:

> Popular people are always healthy. You see it everywhere – the popular people are gay, debonair, full of health, the sickly

ones are just the opposite. Yet often indifferent health and dullness are a simple matter of Vitamin B1 deficiency.

Manchester City News, 13 April 1945

The advertisement went on to reassure that a course of Vitamin B1 tablets revitalises the whole system, drives away fatigue, depression, nerves and gives you the vigorous health, untiring energy and abundant zest for life that everyone wants to possess.

However, the prize for pretentiousness had to go to Milk of Magnesia, whose advertisement appeared to be offering solutions to all the world's woes:

POST-WAR PROSPERITY – THE TRUE FOUNDATION

Most of us are thinking a good deal about the sort of world we are going to have after the war. We have made up our minds that it has got to be a better world.

One of the best hopes for the future lies in the splendid state of the country's health under the stress and strain of war.

Generally the health of the people is sounder than it was in pre-war days.

Milk of Magnesia has done its bit in helping the fighter and the worker to stay on the job. By stopping small digestive troubles becoming big ones, it has saved the country many thousands of working hours. And so in the peace to come, Milk of Magnesia will be playing its part in keeping us well.

We all want prosperity and to secure it we have got to be fit. Remember health counts most.

Quoted in Hylton (1996, 2011), p. 85

If none of the above could rejuvenate you, maybe the advertisement in the *Manchester City News* was aimed at you:

The Convocation of the Church of England has declared that the practice of cremation is compatible with the Christian

> faith. This sets at rest the doubts of those who wonder if cremation is harmonious with their creed … Also increasingly it is felt that precious land must be preserved for the living and public hygiene strictly guarded … Take steps to ensure that your will in this matter is respected.
>
> The Manchester Crematorium Ltd.
> *Manchester City News*, 19 January 1945

German Rations

There were, however, complaints about some rations being excessive. This related to the quantity and quality of food allegedly being fed to German prisoners of war, particularly as the horrors of the concentration camps became more widely known. Complaints about 'chicken-fed Hess' and 'beef-fed Nazis' became increasingly commonplace. As one editorial put it:

> There are good grounds for suggesting that the German prisoners are getting too much food of the wrong kind. It cannot be good for men in prison camps to have too much meat.
>
> *Manchester City News*, 27 April 1945

It was suggested that 'good' German prisoners might be formed into work details and made more responsible for the production of their own food – a form of Dig for Defeat. After all, the newspaper reasoned:

> The average German is an obedient servant; he loves being controlled; he is happy under orders and finds pleasure in carrying out commands to the smallest detail.
>
> *Manchester City News*, 27 April 1945

Britons were being asked to do the same. In 1945 the call went out for people to attend Volunteer Agricultural Camps, to help meet the nation's food needs in a combination of Dig for Victory and Holidays at Home. The advertisements spoke highly of the idea:

> ... a happy, health-giving break from his usual work and help with the country's food supply at the same time ... Living conditions are good, the work interesting and the need for help is great.
>
> *Manchester City News*, 20 April 1945

By the end of the war, digging for victory meant that Britain was over 60 per cent self-sufficient in crop-growing, but some interesting tensions began to emerge in the policy. In the same week that Manchester launched its sixth Dig for Victory campaign, it also announced a programme of prefabricated house-building, as a quick fix to its severe housing shortage. Due to the lack of suitable alternative sites, some of these had to be built on what had been allotment sites.

Profiteering, Hoarding and Other Food Crimes

> Is it equality of sacrifice when the middle- and upper-classes have been free to hoard food in anticipation of rationing, whilst the working-class housewife is at her wit's end to find enough money to pay her weekly grocery bill?
>
> Letter to the *Hampshire Chronicle*, 13 January 1940

Alongside rationing, price controls over rationed goods were exercised, sometimes with near-fanatical precision. The long-established Basingstoke firm of grocers, Messrs H.C. Ody found themselves up before the magistrates for selling butter at above the controlled price of 1*s* 7*d* a pound. Inspectors observed a customer ask for a quarter of a pound, the correct price for which should have been 4¾*d*. They were in fact charged 5*d*, giving the grocer an

Dig for Victory greatly improved the nation's self-sufficiency in food.

illegal excess profit of a farthing (¼*d*), or 5 per cent. In his defence, the grocer said that he could not deal in farthings, since the coins were virtually unobtainable (despite daily requests for them at the bank). He even paid in aid statements from the government confirming the shortage of these coins. None of it did him any good and their ¼*d* transgression cost him a £2 fine.

Before the war, householders were actively encouraged by the government to keep a good reserve supply of foodstuffs in. The start of hostilities was followed by the Acquisition of Food (Excessive Quantities) Order, when anything over a week's supply became hoarding, and subject to fines and confiscation, as a Caversham housewife was to find out:

> FOOD HOARDING PROSECUTION. CAVERSHAM WOMAN FINED. DEFENCE PLEA THAT SHE ACTED INNOCENTLY
> Mrs Elsie Lilian Carter, of 10A Bridge Street Caversham appeared at Reading Borough Police Court on Monday on five summonses of food hoarding. It was alleged that the

This grocer encourages its customers to stock up – or is it hoarding?

defendant had acquired an excessive quantity of preserves and of tinned fruit, tinned steak, fish and milk.

It was stated for the prosecution that these were the first proceedings to be taken by the Reading Borough Food Executive Officer for food hoarding. An excess quantity of food referred to anything in excess of the household's requirements for seven days. In this case, the household comprised two persons. An Inspector was sent to this address in consequence of information received. He asked Mrs Carter to show him his stores, and she opened the door of a kitchen cupboard in which there was a fairly generous supply of household commodities, such as one would expect to find in any normal household. The Inspector asked Mrs Carter if she had any other stores, to save him searching the house. She replied: 'if I have, it has slipped my memory'.

In a recess under the stairs and in an adjoining cupboard the Inspector afterwards found large quantities of food. These included 75lb. of preserves, 196 tins of fish, 82 tins of milk, 81 tins of meat and 98 tins of mixed fruit. Invoices were produced in court to show that the stores were purchased wholesale from Messrs. Kingham since the beginning of the war. On behalf of his client, Mr Berry submitted that none of the goods had been purchased during a period when they were rationed, so there could be no breach of the rationing orders … Mrs Carter had acted innocently under a

> misapprehension that she was doing the right thing, a misapprehension due to taking notice of Government pamphlets.
>
> In announcing fines on the five summonses totalling £36 15*s* the Chairman, Mr A.G. West, said that the bench considered it a bad case of hoarding. In addition to the fines, the defendant would have to pay £10 10*s* costs.
>
> Mrs Carter was allowed one month to pay. Mr Edminson said that the Ministry of food had the power, if they chose to exercise it, to requisition the food stocks upon payment of the wholesale prices. I do not know if that procedure would be followed in the case of Mrs Carter.
>
> *Berkshire Chronicle*, 6 March 1942

A small army of 900 inspectors was sent out to catch those defrauding the rationing system. But their relentless activities were not limited to hunting down rogue hoarders; any shopkeeper knowingly supplying a hoarder could face prosecution. The inspectors would also go into shops with a hard luck story and try to entrap the shopkeeper into letting them have an illegal supply of something, whereupon they would prosecute him. At least one judge asked the inspector what would happen if a member of the public had behaved as he had done. When told they would be prosecuted, he promptly dismissed the case against the shopkeeper. One of them patiently camped outside the Elite Café in East Grinstead for six days, counting every customer who entered the premises. They calculated from this that the proprietor was entitled to claim 828 points. When his claim for 2,150 came in, Mr Bernard Richardson was fined £5 and £10 costs.

Not all cases of hoarding achieved their desired ends. Some families began hoarding early in 1939 but found that, rather than troubling to go to the shop for something for dinner, it was far easier to raid the hoard. By the time hostilities began it had all been consumed. Another family bought two large containers of toilet paper to see them through the hostilities. It turned out to be far more than they would ever need, but they came in useful as Christmas presents during the austerity years of the war.

The public (and the newspaper editorials) got particularly irritated by middlemen wheeling and dealing in foodstuffs and thereby inflating the final retail price. One example quoted was of cans of soup which left the factory at 6*s* 6*d* a dozen but appeared in the shops costing 14*s* 6*d* a dozen:

> The well-fed phrases of the Parliamentary Secretary to the Minister of Food failed to dispose of the facts, which are notorious. The Minister of Food is well aware that speculation in foods is on a colossal scale, and that the middle men who do nothing but hamper the war effort are making fortunes. Yet nothing has been done to check this food ramp except imposing maximum prices on a few foodstuffs.
>
> *Liverpool Echo*, 1 May 1941

The Black Market

Many commodities were in short supply, but most things in short supply could be had – for a price – on the black market. Combs, candles, light bulbs, haberdashery and pencils were among the many items for which there was a steady demand. The public were warned to be on the lookout for traders who did not

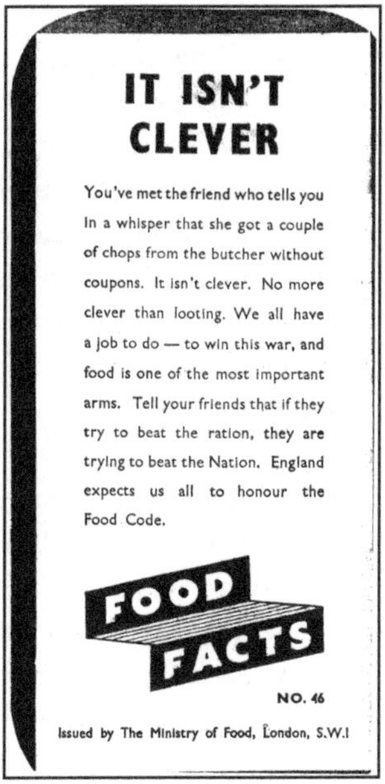

Despite the Ministry's stern warnings, many people saw nothing wrong in a little black market activity.

display the official price regulation signs (though most people would have worked out that someone trading from a suitcase on a street corner was possibly not legitimate). Although black market dealing carried severe penalties – up to two years in prison and a £500 fine – it was an activity that seemed to attract little social stigma. For many, the attitude was 'it's not illegal if you don't get caught'. Headline-seeking Members of Parliament sought even more severe punishment for the offence, up to and including the re-introduction of the cat o'nine tails.

Among the black market's main suppliers were members of the armed forces, who operated their own unofficial army surplus schemes. This got so bad that, at one stage, the army had to dispatch 500 staff with police training to France, to try to stop the problem at source.

Religious minorities, like the Jewish population, also experienced their own shortages in kosher goods, especially when special foods were needed for particular religious events. They developed their own specialised black market. For them the imports of American pork-based canned spam were by no means an acceptable substitute for other meats.

The *Slough Observer* had its own columnist, the outspoken Sweep, whose outpourings the editor felt necessary to cover with the following health warning: 'Sweep's opinions are not necessarily those of the *Slough Observer* – in fact, they are often at variance.' Sweep had his own solution to the problem of the black market, one that would ensure that there were no repeat offenders:

> My own opinion is that there is only one way to stop the national crime of the Black Market – the death penalty. This may sound very extreme, very brutal. But it has often been found necessary as a preventive of looting in wartime, and the Black market is every bit as serious as looting … The Black market is a grave injury to the nation and is nothing less than treason … I would unhesitatingly, but without any regrets,

> pass the death sentence on the rotten, money-grubbing traitors who are weakening the war effort and their country's safety by their dealings in the Black Market.
>
> *Slough Observer*, 12 December 1941

For good measure, he also proposed that anyone caught buying anything on the Black Market should receive a minimum of three years' imprisonment.

Come the end of the war, and even the demob outfit issued to the armed forces as they returned to civilian life became a valuable commodity on the black market. The army put the value of the entire outfit at just £11, but it represented fifty-six coupons' worth of clothing. The suit alone could be sold for £12 and a shirt for £1 5*s*.

'You can't have it' Advertising

Many companies faced the problem of having a much-reduced stock of their products for sale, or none at all. Rather than having the public lose recognition of their brand, they took to what looks today like a curious practice, of advertising their non-availability. Wartime papers were littered with advertisements like that for the soft drink Vimto, announcing that production had been suspended for the duration, but that this was *au revoir* and not goodbye. D-Day gave companies another explanation for non-availability,

Tizer – and no, you can't have any.

Another wartime curiosity – an advertisement that does not actually sell anything.

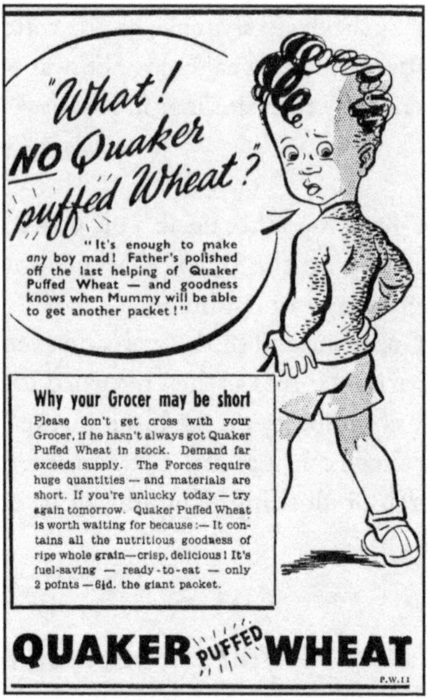

The forces have eaten your puffed wheat.

and the brewers Whitbread ran a series of advertisements saying that as much as possible of their beer was being sent to the fighting forces on the continent, so expect shortages at home. Some even included maps, showing how far towards Berlin their beer had advanced (with some help from the Allied forces).

Salvage

Last week, the railings around Alexandra Park, Manchester, were taken down to the munitions melting pot. Last night, the watchman walked his three-mile beat round the park

Glass – something else in short supply.

with a bunch of keys, locking the six heavy iron gates. He will lock the gates every night until he receives orders to stop.

Daily Express, 20 June 1940

The wartime population (if not the watchman described above) could teach us something about recycling and energy saving, as it struggled to minimise the amount it had to import.

One of the most famous (and possibly futile) campaigns was 'Saucepans for Spitfires', in which the public were invited to recycle their aluminium saucepans as aircraft components. In fact, the government got precious little sufficiently high-grade material from saucepans, but it was felt that it would keep public morale up by persuading them that they were doing their bit for the war effort. For their part, the public were bewildered by the fact that, as they donated their kitchen equipment, aluminium household goods were still on sale in the shops.

At the start of 1941, Mrs Hugh Dalton, wife of the Minister for Economic Warfare, launched a new salvage campaign. She did so by turning an oxyacetylene torch on to the 300-year-old railings at Lincoln's Inn Fields. There was rather more point to the collection of iron railings, for melting down and re-forming into tanks and warships. The country needed 40,000 tons of scrap iron a week to help meet the insatiable demand for the metal. But even this measure was not without controversy. There were claims on all sides for exemptions – for schoolyard

Anything that could be recycled was, in an effort to minimise imports.

Appeal to Householders, Shopkeepers etc.

Hitler's Scraps of Paper

—are worthless

But remember that

Your Scraps of Paper

—are of the greatest valne

Save all your waste paper, cardboard, etc. and the dustman will collect it on his weekly round. Wood pulp for making paper has to be imported. Production can be helped by the utilisation of waste.

Please do your bit and thus help to defeat

HITLERISM

and show him that Britain respects even WASTE PAPER

Public Health Department
TOWN HALL
SLOUGH.

Hitler's name is even used to promote recycling.

railings, to keep the children in for road safety reasons, and around churchyards, to stop farm animals straying into them.

It was claimed that the urban bureaucrats who organised these collections did not understand the realities of country life. Apparently they did not understand the realities of urban life either. Councillors in Manchester complained that the park railings were being removed just at a time when thefts from parks and criminal damage were on the increase, and the loss of domestic railings in urban areas left gardens open to the predation of stray pets. More than that, other railings were needed to stop people falling into deep water, down steep banks or into busy roads. There were complaints that the removal was being carried out by 'hooligans' wielding crowbar and sledgehammer, doing untold damage to private property in the process and leaving behind jagged spikes to impale the unwary in the blackout. It was further alleged that some owners were receiving better treatment than others, even that there was discrimination between one denomination of church and another, with the non-conformists being more likely to suffer a loss of railings. (It turned out that some railings were being left because cast-iron railings responded best to their preferred form of removal – the sledgehammer. The wrought-iron ones required the scarce resource of an oxyacetylene cutter and so had to be left until later.) Last but not least, there were those who sought to preserve their railings because of their historic or artistic interest. For them, the government set up local panels of architects to hear their arguments.

The search for old iron was not just limited to railings. Farmers were sent out to search their fields for old ploughshares or other redundant ironwork that could be recycled. Another valuable resource was to be found in our city streets. An estimated 100,000 tons of tramlines were said to be lying redundant, as authorities up and down the country abandoned their tram networks in the pre-war years (a decision some of them might, with hindsight, have regretted, given the wartime shortages of petrol they were about to face for their buses). London alone was thought to have 40,000 tons to offer up. The body responsible for collecting them offered £6 a ton, twice the going rate, to reflect the cost of ripping them up and repairing the holes in the street they left behind.

It was not just mundane scrap that became a victim of the recycling drive. The British Automatic Company donated no less than 3,000 penny-in-the-slot machines, collected from railway stations up and down the country, which would yield some 250 tons of steel, cast iron and aluminium. In June 1940, the *Hants and Berks Gazette* announced that the twin towers of the Crystal Palace were to be demolished for their scrap value. Survivors of the 1936 fire, they were 284ft tall and offered wonderful views of the surrounding area. Meanwhile, rumours were reaching Britain from France that the evil Nazis were planning to demolish the Eiffel Tower for the 7,000 tons of scrap iron it would yield.

Nothing could be wasted. By 1942, a drive to recycle rags, rope and string was under way, and the Christmas 1943 edition of the *Radio Times* reminded people of their duty to recycle Christmas:

> A word in time about your Christmas salvage. There is bound to be rather more of it than usual, however austere your festivities may be. String and paper from parcels, packing of all sorts, the bones from the turkey, the metal tops of bottles, those extra periodicals you buy for holiday reading, all the litter left about the room after the party – they are all wanted again, urgently. Sort them out carefully and put them in the proper receptacles as a Boxing Day gift to the salvage campaign.
>
> *Radio Times*, December 1943

A Ministry of Information short cartoon film *The Skeleton in the Cupboard* had a more macabre take on the recycling message. In it, a skeleton applies to join the army but, being rejected, seeks some other way to serve his country. He sees a film about the value of recycled bones to the war effort and promptly throws himself into a bucket labelled 'bones'.

Bones were an invaluable ingredient of munitions, as well as having other uses. In 1943, the public were told that they had so far managed to recycle some 35,000 tons; and also learned that this was enough to manufacture 20,000 anti-aircraft shells and 200 broadsides from the 15in guns of a battleship, or 5,370 tons of glue, enough bone meal to feed 68,000 pigs and make 16,000 tons of fertilisers.

The public was forbidden to throw away so much as a bus ticket or a cigarette packet. With the former, littering could attract fines or even imprisonment; with cigarette packets, smokers were invited to decant their purchases into some other

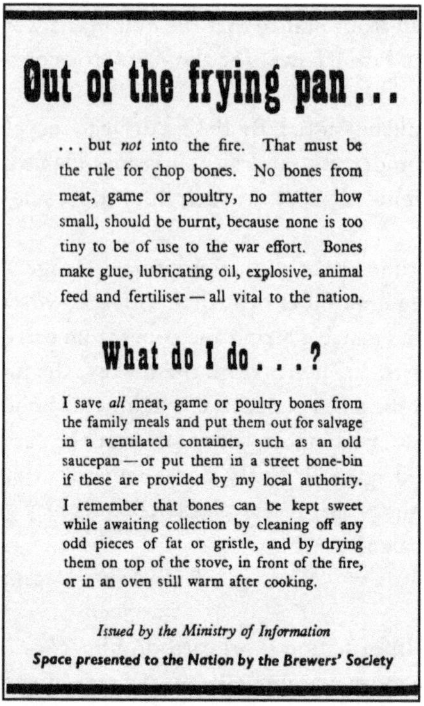

Recycle your bones.

container and hand the packet straight back to the tobacconist for recycling. Grocers were expected to treat the packaging their goods came in with the same reverence they would show to the goods inside them, and return them to the manufacturer for re-use. Even foil milk bottle tops were to be returned to the milkman for reuse.

Anything involving paper was strictly rationed. For grocers, the supply of paper bags for anything other than unwrapped food sold over the counter was made illegal. For all other goods, customers had to supply their own bags. A Reading fish-and-chip shop proprietor, prosecuted and fined £5 for receiving stolen newspaper for wrapping his fish and chips, complained to the court that newsprint had become completely unobtainable

Winston Churchill appeals to the nation to provide reading material for our boys at the front.

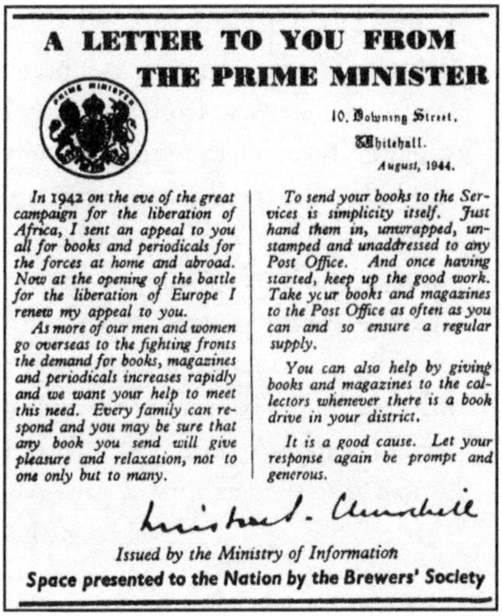

A LETTER TO YOU FROM THE PRIME MINISTER

PRIME MINISTER

10, Downing Street,
Whitehall.
August, 1944.

In 1942 on the eve of the great campaign for the liberation of Africa, I sent an appeal to you all for books and periodicals for the forces at home and abroad. Now at the opening of the battle for the liberation of Europe I renew my appeal to you.

As more of our men and women go overseas to the fighting fronts the demand for books, magazines and periodicals increases rapidly and we want your help to meet this need. Every family can respond and you may be sure that any book you send will give pleasure and relaxation, not to one only but to many.

To send your books to the Services is simplicity itself. Just hand them in, unwrapped, unstamped and unaddressed to any Post Office. And once having started, keep up the good work. Take your books and magazines to the Post Office as often as you can and so ensure a regular supply.

You can also help by giving books and magazines to the collectors whenever there is a book drive in your district.

It is a good cause. Let your response again be prompt and generous.

Winston S. Churchill

Issued by the Ministry of Information

Space presented to the Nation by the Brewers' Society

legally, despite him offering 'fabulous prices' for it. Publishers saw the number of book titles they were able to produce reduced from 17,137 in 1937 to 7,581 in 1941. The government was able to use this as an informal method of censorship; any title of which they disapproved (George Orwell's satire of communism *Animal Farm* being one such) might risk not getting its allocation of paper, with favoured publications like some editions of *Picture Post* getting extra.

Similar controls were in operation when an appeal for books was launched, to restock blitzed libraries and to supply reading material for those at the front. Would-be donors were warned that any titles received which were deemed 'unsuitable' would not go into circulation, but would go for pulping and recycling into something more wholesome. Newspapers were also greatly reduced in size, and at least part of their reduced column space was given over to lamenting their lack of column space at a time when much less worthy causes were being catered for:

A WASTE OF PAPER

Newspaper offices are the receptacles of large quantities of propaganda matters from all sources, and therefore it is easy to gauge how far the wish of the Government that paper should be conserved is being carried out. It is really amazing at a time when newspapers – with all the demands upon them, not least those of backing up the war effort in all its various aspects – are being pared down so drastically, that such a host of really non-vital publications are being produced. If the different bodies concerned are anxious to pursue their propaganda during wartime in this form they should certainly be limited as to the quantity of paper they consume.

Berkshire Chronicle, 2 May 1941

The *Manchester City News* was similarly horrified in January 1944 to discover that free speech had run riot, and that no less than 3 tons of paper had been released for the use of the candidates in the Skipton by-election. Anyone might think we were fighting this war for democracy!

7

Don't Panic! The Home Guard and Civil Defence

> Little boy: 'Oh auntie, you do look funny in your gas mask!'
> Auntie: 'But my dear, I am not wearing my gas mask!'
>
> *Oxford Mail*, 5 September 1939

The newly appointed War Secretary, Anthony Eden, announced the formation of the Local Defence Volunteers (LDV), as the Home Guard was originally known, in a radio broadcast on 14 May 1940. In the first twenty-four hours, 250,000 men nationwide volunteered, totally overwhelming the police stations which had been nominated to receive the volunteers (but not forewarned about it). They could do no more than take names and addresses. The criteria for membership were variously vague (you had to be 'capable of free movement', however that was defined) and minimal – you had to be less than 65 years old, though some extremely blind eyes were turned. One former serviceman turned up at Bromley police station, wearing his medals from the Chitral Campaign; asked his age, he replied 63, which would have made him about 10 years old when he won his medals. When the king toured Home Guard units in the south-east, he was introduced to one company's sergeant major, who freely admitted to being 77 years old and a veteran

The public were constantly being exhorted to redouble their efforts at work, and Oxo clearly saw this as a good marketing ploy.

of the Nile campaign to relieve General Gordon in 1885. One unexpected non-recruit was a man who had been good enough to serve in the British Army in the First World War and who had won the highest award for valour, the Victoria Cross. He was turned down because his parents were not British.

The unpromising nature of some of the recruits did not stop the local newspapers from talking up the new force. According to them, large stocks of rifles were now constantly arriving together with uniforms and other equipment. As for the men themselves:

> BERKSHIRE'S LDV GUARD. CEASELESS WATCH OVER VITAL POINTS. BUT MORE VOLUNTEERS ARE NEEDED.
>
> The night watch … the dawn patrol … silent guards scanning the sunset, keen eyes piercing the morning mists, alert for any suspicious sound … the Local Defence Volunteers are at their posts.
>
> In three weeks, the men of Berkshire have organised themselves into a miniature

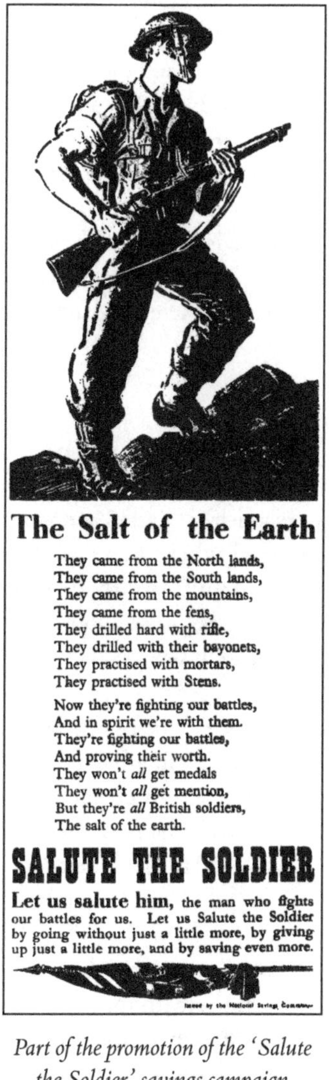

Part of the promotion of the 'Salute the Soldier' savings campaign of 1944.

> army to defend their homes and country from sky invaders – from parachutists and the airborne troops that the enemy might cast on our land.
>
> The Berkshire LDV force has sprung into being swiftly and silently and the efficiency with which its forces have been mobilised has placed it ahead of many other counties …
>
> Their strength lies not so much in their ability to fight like their brethren in the Regular Army, as in their intimate and expert knowledge of the fields, the footpaths, the lanes and the roads in and around their homes … Any one of these men seeing a hostile parachutist or plane descend needs no map to tell him where the danger has come.
>
> *Berkshire Chronicle*,
> 21 June 1940

The public tended to have a rather more jaundiced view of the new force. To many of them, the LDV stood for 'Look, duck and vanish' or 'last desperate venture', and their doubts were not assuaged when they saw the ragtag early units parading, with no more uniforms than armbands and often carrying domestic implements in the absence of rifles. Nor were the regular army best pleased. General Ironside warned that:

> … armed civilians acting independently might well upset the plans of a military commander by their unexpected and unorganised activities. He added that action was needed before civilian residents on the east coast took the law into their own hands and formed their own private defence bands.
>
> General Staff officer to C-in-C Home Forces

For once, the British Army and the Nazi authorities could agree in their disapproval of the new force. On the one hand, the German broadcasts mocked the idea of these untrained men being under arms: 'Under what arms? Broomsticks, or the arms of the local pub, with pots of beer and darts in their hands?' At

Preparing for conscription.

the same time, they hinted at severe reprisals against civilians who took up arms:

> Civilians who take up arms against German soldiers are … no better than murderers, whether they are priests or bank clerks.
>
> Quoted in Longmate

If the authorities regarded the local knowledge of the Home Guard as their strong suit, they saw it as equally important to deny any German invaders such knowledge (in particular knowledge of where they were). 'Blanktown' was an initiative designed to remove any clue as to one's location. The painting out of railway station signs, referred to elsewhere, was one prominent example. In addition, all roadside direction signposting was removed and any shop name that gave a clue as to its location was also painted out. This last regulation could take on ridiculous proportions, such as when the proprietors of shops bearing the name of a town were fined for not painting them out regardless of the fact that the shops were not in the town whose name they bore. The public nonetheless joined in the initiative with enthusiasm, flooding their local newspaper offices with a host of suggestions as to how an enterprising invader could still find out where they were (for example, by looking at which picture postcards or local newspapers the shops sold; displays of bus timetables; even the name of the council on manhole covers

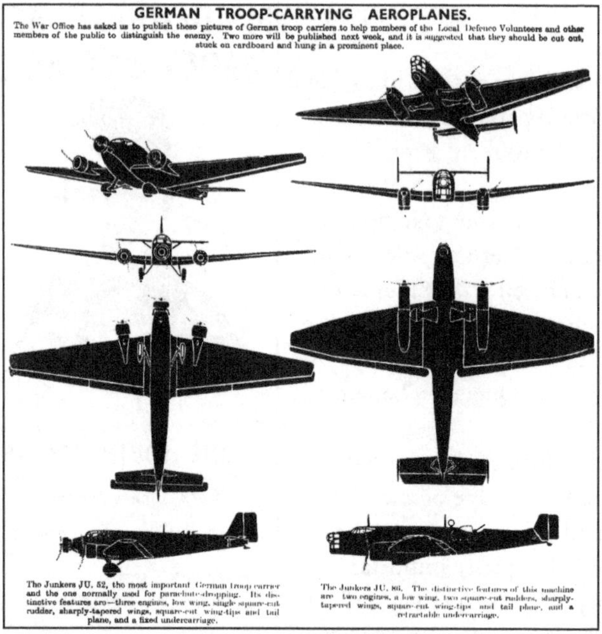

The shapes of German planes were widely publicised, to help the defence forces and the general public distinguish friend from foe.

or council vehicles). There was even a proposal for a novel version of town twinning, whereby all the residents of, say, Slough, if asked by a possible invader where they were, would agree to answer, say, Wolverhampton.

The Weapons of the Home Guard

The new force was competing for a very limited supply of armaments with the regular army, much of whose equipment had been left behind in the retreat from France. At first they had to rely upon bayonets, any shotguns they owned and any domestic appliances with lethal potential they could come up with. J.W. Andrews of the Bath Home Guard made the mistake of asking the Press Association what the correct method was for countering a tommy gun with a bayonet, and was told that he had breached army regulations. He claimed freedom of criticism as a citizen when not on Home Guard duty and told the local press:

> If I am wrong, and I am subject to army regulations twenty-four hours per day, then I am afraid I was badly misinformed when I joined the Home Guard. He said that he had joined the Home Guard to fight for British freedom but if joining the Home Guard takes the freedom away when off duty then I am afraid I shall have to consider my position very seriously.
>
> *Swindon Advertiser*, 15 July 1941

Kent and Sussex were expected to be the front line in the event of invasion and so got priority for such supplies of proper weapons as were available, but the numbers were still pitifully inadequate. The two counties' Home Guards were given a total initial allocation of just 1,500 rifles and 15,000 rounds of ammunition. Distributed to individual units, this led to the ludicrous situation where, for example, the Petworth patrol set out in May and were expected to frustrate any German invasion advance with one rifle (plus ten rounds of ammunition), a shotgun and an otter pole. Worse still, the rifles with which they were supplied had been stored long term in grease and then delivered in sacks that had previously been used to carry sand. Sand and grease were not the ideal storage environment for a rifle, particularly when they were supplied with no cleaning equipment to people with generally no experience of dealing with weapons.

Small wonder, then, that many Home Guards became quite inventive in equipping themselves. The Margate platoon got word of piles of discarded rifles and ammunition still lying around in Dover harbour as the troops evacuated from Dunkirk boarded their trains home. They went down and requisitioned them before the regular army could do so. Despite official protests, they managed to hold on to them until all the ammunition had been used up and the men had learned to shoot.

However, more striking were the improvised weapons developed for the Home Guard. The leader of a Home Guard battalion described these as follows:

> A Home Guard weapon was one that was dangerous to the enemy and, to a greater degree, to the operator.
>
> Lieutenant Colonel J. Lee, quoted in Hylton (2004), p. 42

Among the arsenal of weapons available to the Home Guard were:

The No. 76 Self-Igniting Phosphorous Grenade: or Molotov cocktail. A glass bottle filled with phosphorous, benzene and latex that caught fire when the bottle broke (and, if the wind was in the wrong direction, choked the thrower with poisonous fumes);

The No. 73 Grenade: a lump of gelignite in a tin. It made an impressive explosion (so much so that it was difficult for the thrower to hurl it far enough to avoid being in the blast zone);

The No. 74 Grenade: or sticky bomb. Another glass container, this time filled with nitro-glycerine, covered with a sock and coated with adhesive. It was prone to leaking and breaking, and to sticking to the person throwing it;

The No. 68 EY Rifle Grenade: a rifle-propelled anti-tank weapon. Totally inaccurate and ineffective, and only doing real damage when it went off prematurely;

The Northover Projector: a form of artillery firing hand or rifle grenades with a charge of black powder. It was cumbersome, poorly made, prone to breakage, unreliable and inaccurate above 150 yards. It also let off a huge cloud of white smoke which gave its location away;

The Smith Gun: a 3in smoothbore gun, towed behind a car, and described by its operators as 'a brute of a weapon with a terrifying record for killing its crews';

The Blacker Bombard: or spigot mortar. A combined anti-tank and bombardment weapon. Inaccurate, immobile, heavy and desperately slow to fire;

The Pike: in July 1941 the War Office actually ordered 250,000 pikes for the Home Guard – lengths of scaffolding pole with army-surplus bayonets fixed to the end. These excited outrage from the Home Guard, ridicule from the public and, on delivery, were sent straight into store to avoid demoralising the troops. The junior War Minister Lord Croft was held to be responsible for the debacle, which prompted the following poem in the *Daily Mail*:

> Here lies a victim of them Huns;
> He had a pike and they had guns.
> But now he wonders, gone aloft,
> Whether to blame the Huns or Croft.

Finally, two weapons that were a success:

The Fougasse: a large oil drum, filled with petrol and tar, and set into the bank of a sunken road. It was detonated by a grenade, whereupon it would cover anything near it in an impressive ball of flame and smoke;

The Sten Gun: designed by two officers named Shepherd and Turpin (the EN was for the Royal Small Arms Factory at Enfield), this was a very cheap and simple automatic gun, firing a thirty-two-round magazine at 500 shots per minute. Eventually, some 40 per cent of the Home Guard were issued with these, rather than rifles.

Inventors more generally were doing their bit for the war effort:

> Inventors, professional and amateur, are rallying round, and the Ministry of Supply Research Department reports that it is receiving suggestions to defeat the enemy at the rate of about 400 a week. Some suggestions are hopeless, whereas others are of practical value in developing and improving inventions already in existence. In the hopeless category, we liked the net to catch parachutists. The net should contain pockets, and as the parachutists fell into one of these a bell would ring to indicate a catch.
>
> *Liverpool Echo*, 11 October 1940

In June 1940, the Home Guard were recommended by Lieutenant Colonel J. Ponsonby-Johnson to convert surplus cars into what he described as light tanks. His recipe for conversion was no light-touch operation. It involved converting the vehicle from petrol to diesel, fitting it with caterpillar tracks and armour plating all round, complete with rifle slits for the crew (recommended number of crew – eleven) to fire through. The idea begged all sorts of questions:

- How do you fit a crew of eleven into a typical car, armoured or otherwise?
- How mobile would such a vehicle, weighed down by armour plate, caterpillar tracks and a crew of eleven, have been?
- How much use would it, and its armament of rifles, have been, if confronted by a real armoured vehicle?

Preparing for War

There was a morbid fear of gas attacks by the Germans. Some 38 million gas masks were supplied to the population before the outbreak of war, some of them assembled by schoolchildren in their classrooms. Apparently it was quite a hard task, leaving some of them with sore thumbs for weeks afterwards.

Authorities up and down the country were keen to test their communities' preparedness for gas attacks. To judge from some of the results, it is perhaps as well that Hitler never deployed it as a weapon. In Reading, they chose one of the town's busiest thoroughfares for the test. The exercise went as follows:

> Things went wrong from the outset. A loudspeaker van had been hired to warn the public what was happening. Unfortunately, the organisers forgot that the announcer would also have to wear a gas mask, rendering his warnings totally incomprehensible. Added to this, they failed to use enough tear gas, with the result that members of the public were able to walk stoically, if somewhat tearfully, through the clouds. The end of the event was announced by the loudspeaker van playing 'Roll out the barrel' and other favourites on a gramophone. The gramophone was entirely unaffected by the gas.
>
> Hylton (1996, 2011), pp. 54–55

At least in Maidenhead there was rather more prior warning of a gas preparedness exercise. The public was told in advance that the tear gas would be released in West Street and the immediate residents were told to keep their windows firmly shut. The authorities were understandably vaguer about the extent of the exercise, since that would rather depend upon where the wind took the gas. To be on the safe side, anyone visiting anywhere in the town centre that day was advised to make doubly sure they had their gas mask with them. A similar exercise in nearby Cookham taught the authorities much about the unpreparedness of the local population, and brought down much wrath upon the head of the local ARPs.

Children received coloured gas masks that were supposed to be less frightening to look at, and small boys were delighted to discover that, by blowing sharply into them, the clammy side-pieces could be made to vibrate against their cheeks, making a rude noise. In the week leading up to the declaration of war, the *Portsmouth Evening News* had advice for the anxious mother, worrying about how to look after her baby in the crisis:

> Most mothers imagine that they will be bombed night and day without respite from the beginning of a possible war to the end. This is hardly likely to happen. And the provincial towns have the advantage of knowing that London is sure to experience the first raids. Much will be learned from them about safeguarding both children and grown-ups, so that subsequent raids will not be quite so bad in their effect.
>
> *Portsmouth Evening News*, 1 September 1939

One of the main challenges was seen as persuading a small child to wear the gas mask in the first place, and then to keep it on. Mothers were advised to practise with it before the raids started, to acclimatise them to it gradually. The BBC broadcast similar advice, suggesting she called it 'Mummy's funny face'. The other thing mummy had to do was calm down:

> Children, it should be remembered, are not any more frightened of a gas mask than they are of a fancy head-dress. It is the expression of anxiety on their mother's face, the note of terror in her voice, which makes them associate a gas mask with dire consequences and makes them refuse to wear it.
>
> *Portsmouth Evening News*, 1 September 1939

Military Exercises

Normally, the general public were simply interested spectators at Home Guard exercises, leaving bicycles and prams lying around for the battling soldiers to trip over. However, in the one described below, the public were given a more active role:

BATTLE OF TILEHURST. MILITARY EXERCISES PLANNED. PUBLIC ASKED TO HELP
The residents of Tilehurst will have a chance to cooperate on Sunday May 3 in military exercises between A Company 7th Berkshire Home Guard and troops from an Infantry Training Centre. Operations, which will take place between the Oxford Road and Bath Road, are expected to last two to three hours. The Home Guard will be the defenders and they will resist the ITC soldiers, who will represent an enemy panzer force proceeding in an easterly direction.

It will be the task of the Home Guard force to impose the maximum amount of delay upon the invaders until the arrival of the British field forces. So that the public may easily identify the opposing forces, the defenders will wear steel helmets and the invaders wear forage caps ... Heavy armoured cars will be represented by lorries, and carriers will be used to represent light armoured vehicles ... civilians can help the defenders by reporting as promptly as possible the presence of enemy troops and the direction in which the enemy appears to be going. Civilians are also asked to cooperate in other sorts of ways. For instance, if one of the defenders runs up to the door, let him in at once. If one of the invaders runs up to the door, lock, bar and bolt it.

We understand that fires will be lit at certain points, and that other touches of realism will be introduced as aids to the imagination.

Berkshire Chronicle, 24 April 1942

The press reports following the exercise suggest that these little touches of realism were not universally appreciated by the public:

THE BATTLE OF TILEHURST. PUBLIC SHOW LITTLE INTEREST. DISAPPOINTING LACK OF COOPERATION.

The most outstanding feature of the combined Army and Home Guard exercise was the disappointing lack of cooperation and interest which the civilian population took in the 'invasion of Tilehurst' ... During the mimic warfare little information of the enemy positions was received and defenders were hindered by small groups of spectators at vital points. It must be emphasised that these people were a danger to themselves as well as impeding the troops.

The civilian point of view was put to our representative by Mr Arthur Fenton of City Road, Tilehurst, who complained of brutal treatment meted out by some of the soldiers to certain civilians. He stated: 'During the exercise the invading force had broken through and were sweeping up the road. Quite naturally, many of us were in our front gardens watching the exercise. Suddenly and without warning the soldiers turned into the gardens and commenced to round-up the civilian lookers-on. The front gate of at least one of my neighbours was damaged. Many people were forced to leave their homes, the soldiers urging them on at the point of the bayonet.

'A forces neighbour of mine was on leave and was in civilian garb, when two or three soldiers in civilian garb turned in on him and hustled him into the road. As they passed me, I heard one of the soldiers tell him to "put a ★★★★ jerk into it". I myself escaped being rounded up, as I had recently suffered a fractured rib and I told them that I would stand no tomfoolery. My wife, however, was standing by the front door and she was pushed into the road and had her frock torn by a bayonet.

'One of my neighbours was so taken aback by the sudden assault that he instinctively grabbed the rifle of one of the attackers. There was a bit of a struggle and an officer, on seeing this, stood in the road, yelling like an idiot and shouting "Shoot! Shoot! Shoot!" One soldier actually did fire a blank cartridge and injured his thumb in doing so. I got my car out and took him to hospital in it. Another of my neighbours, Mrs Lightfoot, had a disagreeable experience. Troops dashed into

> the house and rushed upstairs without so much as a "by-your-leave". They forced Mrs Lightfoot downstairs and into the road in her dressing gown'.
>
> Mr Fenton added: 'The whole thing was just like a lot of mass hysteria. At first, some of us thought it was something of a joke, but these soldiers were so much in earnest that they were actually brutal in handling civilians. The whole affair was to my mind ridiculous.'
>
> *Berkshire Chronicle*, 8 May 1942

This reflected a wider national concern, that Home Guard exercises were becoming rather too realistic. One in Windsor culminated in a tear gas grenade being thrown into the crowded bar of a town centre pub, which had to be closed while the victims received medical treatment.

As they got better equipped, the Home Guard took to creating ammunition dumps around their area, to give them rapid access to weapons. One problem was that children broke into some of them, giving them access to real Sten guns, hand grenades and Molotov cocktails with which to play their war games. Four boys, aged between 13 and 15, found themselves up before Newbury County Juvenile Court for letting off a series of hand grenades they had found. The court told them they were lucky to be alive and advised them to join the Army Cadet force, where their dealings with weapons could be properly supervised.

The press were constantly on the lookout for opportunities to publicise the prowess of the Home Guard. When the Manchester contingents of the Home Guard held a march past of 10,000 of its members, the local paper gushed, 'and it speaks well for the preliminary organisation that everything went without a hitch', as if they had just repelled a German invasion attempt. This was somewhat on a par with the coverage of the British Expeditionary Force's departure for the continent in 1939, where the press reported that the entire force had arrived in Allied France 'without a single casualty'.

For a number of months, the blitzed city centre of Manchester gave Home Guard units an ideal training ground for practising urban warfare, and a competition between five battalions was organised there. But one arm of the forces was given a real chance to show what it could do when a gas strike broke out in Manchester in the middle of Salute the Soldier Week. Catering in the city was thrown into chaos; most restaurants could only serve cold meals, some only hot drinks if they had somewhere to light an open fire, and chip shops were closed completely. But hot meals continued to appear without interruption at the Salute the Soldier Show at Piccadilly, where the Army Catering Corps operated 'under desert conditions'.

Communications between units was primitive, generally relying on messages being delivered by hand or them having access to a telephone. In many areas the authorities looked for part-time volunteers with their own cars to act as messengers for the different units. But volunteering was not as straightforward as it might seem: for example, was use of your car for the Home Guard or the ARP wardens covered by your insurance, particularly if it entailed carrying ammunition or other munitions? Drivers were assured by one authority that it was, provided the carriage of those munitions was not a contributory cause of a claim, in which case the matter had to be referred to the War Office. But in Hampshire they took a different line:

> The insurance of cars to cover ARP risks bristles with uncertainties. The Clerk has advised that all owners of cars which might be used during any emergency be sent the actual endorsement recommended, and that they be advised to take steps to see that their insurance companies put it on their policy.
>
> *Hants and Berks Gazette*, 25 August 1939

By the following April, the county council had apparently decided that it was all too complicated, and had obtained group insurance for all vehicles used for ARP work. By this time it was proving difficult to get part-time volunteers for the work, not just because of the insurance, but also the ever-increasing price of petrol (and of running a car generally) and the niggardly amounts of additional ration volunteers could expect to receive.

By September 1944, at just about the time that street lighting was being reintroduced other signs of an approaching normality began to appear. The fire watchers were to be stood down; this would be a matter of regret for some, at the loss of what had for some time been purely social evenings of cards and darts. Compulsory drilling for the Home Guard and other civil defence forces was also discontinued. In the months to come Home Guard units up and down the country would stage their final parades through the communities they stood ready to protect, no longer the objects of ridicule but an equipped and disciplined force of some substance.

8

Is your Journey Really Necessary? Wartime Transport

The Motorist at War

As the last days of peace slipped away, all seemed well on the transport front. Readers looking at their local newspapers may have been forgiven for thinking that petrol supplies were assured. In the very week that war was declared, the *Berkshire Chronicle* announced that:

> In response to many requests, this week we commence our new motoring feature page Monthly Motoring Topics. This will appear on the first Friday in each month and the main article will consist of a report by our special feature writer 'Crankshaft' on an actual road test …
>
> *Berkshire Chronicle*, 1 September 1939

Crankshaft spoke highly in his first (and only) column of the new 1940 Jaguar models, offering up to 3½ litres of air-conditioned, petrol-drinking luxury. Reading Corporation was in the throes of scrapping the last of their electric trams in favour of petrol and trolley buses. Nor did the railways seem to see any clouds on the horizon. All the local papers were full of advertisements for

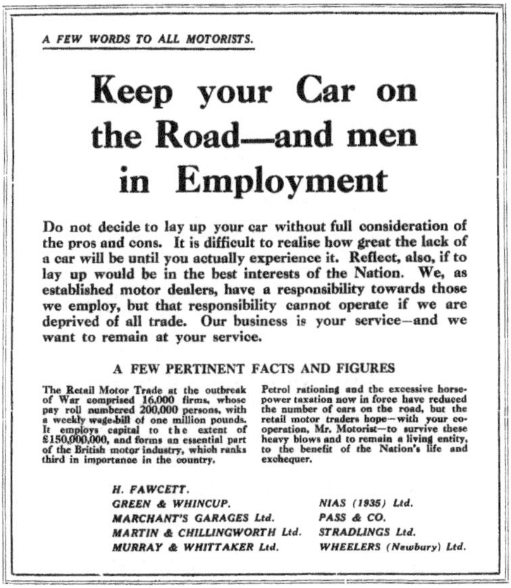

The motor industry appeals to car owners not to take their vehicles off the road for the duration.

rail excursions to seaside destinations, to tempt the late holiday-maker. But things were to change very quickly.

On 23 September 1939, within days of the outbreak of war, petrol became the first commodity to be rationed. The smallest cars were to receive 4 gallons (18.2 litres) a month, rising on a sliding scale to 10 gallons (45.5 litres) a month for the largest (20+hp) models. This gave owners of smaller cars some 200 miles of motoring per month and larger ones 150 miles. The price of official supplies of petrol was set at 1*s* 6*d* a gallon rising to 2*s* 1½*d* a gallon at the height of the war in 1942. The severity of the reductions shocked many motorists and prompted this editorial comment:

> PETROL RATIONING
> Petrol rationing was expected to be severe, for it is necessary to conserve supplies in a petrol war, but there is a general feeling that the present scheme is too drastic and that a more gradual method of reduction would have served best the

> country's interests. Road transport has become so essential a part of the nation's life that it is not surprising that there was some dismay when the basic rations were announced. The General Manager of a well-known firm gave this example:
>
> Our sixteen vehicles have been using 2,100 gallons a petrol per week. According to the basic rations we should be reduced to 240 gallons – not enough to keep our vehicles running one complete day.
>
> *Berkshire Chronicle*, 22 September 1939

The day before rationing came in saw long queues building up at petrol stations; proprietors tried limiting their customers to 2 gallons each, but still ended up running out by mid-afternoon. Those who tried to anticipate rationing by hoarding large quantities of fuel ran the risk of heavy fines. Motorists were also reminded about the strict regulations covering the storage of any fuel they might accumulate, and were warned that it was illegal to try to eke out one's petrol ration by mixing it with paraffin. One alternative for bigger firms was to hoard larger numbers of vehicles than they actually needed, since the ration was made specific to a particular vehicle, and garages were required by law to put the petrol only into the vehicle bearing the registration number on the ration book. There were calls instead for the ration to be made specific to the user and based on a fixed percentage reduction in each user's consumption.

Extra coupons were to be made available for those who allowed their car to be used for essential war work, such as ferrying servicemen about, taking people on hospital visits, distributing essential goods or ferrying evacuees to their new homes. Officialdom required motorists to supply details of their average consumption of motor spirit, the purpose for which they required a supply, the average mileage they covered each month and their average mileage per gallon.

The motor industry, from garage proprietors to car manufacturers, was predictably outraged at the restrictions on motoring.

One of the government's fuel economy campaigns.

They formed an organisation known as the Motor Trade War Executive, which lobbied public opinion through the medium of the local press correspondence pages:

> It appears to be [Chancellor of the Exchequer Sir John Simon's] opinion that such a virile industry as the retail motor trade, with its 16,000 firms normally employing some 200,000 men, to whom a million pounds a week in wages are paid, can be wantonly sunk without trace …
>
> The arbitrary cutting down to almost vanishing point of [motor] transport must result in a decrease of the nation's efficiency just when that efficiency is most needed …
>
> The Motor Trade War Executive ask the Government: Is it in the national interest that one of this country's most valuable economic assets should be destroyed? Is it not the duty of the Government to state in clear terms what it proposes to do with that asset? Has not the motor industry the right to be told?
>
> *Berkshire Chronicle*, 12 January 1940

As the convoys bringing in petrol began to suffer heavy casualties, public arguments broke out about supplying petrol to people for joyriding. The public were asked to choose between joyrides and victory parades and a Member of Parliament said: 'Every gallon of petrol used in this country is mixed with the

Warship week, one of the savings campaigns of 1942.

blood of seamen.' The government's arguments were not unreservedly accepted by the motoring lobby:

> The Ministry of Mines has said that … the economy of use of petrol in this company would release shipping for other purposes. For what, I might ask, might a tanker be used other than the purposes for which it was built?
>
> Letter to the *Hampshire Chronicle*, 27 January 1940

Motor magazine disagreed with the idea of people giving up motoring altogether:

> Love of country is, in war, a necessity as well as a virtue. Nevertheless, those who think that cutting down their tax contribution by, say, £30 per annum, helping to ruin their local garage man, reducing to bare paper value the £150 million invested in a retail motor business, adding to the burden of public transport and, incidentally, denying themselves health and pleasure, is a course well calculated to assist our war effort, are deceiving themselves.
>
> Quoted in Lane, p. 6

However, by July 1942, even the basic ration was scrapped and supplies were limited to those who could prove their journeys were 'essential' (which could cover such things as going shopping in rural areas, going to church or hospital, or taking children to school).

Wings for Victory – one of the many wartime savings drives.

What constituted essential wartime journeys continued to be the subject of considerable and sometimes heated debate in the local press. The police were said to be taking a close interest in cars parked outside cinemas and pubs, with a view to them being prosecuted by the Petroleum Board. In Bray, there was public indignation at a couple regularly seen cruising through the village at the wheel of one or other of their powerful cars (the contents of their garage included a Bentley and a Lancia). This came to a head when they were seen towing a horsebox into a local gymkhana, and the matter was reported in the local paper. The report in turn prompted an irate letter from the couple's London solicitor, pointing out the many good reasons why they merited a petrol ration. These included ferrying their children to school. Even the gymkhana outings were apparently justified, on the grounds that they gave the public much-needed entertainment and raised money for charity.

This just added fuel to the fire, and some of the correspondence over the following weeks took on a decidedly class-war tone. What had become of equality of sacrifice? Or, as one correspondent put it:

> It must be a great consolation to the wife of a merchant seaman serving in a tanker to know that some of the spirit the ship brings is being used to convey children to school and to village horse shows and gymkhanas. No doubt she becomes more resigned to the fact that her own children have to walk or go in a public bus.
>
> *Maidenhead Advertiser*, 7 October 1942

Not even their poor horses escaped criticism. Some correspondents went beyond pointing out that they could perfectly well be ridden to the local horse show; they wanted to know what this family was doing maintaining a string of horses purely for their own pleasure at a time when animal feedstuff was in short supply. The unwritten inference was that a donation to the nearest cats' meat factory would be the patriotic thing to do.

A similar disregard for public opinion was shown by the wife of an air commodore, who was stopped by the police while using her car to go on a shopping trip. It was pointed out to her that there was a half-hourly bus service between her house and the shops, but she explained that, by using her car, she was freeing up a seat on the bus for someone else to use.

Another local scandal centred on an exclusive hotel 3 miles from Maidenhead station, offering 'the world's finest wine cellar' and accommodation costing up to £2 a day. It advertised among its amenities that 'a hotel car will meet patrons at the station'. The paper wanted to know whether this journey was strictly necessary.

For those prepared to take the risk (and who knew where to find it) black market petrol could be bought for 6*s* 6*d* a gallon. In an attempt to prevent the black market, the authorities dyed all fuel not for private use red, but people soon discovered that the dye could be removed by pouring the petrol through a gas-mask filter. Anyone who favoured a particular brand of petrol was doomed to disappointment, as all manufacturers shared their supplies and, whatever it said on the pump, so-called 'pool' petrol came out of it. The motoring

Shoppers are urged to use the overloaded bus services off peak.

correspondents of the local papers tried to persuade their readers that 'pool' petrol was not markedly inferior to the branded varieties to which they had been accustomed:

> I have been running on [pool petrol] for the last 500 miles and have hardly noticed any reduction in performance or extra proneness to knock or 'pink'.
>
> *Swindon Advertiser*, 14 September 1939

The shortage of petrol prompted experiments with alternative fuels, and two forms of gas-powered cars began to make their appearance. One had a device like a giant airbed strapped to the car roof. This was filled with 1*s* 9*d* worth of gas at the local gasworks and gave the car a range of just 20–30 miles (though they could switch to a reserve petrol tank if they ran out of gas on a journey). However, the limited range, along with the instability in winds that the device caused and the limited number of outlets for refuelling, meant that these conversions were not popular; this, and the fact that the taxi companies that introduced them tended to increase their charges to recoup the conversion costs, meant that they soon disappeared from the streets. The alternative was a gas producer plant, in effect a miniature gasworks that was hung off the back of the car. This involved a higher capital outlay (around £65) but offered a rather longer range of about 80 miles. Both types of conversions

Is your journey really necessary? The tank's is.

also involved a loss of 40 per cent to 50 per cent in engine power. Driving styles also changed radically; motorists got used to driving very slowly in top gear, or switching off the engine entirely at the top of a hill and freewheeling down it. This did little for road safety, as pedestrians could no longer hear the cars rolling silently towards them.

The shortage of petrol led to an increased incidence of cars running out of fuel, and prompted the RAC to extend its breakdown service. They would chauffeur the stranded motorist up to 5 miles to a garage where (if they had coupons) they could buy petrol – presumably the RAC man was able to get around

The car roof gas bags were never a realistic solution to the petrol shortage.

the rule of only putting the petrol directly into the car for which it was registered. If the driver was without coupons, their car would be towed to the garage, where it would await their return with the wherewithal to buy petrol.

Hailing a taxi was not an easy option. In London, over a third of the taxi fleet was requisitioned for war work, the fleet's petrol was initially rationed to 3 gallons a day and it was hard to spot the taxis at night, since illuminated meter signs would have breached the blackout.

The supply of cars was initially not cut off as abruptly as that of petrol. Throughout the Phoney War car manufacturers were still turning out some 3,500 vehicles a month for domestic use and a further 5,000 for export. Ford even launched a new model, the Anglia, during this period. The promotional material for this new model, reported in the local press in January 1940, seemed to suggest that it was business largely as usual for the motor industry:

> With the approval of the Government, the British car industry is doing everything possible to supply export markets, and there is plenty of evidence that home demand will continue, although, of course, on a reduced scale …
>
> *Berkshire Chronicle*, 19 January 1940

However, in July 1940, as the reality of war took hold, the government took over all stocks of unregistered cars earmarked for

Ford even announces a new model before controls on the private purchase of motor vehicles were tightened.

export and banned the home purchase of new cars, except for people with a special licence. Most of the production capacity of the motor factories was directed into war work, although, from 1941, the government did authorise the limited manufacture of some small cars, for sale to those on essential war work.

By early 1940, the Motor Trade War Executive had a new slogan:

> Keep your road wheels turning – which was based on the well-known fact that the use of the motor car, so far from being a luxury of that almost extinct middle class known as 'the idle rich', is an essential factor in the efficiency of the nation.
>
> *Berkshire Chronicle*, 26 January 1940

They also had a new target for their outrage – the Chancellor's 'iniquitous' decision to set car tax at the rate of £1 5*s* per horsepower, which had allegedly led to thousands of motorists deciding not to re-tax their cars for the duration.

One man who thought he had the petrol shortage beaten was Mr Norman Sykes, an aircraft designer from Sale, Cheshire. He told his local paper that he had spent three months (and just under £5) building a pedal-powered car that would carry himself, his wife and two children. He, his wife, or both could pedal and the vehicle could reach up to 12mph, though he admitted it was quite hard work until you got used to it. Someone else who at least claimed to have a solution to the petrol shortage was one Thomas Jones. He claimed to have invented a petrol substitute made from decaying vegetable matter, and had allowed several gullible people to buy shares in his 'invention' prior to his appearance before Liverpool Assizes.

One part of the car that was in particularly short supply was its tyres. Following the loss of the rubber-producing areas of Singapore and Malaya in February 1942, the sale of new tyres to civilians was restricted to holders of essential petrol coupons, and even they had to get written permission from the Divisional Petroleum Officer. Naturally enough, a new black market developed, with the owners of mothballed vehicles selling their tyres, until the government made it illegal to dispose of the tyres without selling the rest of the vehicle with them. Local garages were reduced to advertising for donations of worn-out hot-water bottles and other scrap rubber for recycling. For their part, motorists were told by the local press to inflate their tyres to slightly above the recommended pressures. It would give a firmer ride, but would prolong the life of the tyre.

How much tread was there legally required to be left on the tyre? All you were told was that you should return the tyre for re-treading before the canvas started to show through the rubber. Even by these modest standards, three out of five tyres

MG – just one of the makes of car that nobody could buy.

A shortage of rubber forced manufacturers into producing less than ideal synthetic tyres.

returned for re-treading were found to be too badly worn or damaged to be of use.

Manchester hit upon a novel way of storing its supplies of tyres for recycling, after Air Raid Precautions forced them in April 1941 to remove them from city-centre premises. They sunk them in the boating lake of 'a Manchester park', where apparently the water rotted the tyre canvas but did no harm to the rubber itself.

By 1941, anti-freeze had become another motoring essential that was unobtainable. Car owners were advised to drain their cooling systems, if the car was to stand in the cold for any length of time. Generally, spare parts for cars were in short supply and most of the mechanics needed to fit them had been absorbed into the armed forces, so even quite a small accident could lead to a car being laid up for the duration, according to the RAC. But, notwithstanding all the tribulations of motoring, the RAC was also able to report that the prices of cars were up 30 per cent against pre-war values.

A few motorists actually benefited from the outbreak of hostilities: Norman Fairclough of Lymm was one of a number who had his driving ban for dangerous driving overturned, on the grounds that the war meant that there was now a national shortage of drivers.

As the war neared its end, motoring enthusiasts began to look forward to post-war motoring conditions: they foresaw a rapid growth in car ownership, an equally rapid end to petrol rationing and the construction of the 1,000-mile national motorway network planned just before the war by the County Surveyors' Society. In two out of three of these, they were to be sadly disabused.

On the Buses

Nor were things easy for the bus companies. The difficulties of operating a service through the blackout are documented in another chapter, but they had a lot more than that with which to contend. They were subject, like any other business, to petrol rationing; they lost large numbers of their staff to the armed forces as soon as war was declared, and continued to lose conductors to war industries and to other government initiatives as the war proceeded. That same full-employment wartime economy made those conductors difficult to replace. One of the responses, adopted

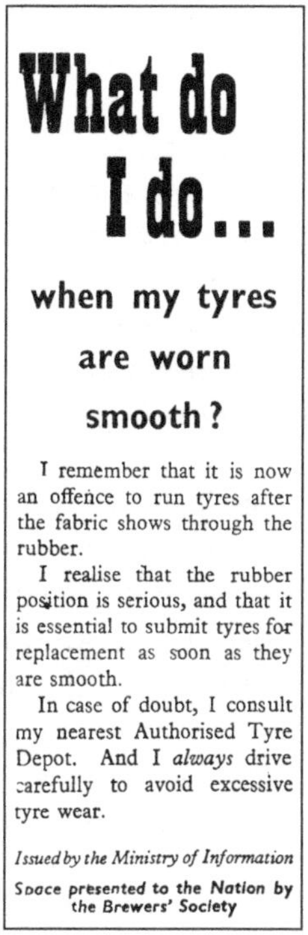

No minimum tread required on tyres – just a covering of rubber.

by most of the bus companies, was to recruit more women bus conductors, but even this came under attack from the *Manchester City News*:

> Our new £3 pounds-per-week bus conductresses are very charming and very efficient. But everyone I meet asks me why young women have been recruited for this unskilled job and I pass the query on to Mr Hill, our Transport Chairman. Can it be that Manchester has no workless men over 40 who are capable of doing a job of simple work? ... I have said before that I am no anti-feminist. But it is still the men who have to carry the family on their shoulders and public departments should think more than once before turning to female labour for an admittedly man's job.
>
> *Manchester City News*, 30 September 1939

This editorial pressure led to Manchester Corporation giving preference to men over 40 above women, in appointing not just bus conductors, but also other jobs for which both sexes might have competed. An editorial in the Liverpool press went further, and seemed to suggest that women were unequal to the task of bus conducting:

> Should Liverpool trams and buses have 'honesty boxes' for the receipt of uncollected fares? Several correspondents of mine are alleging that big sums are being lost to the transport department owing to faulty collection, due to the crowding of buses and the employment of women conductors. The Committee is, I understand, considering the suggestion, and also the idea of inviting volunteers to help on the platforms during busy periods.
>
> *Liverpool Echo*, 14 April 1941

In addition to their core business of carrying the general public, the bus companies were constantly being called upon to support

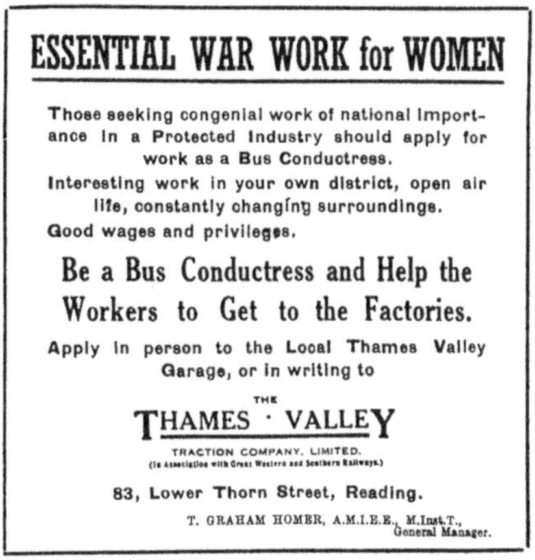

Women are urged to take up an open-air life with constantly changing surroundings – as a bus conductress.

various war initiatives, such as moving soldiers and evacuees about. Their fleet was depleted by breakdowns, due to the vehicles being used so intensively; replacement vehicles were simply not being made to replace them, and those companies that were lucky enough to avoid losses through bombing had to surrender parts of their fleet to companies that had lost vehicles to enemy action. In some areas there were a lot more people wanting to use the buses, because of petrol rationing for private cars and the wartime shifts of population, with both voluntary and official evacuations swelling the population. Small wonder then that bus operations seemed to come in for sustained criticism throughout the war years. If all these tribulations were not enough, bus crews in the Medway area learned at the start of 1941 that they were to be issued with bags of sand and trained to deal with any incendiary bombs they might encounter along their routes.

It was not just the bus journeys themselves that came in for criticism, but also the unseemly scrums that were formed by people desperate to board them. We tend to think of patient queuing being programmed into the psyche of the wartime population, but in Oxford it became such a problem that the city council deemed it necessary to bring in by-laws to enforce queuing. An extract from them is reproduced below, not least as a terrible warning of the meal a bureaucratic mind can make of something so apparently simple:

> 1 When six or more persons are waiting in any street in the City of Oxford to enter a public vehicle in any stopping place, stand or terminus, they shall form and keep a queue or line of not more than two abreast on the footway of such street;
> 2 Where, for the purpose of securing compliance with the aforegoing by-law, one barrier rail or two parallel barrier rails are provided at any stopping place, stand or terminus, the queue or line shall commence against the end of the barrier rail or parallel barrier rails nearest the indication post marked 'bus stop' or 'omnibus stand', as the case may be, and facing the said post, and shall continue alongside a single barrier rail or between parallel barrier rails;
> 3 A person shall not take, or endeavour to take any position in a queue or line otherwise than behind the persons already forming the same, or enter or endeavour to enter any public vehicle before any other person desiring to enter the same vehicle who stood in front of him in such queue or line;
> 4 Etc.
>
> *Oxford Times*, 21 February 1941

In Reading and Swindon they had similar problems. The local press issued a plea for their bus drivers to stop with the entrance to the bus at the head of the queue, so that those who had been waiting longest did not lose their place in the melee which inevitably developed, and a new official was created – a bus queue regulator. They had powers to enforce orderly queuing and prosecute those who failed to cooperate. According to at least one observer, this problem also had a gender dimension:

> The problem is one that, to a great extent, must be left to the general public, for the officials already have their hands

full and an increasing number of women conductors has to be employed.

Swindon Advertiser,
16 January 1941

With queues for everything, there was even a need to ensure one was in the right queue. One couple reported to their local paper standing in line for ages, waiting to get into the Vaudeville cinema, only to find themselves being ushered on board the Three Tuns trolley bus. In Newbury, the cinema queues got so long and dense that they forced other pedestrians out dangerously on to the blacked-out roadway, and Oxford City Council seriously debated banning all queues except those for buses in the city centre. But if undisciplined queuing was not bad – and un-English – enough, things could get even worse once the passengers had fought their way on to the bus:

CROWDED 'BUS TAKEN TO POLICE STATION. READING MAN FINED FOR OBSTRUCTING CONSTABLE
Because people refused to leave a motor 'bus which was overcrowded, the driver drove it off the route to Reading Borough Police Station and asked for the assistance of the police. This unusual occurrence was described to the Borough Magistrates at Reading on Monday when Earnest Hathaway, unemployed paint sprayer of 4, Stockton Road, Reading was summoned for wilfully obstructing Detective Constable Viveash, using obscene language and assaulting a police officer in the execution of his duty. He pleaded not guilty in each case.

Berkshire Chronicle, 17 November 1939

Hathaway's defence for swinging a punch at the constable seemed to hinge upon the fact that he and the police officer had not been properly introduced:

> 'When the policeman came on the bus he called me by my name' said Hathaway, 'and I want to know why he did that. I am not a criminal and it is not nice for policemen to shout out your name. I did not know who he was and I did not know how he knew my name. The evidence is a tissue of lies.'
>
> *Berkshire Chronicle*, 17 November 1939

The magistrates disagreed. He was fined a total of 30*s*.

However, none of this stopped the ladies' page from being relentlessly cheerful about the prospect of queuing:

> There is something friendly about a queue. A cheerful chat-to-your-neighbour atmosphere. You find you soon get to know the woman standing next to you. In just no time you find she's telling you about her problems and you are telling her about yours.
>
> *Berkshire Chronicle*, 30 April 1943

Travel by Rail

Meanwhile, on the railways plans for the hostilities had been in preparation since April 1937, when the Railway Technical Committee was set up to prepare the service for going on to a war footing. They worked out emergency timetables and planned alternative routes in the event of key lines being put out of service by enemy action – for once, the widespread duplication of lines permitted by the Victorian laissez-faire system of railway planning proved a boon.

The Minister of War Transport took over responsibility for running virtually all the nation's railways from 1 September 1939. The public immediately began to notice differences in the services. Armed guards were placed at strategic points around the network, services were curtailed and trains reallocated to the mass evacuation and other war-related activities. Pullmans and restaurant cars were (at first temporarily) withdrawn, but other forms of class distinction were slower to disappear; first-class travel was scrapped on the Underground from February 1940, but was not abolished on London suburban services until October 1941. As part of this process of democratisation, the Southern Railway also took the carpets out of the first-class compartments and raised all the armrests, so that more third-class passengers could be squeezed on to the ample first-class seats.

There was also a good deal of confusion; notices announcing 'services cut' would appear alongside contradictory ones saying 'services restored'. Supplies of locomotives were moved around to meet the differing needs of a wartime service; the Southern Railway, being primarily a passenger railway, many of whose customers would be going into the armed services, was one that was able to loan locomotives to many of the other companies.

The first big test for the railways was the evacuations – both the official and the unofficial ones – in which hundreds of thousands of vulnerable people left London and other big cities. The railways had had a dry run of their evacuation plans at the time of the Munich crisis in 1938, at which time they ran 200 trains, compared to the 4,000 or so of the full 1939 exercise. Between July and early September 1939 the railways – despite other

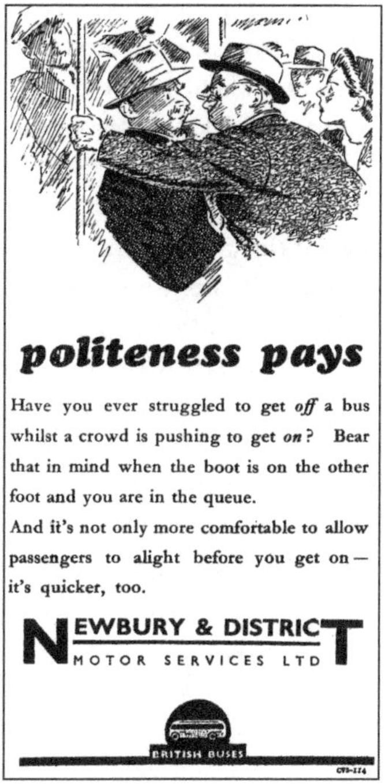

It was felt necessary to pay for advertisements to tame bus queues.

pressures on them, such as delivering hundreds of thousands of Anderson shelters around the country, getting returning holidaymakers home, laying on any number of government special trains and coping with evacuees who were not part of the government scheme – managed to put on 2,345 additional government evacuee trains. Some of the biggest volumes in traffic were heading westward out of London, along the Great Western main line. Evacuee trains were leaving Ealing Broadway at a rate of up to sixty a day, loading up as many as 800 bewildered evacuees and departing at nine-minute intervals. In total, some 112,994 evacuees passed through this station alone in four days. The exercise had been planned with military precision beforehand (at least so far as the transport aspects were concerned); the final decision to go ahead was only made on 31 August and the first trains left at 8.30 a.m. the following morning.

Much less planned was the arrival, the following May, of some 300,000 troops, evacuated from Dunkirk, at seven south-eastern ports. Some 620 special trains were needed in the space of a few days, and 186 locomotives and over 2,000 carriages were called upon to take the exhausted troops from the southern coastal ports to every corner of the country. The Ministry of Transport called it the greatest unpremeditated railway move in history.

Invasion threatened after Dunkirk. Hundreds of railway bridges were mined, ready for destruction if the Germans came; other key parts of the rail infrastructure were painted red, to indicate that they should be immobilised in the face of an enemy advance. The Home Guard was formed, one of whose duties was to guard strategic points on the rail network. Some of the Home Guard battalions were made up of railway company staff. Armoured trains were built to patrol coastal lines in the south-east and in Scotland, including the narrow-gauge tourist line, the Romney, Hythe and Dymchurch in Kent.

Final preparations were made for the anticipated Blitz. Large quantities of materials for repairing damaged rail infrastructure, or for propping up bridges that had been left unsafe, were accumulated. Railway control rooms were duplicated in secure locations and signal boxes were made as bomb resistant as their designs permitted.

The blackout posed particular problems for the railways. The government accepted that they could not function in a total blackout, but the low-wattage greenish-blue lamps that stations, depots and yards were allowed to show – known to the staff as 'gloomy glim' – came very close to the genuine blackout. It led to thousands of accidents to passengers, falling over items in the station or off the platforms altogether, and made the jobs of many railway staff very dangerous. In train compartments, passengers were initially limited to the equivalent of a 15-watt blue bulb, shrouded in a metal tube, which was not even bright enough to read by. After widespread complaints, the railways did at least allow a low-wattage white bulb in compartments with proper window blinds.

Equally problematic was the blacking out of steam engine footplates, given the need for the crew to see where they were going, and various partial blackout measures were tried, such as suspending a tarpaulin from the top of the cab to the tender. The partially blacked-out cabs of steam locomotives became stiflingly hot and it was extremely difficult for the crews to spot signals and the right places to stop in the blackout.

In the stations, the near blackout meant the rail passenger had much the same problem as the bus passenger, in knowing where they were, though at least in major stations they had the benefit of station announcers. Their confusion was not helped by the practice of painting out station names, to fool invading forces. In daylight, the painting out of station names was less effective, since these were often spelt out in relief on the signs, making it perfectly obvious where you were, painted out or not. On the Southern Region, the railway company tried getting round the station identification problem at night by cutting the name of the station out of the blinds of the waiting room windows and allowing these to be illuminated by the waiting room lights.

As with other parts of the war effort, the role of women was vital, as they took on a wide range of railway work that was new to them, including heavy manual work such as portering, track maintenance and concrete mixing:

> The British railway-woman has adapted herself quickly to new surroundings and work which is very different from her pre-war occupation, and she has taken her share of night work. In many cases her husband is in the forces, and she has shown a marked devotion to duty, sometimes in difficult circumstances during and after enemy air activity. She does her turn of duty and goes home to the cares of a house and children. She is making a vitally important contribution to the war effort.
>
> British Railways Press Office, 1943

Maintenance and renewal were cut to an absolute minimum, as much of the capacity of the railway workshops was given over to manufacturing war equipment. The Swindon workshops of the Great Western Railway, for example, were converting passenger coaches into ambulances, manufacturing parts for nine different types of aircraft, mountings for naval guns, searchlight projectors, parts for miniature submarines and bomb cases, not to mention cudgels for the Home Guard made from steam engine boiler tubes.

It is not as if all this additional activity was achieved on a stable network; the service constantly had to work around serious damage to its infrastructure. The railways were a strategic target for the Luftwaffe and between 1939 and 1944 they suffered over 10,000 attacks, 250 of which put lines out of action for a week or more. The most bombed section of line was claimed to be that between Waterloo and what became Queenstown Road station, which was bombed no less than ninety-two times between September 1940 and May 1941. During the infamous raid on Coventry in November 1940, one 3½-mile stretch of track suffered forty-two bomb hits in one night. Over 1,000 flying-bomb incidents were also recorded during the latter years of the war. In addition to damage caused directly by enemy action, the blackout, and overstretched and under-maintained infrastructure all added to the likelihood of other railway accidents. When these occurred, they could be further exacerbated by the large amounts of dangerous cargo the railways had to carry – notably munitions and fuel. At Soham in June 1944, a fire in one of the wagons detonated its cargo of bombs, killing two railway workers, whose bravery only narrowly averted a much larger death toll among the residents of the village.

The railways became highly adept at repairing or working around damage quickly. In one bombing raid a station building was hit, four through lines were severed and a train on one of them was damaged. A series of shuttle buses was laid on within fifteen minutes, the damaged train removed within a few hours and the tracks re-laid and back in operation within two days. In another, a major signal box, destroyed by a direct hit, was replaced overnight by one housed in temporary buildings. In a London terminal, a bomb exploded between the tracks with such force that it lifted a train on to the platform and blocked all lines in and out of the station. Again, normal service was restored by the following day. In the case of the Coventry raid, mentioned above, the railway managed to repair all forty-two areas of damage (one of which was a 60ft crater) and get the main line running again within four days. As well as repairing the physical infrastructure, there was also some important paperwork needing to be done:

> The planning of train services in normal times is a long operation. In these days new timetables are drawn up in a night; indeed, in one night three new timetables were drawn up as additional details of damage made it necessary to change plans.
>
> *Swindon Advertiser*, 1 January 1941

Operationally, the demands of a wartime service taxed the railways at every turn: giving priority to slower goods trains created bottlenecks; a single coal train making its leisurely way through the Severn tunnel would displace three faster passenger services; and passenger services had to be amalgamated to free up more timetable space for military trains. On the Southern Railway this meant passenger trains of up to twenty coaches, which were so long that they blocked the entrance to the other platforms at Waterloo while they were standing in the station. These weighty trains, inevitably packed full, also put greater stress on the overworked locomotives.

Nevertheless, the greatest effort of all was invested by the railway in supporting the build-up to D-Day itself. The quiet rural station of Micheldever in Hampshire had no less than 14 miles of sidings built around it, to store many of the weapons and supplies to be sent to France. So many varieties of military hardware were to be found in its sidings that it came to be nicknamed 'Woolworths'. The year of the D-Day landings saw the greatest demands on the service, with an extra 178,362 special trains being called for. The month following D-Day was said to have been the busiest in the entire history of the railways. By May 1945 the railways had run 451,765 wartime special trains for the armed forces.

However, much of these heroic efforts to keep the service going would not have been immediately obvious to the local newspaper reader or the average rail traveller. For them, the wartime experience was of slow, crowded trains, sometimes having to give way to the demands of wartime traffic, the inconveniences of the blackout, and the lack of sustenance on a long journey (restaurant cars were first reduced in number then withdrawn completely in May 1942). Even such basic amenities as towels, soap and toilet paper were in short supply on the trains – more general wartime shortages of them made them attractive to thieves. The growing inconvenience of rail travel – including the disappearance of attractive venues to travel to – meant that

Yorkshire Relish ensures at least one happy railway traveller.

One of the many attempts to discourage the public from using the railways at holiday times.

people did tend much more to take only necessary journeys. It also meant that they grumbled a lot, which sometimes left the railway staff feeling unappreciated:

> I have noticed … a lot of people who earn their living in Swindon and district and who are not connected with the railway or the works who take a delight in destructive criticism of both, when in the presence of railway folk.
>
> A lot of it is no doubt meant in a jocular way, but much more is said in a vindictive spirit, and if these people had their own business criticised in the same way by railway employees they would probably resent it …
>
> Healthy criticism, coupled with facts, is good and necessary for progress in all spheres of life, but no sane person wishes to listen to the vitriolic contumely of artificial zealots.
>
> Letter to the *Swindon Advertiser*,
> 2 January 1941

One of the local press' main contributions to the war effort, so far as the railways were concerned, was to appeal to the public not to make unnecessary journeys in peak hours and holiday periods. The following was typical:

> To stay put this Whitsun is both good citizenship and good sense. Goods traffic in wartime is more important than passenger traffic. Extra demands by holiday-makers place an unfair burden on transport workers, who have already been under a heavy strain during the past 'blackout' months. They have done magnificent work in keeping the lines open, so that vital supplies can get to where they are most needed with the least delay.
>
> *Berkshire Chronicle*, 30 May 1941

The possibility of introducing a travel permit system had been considered but rejected, because of the vast number of staff needed to run it and the delay and inconvenience it would cause for those with a legitimate need to travel. In the week before Christmas 1940, the Minister of Transport published the following, very friendly, appeal in the newspapers:

> I wish I could be a Santa Claus this Christmas and produce out of the bag hundreds of extra trains, miles of additional track and thousands of additional railway workers, so that you could travel where and as you wish – and in comfort.
>
> Indeed, I have to curtail Christmas passenger trains and try to persuade you not to travel at all. You know this must be a stern Christmas-tide – one during which we must work for victory. The enemy won't wait while we take a Christmas holiday and therefore railways must continue to devote all their energies to vital war transport.
>
> No extra holidays for railway workers – for you no extra travelling facilities. Forgive no presents this year, but best wishes for Christmas and the new year.
>
> Government press release

His message was widely ignored. On the Saturday before Christmas:

> ... platforms seethed with people ... most of the travellers were women ... at Euston, hundreds of people were queuing up before 9 am to get onto the platform for trains going north.
>
> Brown, p. 57

In future years, the authorities dispensed with the niceties and variously gave harder-hitting messages, along the lines of 'don't think about travelling – you might not be able to get back again', or looked for compromises: 'Lighter luggage please if you must travel.'

Last but by no means least, the railways feared with some justification from the outset of war that their income would be squeezed at a time when their costs were increasing. Over the course of the war, the railways' running costs would increase by at least 70 per cent, whilst their income was only permitted to rise by 16 per cent. They were not allowed to increase their costs in line with inflation; they had to carry government traffic at a 33 per cent discount and had to share any additional revenue the extra traffic generated with the government. Even so, the increases they did secure were enough to set off another wave of grumbles:

> Yesterday railway charges were increased 6% – the second advance, thus bringing the chares up to about 15½% above those prevailing at the outbreak of war. A proposal for another increase in charges is to be lodged by the Railway Executive Committee with the Minister of Transport ... The Government's arrangement with the railway companies has been condemned on all sides ... The companies have no inducement to practise economy and provides a spiral which will bring about inflation and give rise to many economic problems.
>
> *Liverpool Echo*, 2 December 1940

The road haulage industry was notably free from any similar controls; they even made a considerable profit from hiring 2,500 lorries to the Ministry of War Transport, and were able to charge the government commercial rates for services the railways had to provide for free. All of this left the railways far more vulnerable to competition from road transport once hostilities ended. As if to add insult to injury, petrol rationing meant that much of the additional business the road-haulage industry had won from the railways during the 1930s had to go back on to rail, further burdening the wartime network. In similar vein, much of the coal and other bulk cargo that before the war was moved via coastal shipping was forced back on to rail. It was ironic indeed that, before the war, the four big railway companies had already been running a campaign under the slogan 'Fair Deal', the aim of which was to secure a leveller playing field for the railways relative to the road-haulage industry. For their part, the road-haulage industry also pleaded hard times during the war years. They told readers that, before the war, one in nine men had been employed in the industry and that they too had been hard hit by conscription.

Movement Restrictions

Regardless of the method of transport chosen, from the middle of 1940 onwards it became a lot more difficult to travel to some parts of England. The *Hants and Berks Gazette* reported that, from 21 June, a coastal strip from the Wash to Rye was to be designated a prohibited area. From that date, it was forbidden to go there, or to stay there, for the purpose of 'a holiday, recreation, pleasure or as a casual wayfarer'. Travellers arriving there should expect to have to justify their visit to the police or military authorities. Readers were, however, informed that visiting close relatives in these areas did not constitute pleasure in official eyes, and that this remained one of the acceptable purposes for a visit. One family found themselves prosecuted for going to visit

The wheels of industry continue to be advertised in wartime.

their son at his boarding school just outside a prohibited area and taking him to lunch at a venue just within it.

Aliens living there, even if long-standing residents, had to obtain official permission to stay there or else be forcibly moved out. For those aliens that did go to or stay within them, there was a list of things they were not permitted to possess, such as cameras, binoculars, telescopes and maps. Aliens generally found their freedom of movement seriously restricted. In one typical case, Anna Schiefer, a German subject who had been evacuated to Haddenham from Chiswick, found herself before the court for travelling more than 5 miles from her registered address without a travel permit. These had to be obtained from the police, who would refuse them if the purpose of the journey could not be justified. In another, a Czechoslovakian alien, Frank Heumann, found himself fined 15*s* for being out after the 8 p.m. curfew to which he was subject. This despite the fact that he had been engaged on what might be regarded as work of national importance – repairing a tractor needed for food production.

In the month following the designation of prohibited areas, the papers reported a further order which made it illegal to leave a vehicle unattended without immobilising it, lest it be commandeered by invading forces. As ever, the authorities (probably quite properly) anticipated interminable arguments about what constituted 'attended' and what 'immobilised' meant, and sought to close the loopholes. So 'attended' was defined as there being a person of 14 years or more in or near the vehicle, and that they could not be attending more than one vehicle at the same time.

As for 'immobilised', during the daytime it was deemed sufficient to remove the key and lock the vehicle's doors. By night, stricter precautions were required. The vehicle had to have a locking device fitted or be in a locked yard. Failing that, it should have a key part of its mechanism removed to make it impossible to start. Wilfred Sherwood thought he had immobilised his car by putting a fierce dog behind the steering wheel whilst he went about his business. Sure enough, the policeman that went to investigate was intimidated from getting into it, but it did not stop the court from fining Mr Sherwood for not immobilising it within the letter of the law. In another case, the question was raised (but not answered) as to whether fitting a secret immobilising switch complied with the regulations.

All vehicles, including those needed for the war effort, were in short supply.

The regulations gave a five-minute dispensation to vehicles making deliveries to be left unattended. In the event that invasion did actually take place, people were warned that the use of private cars or motorcycles by local residents would be forbidden in the areas concerned. This would particularly have upset the many coastal residents who, according to the papers, had bought trailers to facilitate their flight from invaders.

9

Dressed to Kill: Wartime Fashion

> You are, no doubt, feeling in need of a tonic. Who isn't? So, for a pleasant change, let's think about something as frivolous as hats.
>
> *Portsmouth Evening News*, 5 September 1939

> Miss Jones: 'Whenever I am down in the dumps I get a new hat.'
> Miss Smith: 'I often wondered where you got them.'
>
> *Liverpool Echo*, 29 June 1940

Clothes Rationing

Clothes rationing was introduced in June 1941. It appears to have been done in something of a hurry, since the public were told that, until the new clothing ration books were ready, they should use margarine coupons instead. The authorities explained its purpose thus:

> Rationing has been introduced not to deprive you of your real needs, but to make more certain that you get your share of the country's goods – to get fair shares for everybody else.

The exertions of the wartime economy threaten to bring on an attack of the dreaded 'B.O.'

When the shops reopen you will be able to buy cloth, clothes, footwear and knitting wool only if you bring your food ration book with you. The shopkeeper will detach the required number of coupons from the unused margarine page. Each margarine coupon counts as one coupon towards the purchase of clothing and footwear. You will have a total of 66 coupons to last you a year, so go sparingly. You can buy where you like and when you like without registering.

Government press release

By this time, imports of cotton and wool had fallen to 20 per cent of their pre-war levels and there were fears that the first signs of a shortage would lead to panic buying by the better-off that would strip the shops bare. Each item of clothing was worth a given number of coupons. In addition to paying the cash price for the item of clothing, you would have to hand over the requisite number of coupons. The annual allowance of sixty-six coupons was reduced to forty-eight by the middle of the war and to thirty-six by 1945, and clothes rationing would not end until 1949. The government encouraged ladies in particular to exercise restraint, including this appeal from one of the few female MPs, Dr Edith Summerskill: 'This is not the time to buy extra clothes when our soldiers are asking for guns, aeroplanes and tanks.' Asking women not to discard a frock, in wartime, for the reason that some of their friends might have seen them wearing it last year, Dr Summerskill went on: 'I am not advocating shabbiness or dowdiness. I like women to look as charming as possible' (*Liverpool Echo*, 14 June 1940).

Applying bureaucratic control to the vagaries of fashion was like trying to harness deer to the plough. It greatly exercised the creativity of civil servants, and resulted in some infinitely detailed regulation. For example, a lined ladies' mac or coat of over 28in cost fourteen points, while a shorter one required just eleven. A woollen dress cost eleven coupons, whereas one of any other fabric was seven. Officials were asked to adjudicate as to whether a bolero jacket counted as part of the dress it accompanied or if it was a separate item of clothing. (If they could be worn separately, they had a separate points score.) Did shirts that came with two collars require extra coupons? (No.) Was any clothing or other material exempt? (Yes, baby clothes for those under 4 months; boiler suits and other work clothing; hats; clogs; blackout material.) Why should scarves, which were often worn as turbans, and thus served the same purpose as hoods, be rationed, whereas hoods were not? (Good question.) In an effort to clarify things, the government issued clothing coupon quizzes. The press release for the second edition of the quiz whetted the nation's appetite as follows:

> How many clothing coupons for a non-woollen sleeveless dress, for a baby's matinee coat, or for lined woollen shorts? These and other questions about clothes rationing can quickly be answered with a copy of the new revised 'Quiz', which replaces the first edition, now out of date.
>
> Quoted in the *Berkshire Chronicle*, 16 January 1942

The government warned that traders who failed to demand coupons when they were required could be prosecuted and that, if an item was not on the rationing list, it should be treated as the nearest equivalent item on the list. Thus, it explained (perhaps unnecessarily) that plimsolls counted as shoes and blackout material would not be rationed, but it had to be black to qualify.

Clothes rationing had to respond not just to availability, but also to seasonal and other market demands. Non-woollen items got a lower points rating than their woollen counterparts during the summer months, coupon rates were reduced during August to help retailers clear their summer lines and khaki wool was removed from the ration entirely for a six-week period, to encourage the knitting of comforts for the armed forces.

On day one of rationing, shop assistants were constantly asking their managers questions they could not answer about the correct coupon rating for items. Retailers were also at a loss to know how they dealt with items that were purchased and then returned (could you/should you refund the coupons, and if so how?) or what to do with seconds, or goods that were salvaged from bombed premises (would the customer really have to really have to pay the same number of coupons for them as for perfect goods? Official answer – above a certain price, yes). Nonetheless, the stores did good business as rationing came in.

As with other parts of wartime regulation, its complexity caught out even those whose job it was to uphold the law. In Reading in 1944, a second-hand clothes dealer was brought before the magistrates for selling a second-hand coat for £10 10*s* without receiving the necessary coupons. The magistrates themselves were unaware that second-hand clothing above a certain value required the same tokens as new goods, but it did not stop them fining the accused £5. Families with growing children faced particular clothing problems, and the WVS introduced an exchange scheme for outgrown children's clothing.

A different unforeseen problem faced that dwindling band of women still employed as domestic servants. The introduction of rationing meant that their employers could no longer supply them with the aprons and other regalia of their calling. It was left to any domestic servant wishing to keep up pre-war standards to buy them for herself, out of her own rations. A plea was made for such working clothes to be given the same non-rationed status as men's bib and brace overalls. Another group facing particular complexities were pregnant women. They had to buy whatever their baby would need from their own ration allocation (which could consume most if not all of that allocation). Once the baby was born, it would be issued with its own ration book, which the mother could then use to replenish her own supplies.

In 1942, the British Civilian Clothing Order gave birth to utility clothing. This was designed to do away with excess ornament and minimise the use of material. Leading lights of the fashion world such as Hardy Amies and Norman Hartnell created thirty-four clothing designs that complied with the rules of utility (such as a maximum of three buttons, no turn-back cuffs and skirts that were 19in from the ground). Like many wartime regulations, this one impacted unequally on the rich and the poor. Luxury items like fur coats were exempt from rationing and those who could afford it could still had clothes custom made to whatever design they wished. Fashionistas entered into battle with the bureaucrats over the utility clothing regulations, arguing for example that the privations of war were bad enough without having to do without turn ups on trousers, and that men should be allowed a double-breasted suit if, in return, they did without a waistcoat.

War or no war, people's interest in fashion was not going to go away. It simply presented the fashion conscious with new challenges and new contexts in which to apply their fashion sense. It was also seen (at least, by the advertisers) as a woman's patriotic duty to look her best:

The better-off you were, the more durable your rationed clothes were likely to be.

NEW CLOTHES ARE A WONDERFUL TONIC and we all need a tonic just now. Don't put off getting that new coat, or costume or hat, or frock you were going to have this autumn. BUY IT NOW and find out for yourself what a difference it makes. You will face your problems with a lighter heart and your smile will help others less fortunate than you are. TRY IT.

Berkshire Chronicle, 22 September 1939

In the very first weeks of the war, before a single air raid had taken place, this same newspaper column turned its mind to what the well-dressed woman should be wearing while being bombed:

> Slacks ideal in an air raid
>
> Having recovered from the first shock of knowing that the nation is at war, women are resuming their interest in clothes, although with different views from those they held when the Paris collections were launched. The result is that the day clothes which are most sought are those which are strictly practical … Many women have invested in an outfit which can be slipped on at a moment's notice, should there be an air raid at night. If the sirens did waken you from sleep, would you have

Utility chic.

warm clothes at hand which could be rapidly slipped on? There will be no time in an emergency to don lingerie, but feminine night attire would be quite unsuitable, so I think the best thing to do is to invest in a warm pair of tailored slacks – perhaps in navy flannel – and a thick woollen jumper. A zipp fastener on the slacks and another on the jumper would be much easier than buttons, so bear this in mind if you are buying such an outfit … A man-tailored dressing gown in dark woollen, cut shorter than ankle length, is the third essential for this quickly-donned emergency outfit, which is practical enough to keep you warm and neat, while allowing you full freedom to make yourself as useful as possible. Keep this outfit handy in your bedroom, particularly if, in the event of an air raid, you would go to a communal shelter.

Berkshire Chronicle, 22 September 1939

Not everyone was delighted with this idea:

A serious epidemic seems to have broken out in Henley among women, namely trousers. At first one is only disposed to laugh

> at them as they are really very comical, but this feeling soon gives way to disgust. How is it that apparently women may with impunity copy a man's dress, while should a man ever parade the streets dressed as a woman, he would be quickly run in?
>
> *Henley Standard*, 8 August 1941

Predictably, this drew the response that skirts were hardly suitable for climbing ladders or trees, or doing any of a hundred other jobs required of women engaged in the war economy.

One Ramsgate dancehall had its own idea of what should not be worn in the shelter. They banned long skirts from their establishment, for fear of them causing people to trip while running to take cover. As the nation faced possibly the greatest peril in its long history, this ladies' page had its eye on their big issue of the day:

> This season will be an important one for accessories and, if our choice in clothes is to be severely limited in the next few months, as seems very likely, accessories will be more vital than ever. Check over your own wardrobe and see where you can fill gaps with inexpensive yet pleasing oddments.

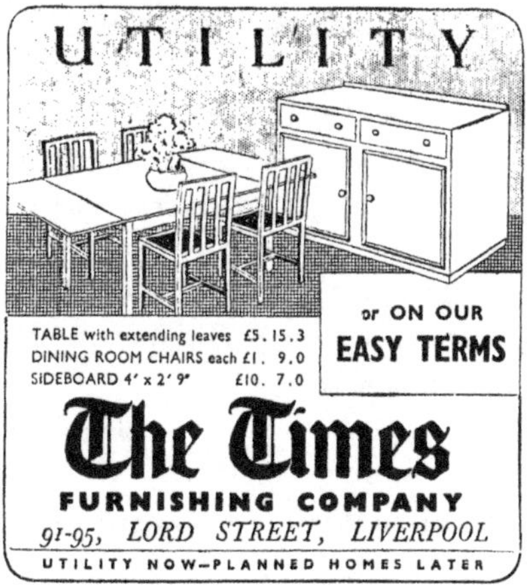

The concept of utility was extended from clothes into furnishings, providing a limited range of basic, but well-designed and made, furniture.

The bus conductress seems to have become something of a wartime heroine, if this soap opera is to be believed.

I think that the question 'Will it stay fashion-right for several seasons?' is the most important one to us all at the moment.

Berkshire Chronicle, 20 October 1939

The theme that it was women's patriotic duty to buy new clothes resurfaced during the darkest days of the war. It seemed an army did not (as the saying goes) march on its stomach, but rather on the clothing worn by the women who cheered them on:

> Women can help win the war. Bright clothes create cheerful atmosphere.
> That clothes make the man is not really true, because many of the best men wear the worst clothes and it is no easier to judge the real quality of a man than a baked potato by its jacket.
>
> That women's clothes make the man is, however, undoubtedly true. If they are the right kind of clothes, snappy and bright and smart, they will make him cheerful and bright, too; if they are stuffy and dowdy and uninteresting they will be as depressing as an empty tobacco pouch to an air raid warden on a cold and foggy night. This aspect of the question is surely more important at wartime than at any other.
>
> Modern wars are fought psychologically as well as physically, and no psychological campaign will achieve a greater victory than the campaign for brightness and cheer. This is a battle that women can fight as well as men, and it is fought not with guns and tanks and suchlike nasty rough things, but with lovely crepe, satin and fascinating moiré, which can provide a variety of life and brilliance of colouring that will put miles into the marching power of the British army.
>
> Quoted in Hylton (1996, 2011), p. 31

Not only was it women's patriotic duty to look attractive, it was also a Christian imperative. News of this emerged after the popular radio programme *The Brains Trust* had the temerity to criticise women for their use of lipstick. This prompted editorial comment:

> A well-groomed man and a well-dressed, well-tended woman pay tribute to the body and thus honour the creator. It is a Christian duty to look as nice as possible.
>
> *Manchester City News*, 26 January 1945

However, the author of this editorial chose not to quit whilst he was in relatively uncontroversial territory. He went on to offer his views on what constituted beauty in a woman. 'A graceful carriage', as opposed to waddling like a duck, was one thing. A voice which was 'gentle, sweet and low' was another. He ventured the view that women's voices had grown shriller over the war years due to 'increased nerve tension'. He advised his lady readers to 'learn to speak in a gentle, cadenced voice … and you will really begin to be attractive'. Stepping further on to the thin ice, he dared to lecture his lady readers on fashion. He told them they should not slavishly follow every fashion, however unsuited to them it was. Women with fat legs should not wear short skirts with horizontal stripes. Finally, inner beauty requires wit, vivacity and 'the sunshine of your expression' – a sullen, discontented, selfish, bored woman could never be beautiful.

The Lure of a Uniform

As the war progressed, more and more women found themselves in one or other of the uniformed services. The ladies' page of the newspapers naturally did their bit to promote this trend, but in some cases it was not so much the war work as the uniform that was celebrated:

> <u>Lady ARP warden</u>
> When I called on Mrs Wintle to ask her about her work as a warden, I found her dressed, ready for immediate duty, in a smart one-piece trouser suit of navy blue. The gleaming silver buttons and the red embroidered letters ARP are the only notes of contrast, yet the tailored uniform is becoming as well as very practical.
>
> <u>Bus conductress says she likes her job</u>
> Miss Devoy was wearing the summertime uniform issued to the conductresses – a neat coat overall of dark grey with red

Women are called upon to help meet the demand for munitions.

facings and pocket tops and a jaunty peaked cap to match, but she told me that she had been measured for the permanent uniform, which she is looking forward eagerly to wearing. This comprises a trim skirt and double-breasted jacket in the same dark grey cloth as is used for the men's suits. The jacket has facings of red, and a smart red stripe runs down the side seam of the skirt.

Ambulance driver
The uniform which the ambulance drivers wear is one of the smartest designed for women. It consists of navy blue slacks and blouse, or dungarees, a navy coat and a trim peaked cap. I expect you have seen women dressed like this and thought that it looked like a smart skiing outfit.

Berkshire Chronicle, various, 1940

However, the fashion editors must have thrown their hands up in despair when they went to meet:

Ladies who operate machines
Mrs Martin was wearing the workmanlike navy blue boiler suit and blue cap that are supplied to each trainee by the

> Ministry of Labour, and when I asked her if she found the work hard on her hands she said although they looked black while she was at work the grease soon came off with soap and water ...
>
> *Berkshire Chronicle*, 1940

Nevertheless, even this outfit would have seemed feminine compared to the boiler suits issued to female air raid wardens in London just before the war. Their crotches hung down to their knees, and when they tried to organise test drills they looked so ludicrous in them that the public refused to take them seriously. It was said that the appearance of the uniform was an important influence over the service women chose to enter, and the Wrens brought in elite fashion designer Edward Molyneux to design theirs. His design, consisting of 'a smart double-breasted tailored jacket, svelt skirt and pert tricorn hat', produced a huge surge in the number of volunteers. (After the war, the British Overseas Airways Corporation bought up surplus Wrens' uniforms for use by their air hostesses.) The ATS and WAAFs, by contrast, allowed function and not appearance to dictate their uniform design, and came up with belted outfits that were widely regarded as making the wearers' bottoms look huge. Nicholson gives this account of an ATS recruit's first unhappy encounter with her uniform:

> [It] fitted me about as well as a bell tent, trailing on the floor behind me while my hands groped in sleeves a foot too long. Evidently the army expected its women to be of Amazonian proportions. I was to find that the army had a genius for issuing absurd garments and expecting one to take them seriously.
>
> Quoted in Nicholson, p. 145

The Woman's Army even saw fit to publicise its make-up code:

> The Woman's Army is a very human institution – the use of powder is allowed, and even a touch of natural lipstick ... Not an easy life, perhaps, but a healthy, friendly one.
>
> Quoted in Nicholson, chapter 1

Although uniformed women became iconic wartime images, appearing in a range of advertisements, the idea of women wearing uniform was never generally popular – it came top of a list of wartime dislikes among *Daily Mail* readers. It was associated in many people's minds with coarseness and loose morals, as was reflected in the nicknames given to the various women's services:

- ATS – officers' groundsheets
- WAAFs – pilots' cockpits
- Land Army – backs to the land
- Wrens – up with the lark and to bed with a Wren.

For those wishing to be stylish in uniform and who could afford it, there was the option of having it made to measure. Throughout the war Cliftons of Winchester, an up-market outfitter, was advertising bespoke suits and uniforms in the *Hampshire Chronicle* with a shameless appeal to elitist sentiments:

> Those who have always worn the best never wonder, even in these days, if they have spent wisely. They know that Service Dress, both for ladies and men, cut from good cloth and individually tailored is worth every penny paid for it.
>
> *Hampshire Chronicle*, 9 September 1939

In fact, military officers could obtain uniforms without coupons, simply by signing a statement on the back of the bill that they were for their own use. The same privilege was not available to other ranks, except naval ratings (although they needed prior approval of their officer). It was one thing to have a uniform tailored and quite another to be entitled to wear it. In the days when the likes of fighter pilots and naval officers were the height of glamour, posing as one could give one a flying start with the ladies, or in obtaining credit. Darcy Wilson, a 29-year-old barman, was one of many who succumbed to the temptation. He found himself up before the Bow Street Magistrates Court in September 1940 for impersonating a flight lieutenant. The court accepted that he wore the uniform purely to impress women and that there was no subversive intent. They heard how he had deserted his family and 'victimised' a number of women (in the sense of taking money from them). He was about to marry an 18-year-old who thought he was a test pilot and, more to the point, single. He told the court he wore the uniform to get away from his wife, and he was able to do just that, as he served his two months in prison.

A 17-year-old Reading youth dispensed with the expense of a bogus uniform and simply posed as a secret agent:

> He gave a young lady of his acquaintance a 'secret' letter to take care of, and later phoned her, pretending to be an air commodore. He told her that the secret agent had been killed parachuting into enemy territory and that she should bring the secret letter and meet him (the air commodore) at a special rendezvous. She very wisely sent a policeman in her place.
>
> Hylton (1996, 2011), p. 75

However, the prize fantasist must have been Lord Kilmarnock, or rather David Fisher, a 21-year-old former errand boy who adopted that title. His fictitious lord purported to have been educated at Eton and Oxford, and have estates in Scotland and Dorset and a town house in London's fashionable Berkeley Square. He also 'owned' an aeroplane and three boats (in one of which he claimed to have carried out heroic rescues at Dunkirk). He tried to use this CV to obtain a directorship of a firm, the post of instructor in the ATC and the juvenile lead in an opera company, but all it got him was an appearance before the magistrates.

Britain mobilised the female labour force far more effectively than Germany.

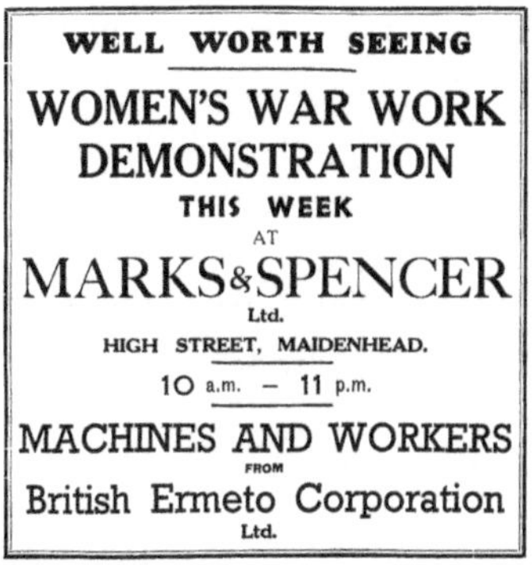

Like every form of wartime shortage, clothes rationing prompted its share of criminal activity. One group of racketeers took to buying up old travelling rugs at knockdown prices and remodelling them into overcoats, which they sold on the black market for a high price but requiring no coupons. Although the rugs themselves were exempt from rationing (possibly on the grounds that nobody was making them in wartime) any clothing made from them did require coupons, and they were prosecuted.

Where did you get that Hat?

If the clothes worn by the devotees of the ladies' page were increasingly dictated by the branch of government that employed them, at least their choice of off-duty headgear was purely for their own pleasure:

> To know that one is looking attractive, in these times more than ever, helps a woman to face the day's problems in a way that only a woman can appreciate. Our newly-arrived SPRING HATS are calculated to brighten your outlook.
>
> *Maidenhead Advertiser*, 5 March 1941

If you could not manage a new hat, why not recycle an old one?

> Why not cover the brim with a little veiling? Net has a very becoming effect. Why not remove that flower and replace it by another at a slightly different angle?
>
> *Berkshire Chronicle*, 23 April 1943

You could even try making a pillbox hat out of a scarf – if you were feeling lucky:

> You can try it if you like – but it is not very easy to manage.
>
> *Berkshire Chronicle*, 23 April 1943

As the war progressed, shortages of everything got worse and, by 1943, 'make do and mend' was the order of the day (though it had been so for poorer members of society since time immemorial). The Ministry of Information produced booklets showing how to convert a man's suit into a tailored dress and his shirts into ladies' blouses. They included the health warning:

> Once a woman develops this habit, nothing can be safe from her mutilating scissors, her busy needle and thread.
>
> Quoted in Hylton (1996), p. 88

Pity the man who returned home to find his wardrobe had been subjected to this treatment. At least it would give him an opportunity to make a whole new circle of friends. Nothing was spared: pillowcases became white shorts and wedding dresses, and once they had done the rounds of several brides they were cut up to make underwear. Weddings generally lost the opportunity to become fashion displays, as witnessed in this rather sad little item, reporting a wedding that had been brought forward due to the imperatives of war:

> The bride, who was simply attired and had no bridesmaids in attendance, was given away by her father. There was no best man.
>
> *Manchester City News*, 30 September 1939

Wives are encouraged to cut up their husband's clothes in order to dress their children.

The newspapers were less likely to report what the key players at the wedding were wearing than whether or not they were carrying their gas masks. No clothing materials – or potential sources of clothing materials – could go to waste. The public were urged to gather the scraps of sheep's fleece that were found on farm fences and hedgerows.

Make-up was also in short supply. This was a particular problem for women working in munitions factories, since the chemicals in the munitions caused their skin to go yellow and they were encouraged to wear barrier creams to prevent it. Max Factor used to test out new cosmetics by giving supplies of them out to munitions workers. Manufacturers even made a concession to the war economy by producing a new shade of make-up – called burnt sugar – designed to go with khaki. The government recognised the importance of make-up to women's morale and made strenuous attempts to obtain additional supplies, but a good deal of ingenuity was still needed to get round the remaining shortages. Sugar water was used to set waves in the hair; Vaseline gave a sheen to the eyelids; shoe polish served as mascara; bicarbonate of soda for underarm deodorant; and starch for face powder. The very last traces of lipstick were extracted from the tube using warmed almond oil. Again, shortage produced its own black market. The dearth of cosmetics led to the sale of fakes, some of which contained very toxic substances. Women were warned against face cream containing harsh abrasives that could result in permanent scarring and nail polish that caused dermatitis.

The chronic shortage of silk stockings led to a number of ingenious substitutes (including the use of gravy browning, which undoubtedly made the wearer more attractive – to dogs). But the cosmetics industry came up with its own solution:

> Miner's liquid stockings make-up – in two new stocking shades, grape mist and gold mist. Just smooth it on … looks like gossamer silk stockings … it doesn't streak and it's waterproof … no more ladders … no more holes … no more silk stocking bills.
>
> Advertisement in the *Liverpool Echo*, 27 June 1940

In case it offered some crumbs of comfort, the authorities reminded newspaper readers of the worthy wartime uses to which their consumer goods were being diverted. The materials needed to make corsets were also required for parachutes; net curtain manufacturers had now turned their hands to making mosquito netting for our boys in North Africa; face cream manufacturers were producing anti-gas ointment; and golf balls were competing with gas masks for the same raw materials.

The wartime shortage of rubber also had fashion consequences, in the form of a dearth of knicker elastic, leading to a lot of embarrassing episodes. The contemporary joke about utility knickers, following the American entry into the war, was 'one Yank and they're off'. Officialdom's response to this crisis was to issue the Making of Civilian Clothing (Restrictions) No. 11 Order, which set out in minute detail the permissible levels of ornamentation (and elasticity) in women's and maids' underwear.

Looking Forward to Peace

By 1945, the ladies' pages could look forward to a relaxation of the constraints the war had put on fashion:

> It cannot be such a very long way from the end of the war. Women want and deserve to go back to their old femininity. Women will choose this year the high hat with the flowers and the feathers. They are tired of the tight skirt, like bloused backs, waists as narrow as possible, rounded hips, unpressed pleats, flares, gathers and necklines that are soft and rounded.
>
> *Berkshire Chronicle*, 9 March 1945

10

Them and Us: Divided Nation

By no means was everyone in Britain equally committed to the war effort, or at least to the official version of it. For some, victory only pointed towards a continuation of the situation that prevailed before the war, of inequality, mass unemployment and hunger marches. To them, a German-dominated regime could scarcely be any worse, and might even address some of the injustices that had afflicted those at the bottom of the pre-war heap. Some – a relatively small number – were positively committed to pro-fascist ideologies, while others were, to varying degrees, supporting a socialist agenda which seemed the antithesis of fascism but which, through Russia's pre-war policy, seemed to have become allied to it. Others, for reasons of religious conviction or a variety of other motives, were opposed to the very idea of war – or, at least, to their participation in it.

Class War

Britain certainly entered the war as a society deeply divided by class. Lloyd George's broken promise of a land fit for heroes to live in, made at the end of the last war, was not forgotten and the

General Strike of 1926 was still particularly fresh in many minds. This had seen Churchill far exceeding his mandate as Chancellor of the Exchequer and trying to move into dictatorial mode, with proposals to take over the BBC, calling for tanks and machine guns to escort food convoys and producing his own propaganda sheet, the *British Gazette*, to replace the striking newspapers. He was aided and abetted in this by a positive army of strike breakers, who got to fulfil their childhood dreams of running the railways or driving lorries or trams.

American GIs were particularly struck by the extent to which British society was riven by class. This from the wartime diary of American air force man Bob Raymond:

> I sometimes feel that England does not deserve to win the war. Never have I seen such class distinctions drawn and maintained, in the face of a deep effort to preserve a democracy. With powers of regulation and control centred in the hands of a few, the abuse and preservation of the Old School Tie is stronger than it ever was on every side … it has been well and truly said that General Rommel of the German Army Afrika Corps would never have risen above the rank of NCO in the British army. This nation seems inexplicably proud of defects in its national character.
>
> Bob Raymond, Diary

The American authorities foresaw this as something that would sit uneasily with their troops and tried to play it down:

> Old-time social distinctions are being forgotten as the sons of factory workers rise to be officers in the forces and the daughters of noblemen get jobs in munitions factories.
>
> *Instructions for American Servicemen in Britain*, p. 22

The truth was far less clear-cut. The BBC, the nation's monopoly broadcaster, was a living embodiment of the class system in action. Before the war they had a strict rule that the only people with regional accents who could broadcast were comedians. They even had a pronunciation panel to advise on the correct way to say words. As Wilson recounts, one panel member, confronted by the word 'sausage', insisted that it should be pronounced 'sorsidge'. J.B. Priestley was the first person with any hint of a regional accent to be recruited as a broadcaster and, though the regional influence in his voice is not particularly strong to modern ears, it was still seen by some as a sign that he was preaching left-wing politics. The American authorities also saw accents as a potential source of misunderstanding between their troops and the host population:

> In England the 'upper crust' speak pretty much alike. You will hear the news broadcaster for the BBC … He is a good example because he has been trained to talk with the 'cultured' accent. He will drop the letter 'r' (as people do in some sections of our own country) and will say 'hyah' instead of 'here'. He will use the broad a pronouncing all the a's in 'banana' like the a in 'father'. However funny you may think this is, you will be able to understand people who talk this way and they will be able to understand you. And you will soon get over thinking it is funny.
>
> *Instructions for American Servicemen in Britain*, p. 26

The war presented many more opportunities for the classes to mix, and the experience did not always lend itself to greater tolerance and understanding. They often mingled in the food queues, leading to accusations that favoured customers got special treatment with 'under the counter' goods from the shopkeepers. In any event, for those with enough money the black market and the possibility of eating out regularly offered a lot more choice. Housewives, standing in the interminable queues for rationed goods, also used to get incensed by the upper-crust families, who simply placed their orders by telephone and demanded that they be delivered, as this correspondent testifies:

> My wife makes an early-morning pilgrimage to the shop which has supplied us for years, either to see the day's supply already wrapped for delivery and be blandly told 'there is no fish today', or alternatively, if the fish is in sight 'It is all wanted for orders already booked'.
>
> Now I am quite certain that Lord Woolton did not mean to reserve our limited supplies for telephone subscribers and leave the hoi polloi with nothing!
>
> *Henley Standard*, 15 January 1943

As the wartime food shortages grew tighter, official censors had to discourage newspapers from printing 'inflammatory' photographs of the rich enjoying themselves at lavish banquets. They certainly inflamed some parts of Parliament, who held an inquiry into the amount of conspicuous consumption that was going on under rationing. But, if one was to believe the catering manager of the Grosvenor House Hotel in London's Park Lane, who was called to give evidence to the inquiry, luxury dining was a mere figment of the imagination:

> There is no demand for 'luxury food' ... People now don't want such delicacies as caviar and oysters and conditions are such that early asparagus is as cheap as cabbage, and is being served as an ordinary vegetable ... Take oysters, which are produced in this country, for example. The consumption of oysters during the season was only 40% of what it is in normal times ... the demand for early strawberries, which are grown under glass for well-to-do households and hotels, has also been negligible.
>
> *Oxford Mail*, 20 May 1940

Rationing generally did not impact on the classes equally. Taking clothes rationing, the better-off would have started the war with a much larger and newer wardrobe than their poorer counterparts, for whom making do and mending had been a way of life for many years. They could afford to buy better quality (and therefore more durable) items of clothing with the same points allowance. West End stores reported booming sales of 'indestructible' tweed suits as clothing restrictions began to bite. As we saw, the really well-off could afford to buy unrationed fur coats and couturier clothing that was not constrained by utility styling, while the really poor could not afford to buy even the amount of basic clothing to which their ration allocation entitled them.

Class feeling came into the ill-fated Children's Overseas Reception Board (CORB) plans to evacuate children overseas, after the scheme firstly got hugely oversubscribed and then suffered the sinking of the *City of Benares* with the loss of seventy-seven would-be child evacuees. It was claimed that the scheme had been run for just long enough to allow the rich and influential to get their children out of harm's way, and then scrapped.

Class also opened the door to privilege in the field of war service. Middle- and upper-class young ladies who wished to avoid the unpleasantness of heavy manufacturing or munitions could instead join the Voluntary Aid Detachments (VADs), which carried out basic nursing and other duties for the armed forces. Attempts to merge them with the more proletarian Auxiliary Territorial Service (ATS) led to a flurry of protest in high places that soon saw that idea knocked on the head.

The armed forces themselves were bastions of privilege: pilots of the officer class received different treatment (ranging from different ranks, to different medals for the same acts of heroism, to different classes of rail warrant when going on leave) to working-class pilots who had risen on merit through the ranks. In the army, public schoolboys were fourteen times more likely than their state-school counterparts to be commissioned as officers and the navy reserved half its naval cadet places for those from public schools. Conscription meant that a much wider cross-section of the public was exposed to these long-standing inequalities.

Nor was the Conservative leadership of the coalition government through the war years likely to heal the breach between the classes. Neville Chamberlain cordially loathed socialism and socialists, and made no effort to disguise the fact. To some on the left, he and his followers were held to be almost as responsible as Hitler for the hostilities. The Honourable Wogan Philipps, prospective Labour parliamentary candidate for South Buckinghamshire, offered this analysis of the rise of fascism:

> The Government now standing for freedom and democracy is the most imperialist and reactionary government the country has had for ages. It was under this Government that Hitler and fascism gained the upper hand ... Germany was at one time pretty nearly 'red' and real freedom was at hand when the moneyed people in this country put Hitler in power. English capital was in every country in the world and that capital could dictate the policy of the country concerned. That capital was always on the side of keeping labour down.
>
> *Henley Standard*, 27 October 1939

For good measure, Mr Philipps offered the view that Chamberlain had only intervened on Poland's behalf because Hitler's eastward thrust had in some way threatened the British Empire. Home Intelligence picked up the following views from some of their working-class respondents about the consequences of Hitler invading:

> He won't hurt us; it's the bosses he's after; we'll probably be better off when he comes; he robs the rich to pay the poor; German victory would only harm the wealthy.
>
> Quoted in McLaine, p. 94

Churchill, too, was a noted class warrior. In addition to his inflammatory action during the General Strike, he was widely (if incorrectly) blamed for calling on troops to open fire on striking Welsh miners in 1910.

One of the earliest Ministry of Information poster campaigns played right into the hands of the class conflict. Devised by a career civil servant with no experience in public relations, it read: 'Your courage, your cheerfulness, your resolution will bring us victory.' This was widely taken by the British public to mean that the many would make sacrifices from which the elite few would benefit.

Conscientious Objectors

During the First World War, conscientious objection was limited to grounds of religious belief, and the treatment of objectors was often harsh. Around 6,000 of the 15,000 or so who sought exemption between 1914 and 1918 ended up serving time in prison and over seventy of them died from the treatment they received there. But for much of the Second World War, the Home Secretary was Herbert Morrison, who had been one of those objectors in the earlier conflict. The criteria for exemption were extended to cover philosophical and political objections to the conflict, and the tribunals were able to test the limits of each individual's willingness to participate, given that, in a total warfare economy, virtually everybody makes some sort of contribution to the war effort. Over the course of the war, some 59,000 people applied to be registered as conscientious objectors. Among those appearing before the tribunals were 1,072 women, 257 of whom would eventually be imprisoned for their unwillingness to serve.

They tended to receive little sympathy from the local media. Sweep, the columnist in the *Slough Observer*, thought conscientious objection was some kind of mental illness:

> Conscientious Objection is obviously a disease of the young and callow. What a pity the patients, whom I personally regard as mentally abnormal, can't be injected with a few more years, when the majority of them would become normal men and lose their mental abnormality.
>
> *Slough Observer*, 2 May 1941

The following editorial attempt to associate pacifism with communism provoked an angry rebuttal from the Peace Pledge Union and others:

> PACIFIST PROPAGANDA
>
> While acknowledging that many pacifists are sincere (though their attitude to the fight for freedom is, to say the least curious) it is unfortunately true that a great deal of the pacifist propaganda circulating in this country, and intensified in some respects since the war began, is inspired from political, rather than anti-war motives. The curious position today is that organisations which, in the ordinary way, are diametrically opposed to each other are now adopting more or less the same slogans and working to the same immediate end. That end is the stopping of hostilities, leaving Germany in possession of the field.
>
> The arguments employed are not convincing. The Communists, on their toes for years past to bring the Nazi regime to book and uncompromisingly critical at all times of any words or action of the Government which might be likely to put off the day, are now most anxious to convince us that the German-Russian deal is the best of all possible arrangements for the peace of Europe and for the workers of the world. The pacifism of the Peace Pledge Union, on the other hand, finds its expression in leaflets urging the stopping of war because Hitler has conquered Poland and nothing can be done about it … Truly a one-sided brand of pacifism.
>
> The Communists urged an allied pact with Russia to defeat Hitlerism. Now we are asked to accept a pact between Stalin

> and Hitler as being quite consistent with the Communist outlook on life. The organised pacifists wanted peace all round, in any circumstances. When it failed to materialise, despite the prolonged efforts of the Allies, the Allies are criticised for wanting to prolong the war so as to ensure justice for the oppressed and a Europe freed from the nightmare of recurring war ... There is every indication, however, that the immense majority of the people are firmly behind the Government in their determination to end Nazi aggression.
>
> *Berkshire Chronicle*, 3 November 1939

However, for most would-be conscientious objectors their grounds for objection were founded not in communist but in religious beliefs, and it was left to the tribunal to decide on the sincerity of those beliefs. One self-styled Seventh Day Adventist was asked when he had last gone to church. He replied: 'When I was fourteen. Since then I have been too busy.' Another claimed that his unique religious creed was a mixture of Christianity and Buddhism, though he could not claim to be precisely a Christian or a Buddhist. One Frederick Kew tried unsuccessfully to argue conscientious objection, in that he objected to bloodshed on 'slightly religious grounds' and Harry Taylor had no more success in arguing that 'war was too much of a filthy mucky job for me'. Even less conventional was the creed of the applicant who claimed to have undergone a series of mystical experiences, variously while reading *King Lear*, listening to Beethoven's *Ninth Symphony* and sitting on top of a mountain. Another seemed to get religious and political objections rather muddled:

> I felt sort of queer when I registered at the Labour Exchange. People seemed to think I was a coward. I am only going on one thing, and that is the Bible, although I have only read one or two pages. This war is the fault of the Government and not of the working class. What is a Government for, anyway?
>
> *Berkshire Chronicle*, 10 May 1940

The tribunals heard many differing interpretations of God's view on the war. One said that the war had been brought about by God as a punishment for mankind and their wickedness, while another volunteered to fight in Jehovah's army, but not that of wicked humans. Joseph Butler, a member of the Four Square Gospellers, believed that the war was far from being of God's making, and took a rather unworldly position:

> I have renounced worldly pleasures and worldly policies and I do not intend to be unequally yoked together with unbelievers in the execution of Christ-rejecting policies of men.
>
> *Swindon Advertiser*, 11 April 1940

However, all of these differed markedly from the bloodthirsty voice of Christianity offered by the Revd C.W. Whipp in the parish magazine of St Augustine's, Leicester:

> There should be no RAF pilot returning home because he cannot find a military objective for his bombs. The order should be 'Wipe them out' and to this end I would concentrate all our science towards discovering a far more terrific explosive. His hope was that the RAF will grow stronger and stronger and smash Germany to smithereens.
>
> Quoted in the *Swindon Advertiser*, 5 September 1940

A few of the applicants reached their decision to object by totally non-religious routes. A number claimed exemption on the grounds that they needed to care for sick or elderly relatives, which may well have been conscientious of them but not in the terms meant by the legislation. No more successful were those who pleaded exemption on the grounds of socialism, vegetarianism, membership of the Boy Scout movement or the fact that they were orphans. One young man spoke loftily about the prior claims his chosen vocation made on him:

> I cannot permit any responsibility to my country to take precedence over my loyalty to God. My loyalty will not allow me to be transferred from the career I have accepted.
>
> *Berkshire Chronicle*, 7 June 1940

And what was this overriding vocation? He was a clerk at the London County Council. Equally lofty were the views of Ronald Moss, who declared himself to be a Christian pacifist and a socialist who recognised no nations. To him, all wars were civil wars and he could not bring himself to fight against his brothers.

Another applicant, Edgar Priddy, had been a furniture sales man until he took a short vacation 'to improve his mind' and ended up reading up on pacifism. Richard Diment of Devizes sought conscientious objector status, not because he was a pacifist but because of his rooted objection to conscription. A Reading man, Arnold Greenwood, told the tribunal at Maidenhead that 'I object to taking part in this war because I do not believe that it is being fought for the ideals of peace, freedom and democracy'. He rather undermined his own case when he admitted that he would have no objection to killing Germans if he thought it would bring freedom to the German people (or, at least, to those who survived his efforts). Horace Goodlife told the tribunal that 'I would not care to be shot at or have cold steel run through me or be blown up' (a sentiment he no doubt shared with a good many conscripts, except that he concluded 'so I could not do the same to others').

Some claimed exemption because they had been traumatised by militarism at an early age. Charles Hutchen told the tribunal:

> My father was in the army for twenty-one years and I spent most of my childhood in barracks. I absolutely detest the sight of a uniform and the ordering of men about.
>
> *Berkshire Chronicle*, 2 August 1940

Tribunals often resorted to 'What if ...?' questions. One applicant, Leonard Offor, was asked what he would do if confronted by a German paratrooper with a rifle. He replied that he would try to talk with him. Asked if he could speak German, he said no, at which point, the tribunal suggested that the dialogue might be rather pointless.

Another individual preached a strange mixture of pacifism and fascism, arguing that:

> The fascist creed is the only thing to bring peace to this country. I believe all war is wrong because it leads to the destruction of man. I believe we are wrong in taking up arms against Germany because it was not Britain's responsibility.
>
> *Berkshire Chronicle*, 12 April 1940

It was established that he was a known activist for the fascists and his application was refused. Reginald Reader, a clerk from Kensington, had some fairly unconventional views about the causes of war:

> I think that the main cause of all wars is the love of man for woman's body. You may think I am mad, but I am no prude, indeed I am no different to any other man.
>
> *Swindon Advertiser*, 8 April 1940

His analysis failed to win him exemption. Another would-be objector in Manchester, having failed to persuade the tribunal of his deeply held pacifist tendencies, stabbed the chairman of the tribunal six times with a sheath knife; another opted for passive resistance:

> A 'conchie' had a grievance against the Ministry of Labour, so, instead of turning the other cheek, he thought he could air the grievance by staging a 'sit down' strike at the Labour Exchange. The manager said this opponent of force clung

> to tables, chairs, etc. and had to be forcibly ejected. Then he bought a summons against the manager for assault, alleging that the latter had used unnecessary force in ejecting him. The Chairman's comment was that the complainant was fortunate that he was not knocked about more.
>
> *Berkshire Chronicle*,
> 18 July 1941

Many would-be objectors were offered the option of registering for non-combatant duties. One such refused to engage even in such activities as road-building in case an army marched along it. He said his creed was based upon his surroundings:

> I find myself influenced by the countryside: fields, hills, plains, rivers, the sky and the natural life to be found there. Cycling about the country, not only in Britain but in other countries, getting to know the people and to realise more than ever the futility of wars and how unnecessary and undesirable they are.
>
> *Manchester City News*,
> 10 August 1940

The reactions of the tribunal can be predicted: 'Nobody is proud of you, run off home out of my sight', they told him, having registered him for non-combatant duties. Another would-be objector in Manchester went even further, claiming that he would not use an air raid shelter or a gas mask in the event of an air raid. 'You are quite a sincere young man', the tribunal told him, 'but we haven't a doubt that you possess stupid views'.

To help would-be objectors prepare for the rigours (or vagaries) of a tribunal, organisations like the Peace Pledge Union held test tribunals in which their own members played the roles of the inquisitors. It was reported that:

> Young men formed a large part of the audience and there was an atmosphere of intense seriousness throughout the proceedings.
>
> *Berkshire Chronicle*,
> 10 November 1939

The *Daily Express* reaction to these was 'Conchies learn the answers: mock tribunals teach them what to say'. Employers – in particular local authorities who felt more publicly accountable for their actions – agonised over what to do about any conscientious objectors on their payroll. Some were simply sacked or given unpaid leave of absence for the duration and told to find jobs in the war economy. For those who remained, there were a variety of options. They could be paid no more than they would have earned, had they been conscripted, on the basis that they should not benefit financially from their refusal to fight. They could be denied promotion, so that they did not advance their careers at the cost of their conscripted colleagues (though this did not address the question of them strengthening their CVs through the experience gained during the war years).

At the same time, those same employers had to consider whether to compensate their former employees for taking the patriotic step of signing up for a much less well-paid National Service. In Hampshire County Council, after much agonising, they came up with the formula of supplementing the army pay of their married conscripts (but not the single ones) up to half of their loss of income (the rationale for this was based upon the fact that the conscript would at least receive free uniform and lodging, representing a cost saving).

Hostility towards conscientious objectors sprang from the most unexpected quarters, such as the annual meeting of the Wiltshire, Hampshire and Dorset Beekeepers Federation. The report of a marked increase in the number of beekeepers since hostilities commenced prompted Mr H.F. Moore to ask:

> Are people to remain members of the Federation when they register as conscientious objectors? Some of us feel rather strongly about it … I don't think we like people like these in our midst.
>
> *Swindon Advertiser*, 8 April 1940

Members were urged to look after the hives of those colleagues who volunteered to fight, rather than let the bees fall into the hands of pacifists. It was left to meetings such as those of the Swindon Pacifist Groups to make the general case for conscientious objection:

> Revd. C.H. Cleal denied that the crushing of Germany by military force was the only method by which the true independence of Poland could be safeguarded, and pointed out that a lasting peace could only come about as a result of the willingness of governments to come to the conference table and to share their resources in the interests of the common people …
>
> Pacifists would be the first to desire to give every assistance to the evacuees, and many would … offer their services in ambulance and hospital work.
>
> *Swindon Advertiser*, 16 September 1939

There was no shortage of suggestions in the letters pages – most of them hostile – as to what to do with conscientious objectors. One called for them to be employed in repairing bomb damage, while others – in a chilling echo of what was going on in mainland Europe – called for them to be made to wear distinctive badges or armbands. Some even wanted them to have their own concentration camps.

Friends of Hitler and the Fifth Column

Those on the far right were left floundering by developments, though they were largely a spent force, even before the final scenes of the build-up to war were acted out. Oswald Mosley's British Union of Fascists (BUF) was the only far-right organisation of any size, and even their membership was just 22,500 by 1939, of which only some 8,000 were active. This shrank still further as hostilities grew closer. The mainstream had had a brief flirtation with Mosley in the early 1930s, with car manufacturer Lord Nuffield funding what was then called his New Party to the tune of £50,000 and the *Daily Mail* running an article praising Mosley's 'sound commonsense Conservative doctrine' under the headline 'Hurrah for the blackshirts!' But people had been alienated by the violence that attended the events they organised and the increasingly shrill anti-Semitism of their policies.

Nevertheless, how were they now to reconcile their support for the policies of Hitler with their patriotic instincts as Englishmen? Some, notably William Joyce, the future Lord Haw-Haw, voted with their feet and left for Germany. Others, such as Admiral Sir Barrie Domville and his far-right organisation The Link, went down the patriotic route, declaring (as they wound their organisation up) that the king's enemy is our enemy. Unity Mitford was so divided in her loyalties that she shot herself in the head; and I summarised Mosley's shifting stance as follows:

> Once war broke out, Mosley tried initially to maintain a relatively neutral stance, calling on supporters not to be dragged into 'an alien quarrel' caused by 'the dope machine of Jewish finance'. They should instead engage in civil defence activities and 'do nothing to damage our country or to help any other power'. By May 1940 Mosley went further and put his supporters at the disposal of the British defences, in the event of an invasion. He even condemned members of the Nordic League as Nazi traitors. It later transpired that he was not, unlike some of his fellow extremists, on the Nazis' list of potential collaborators.
>
> Hylton (2010), p. 89

The BUF party rank and file did not always follow Mosley's lead; it emerged that the Westminster branch of the BUF were stocking up on ARP helmets and badges with the aim of distributing them to their supporters in the East End, who in turn planned to pose as wardens and go out beating up Jews during air raids. Some complied with the letter of Mosley's changed policy, arguing that people should do their duty (largely as a means of trying to avoid the party being proscribed) whilst spreading pacifist and defeatist propaganda. Others took up membership of the Peace Pledge Union as a convenient vehicle for campaigning for a negotiated peace with Hitler. The Phoney War period to some extent played into their hands, offering evidence that Hitler had no evil intent towards Britain. But their shifting stance did neither the party nor its leader any good; the BUF was the only organisation (as distinct from individuals) to be proscribed under the Defence Regulations and Mosley himself was interned. Once hostilities got under way in earnest, the views of the far right carried little weight in the mainstream of public opinion.

At the same time there remained concerns about fascist sympathisers forming a Fifth Column. Two of the most fruitful sources for these concerns were the German propaganda broadcasts of Lord Haw-Haw and the government's rather panic-stricken actions in its ill-judged Silent Column campaign, and in rounding up all enemy aliens. More precisely, the concerns about Haw-Haw were more about what he was alleged to have said, for his supposed knowledge of the minutiae of the British domestic scene tended to improve with each retelling. In Slough in May 1940, rumours began to circulate about remarks Haw-Haw apparently made about the town. Allegedly he complimented the town clerk on the display of tulips outside the town hall (which he said would not be left standing for long) and pointed out that the clock at the Finefield Garage was running slow. (There were several versions of these stories in circulation, involving different beds of tulips, different clocks and different targets around the town.)

The trouble was that nobody could be found who had actually heard the broadcasts – all the reports were second- or third-hand. The *Slough Observer* challenged any of its readers who had actually heard the broadcasts to come forward. Meanwhile, correspondents began to speculate about a possible Fifth Column in Slough, spreading rumours to destroy morale:

> Before the war, Slough had a German club with a large following. At one of their social functions at the Good Companions, more than two hundred attended, and at that time the swastika was hung over the platform in the hall. When Hitler forced all Germans living outside the Reich to join the party or lose their passports, Slough German Club members embarked on a 'strength through joy' ship and celebrated their link with the party to the tune of a German band … It would appear that, in the Slough German Club before the war, there was the machinery for forming the nucleus of a Fifth Column.
>
> *Slough Observer*, 17 May 1940

In the event, no one who had actually heard the broadcasts came forward and the paper was able to establish authoritatively through the Ministry of Information that Haw-Haw had made no such references. None of this stemmed the nationwide obsession with the supposed Fifth Column (for whose existence precious little evidence was ever found). Official sources warned their readership that the first task of the German parachutists (who were mostly 'young men of the desperado type, armed with machine pistols') would be to organise and arm the local Fifth Column. In Holland, readers were told, the Fifth Columnists carried identity cards and had a special code word to identify themselves with the invaders.

However, if Haw-Haw lacked a Fifth Column, there was another source of intelligence open to him. In June 1940, the Germans were alerted (via the British press) to a valuable new source of intelligence about the Allied war effort – the parish magazine. It appeared that these innocent documents were betraying all sorts of secrets about troop concentrations and their embarkation points, and about the location of new war industries, simply by describing the clergy's efforts to minister to these new flocks.

Those of foreign extraction – no matter how unimpeachable their anti-Hitler credentials might be – were particularly suspect as Fifth Columnists in some eyes. The Member of Parliament for South Oxfordshire received this petition from 285 of his constituents:

> We have seen with alarm reports of the activities of enemy alien women and children in Holland and Belgium, and of the effective assistance given by them to German parachute troops. In view of the imminence of this peril to us and our cause, we are of the opinion that all enemy alien women and children, over the age of twelve years, should be interned immediately, together with all males of whatever category.
>
> *Henley Standard*, 31 May 1940

The editorial response showed that they were far from alone in their views:

> We have had many similar expressions of opinion from our readers in Henley and district … Even stronger measures are advocated. No action can be too drastic for the Government to take to endeavour to save us from the evils of spies in our midst. In this connection Belgian refugees will want very careful watching, many of them may be the agents of our enemy.
>
> *Henley Standard*, 31 May 1940

If they were not incarcerated, was it acceptable to employ aliens as domestic servants? One reader's letter asked his fellow countrymen:

> … whether they consider it a wise or patriotic thing to harbour aliens amongst their households. An alien may not be pro-Nazi, but nearly every one of them is pro-country. Holland, Belgium, Norway and France have all suffered from 'Fifth Columnists', many of whom have been alien servants. Why should we flatter ourselves we are immune from this dangerous pest?
>
> I appeal to all employers of alien servants within this country whether they would not be willing to forego some of the domestic comforts brought into their homes by these people, if it were for the national good that they be cleared out. Safety first!
>
> Letter to the *Hampshire Chronicle*, 22 June 1940

Aren't we Doing Badly/Well?

The Allied authorities were very concerned at the potential for propaganda and defeatist talk to undermine public morale. In June 1940, Sir Arthur Willert, the Southern Regional Officer for the Ministry of Information, found himself making a tour of Reading's largest employers, giving five-minute pep talks on the danger of spreading rumour and gossip. He told the 5,000 workers at the Huntley and Palmer biscuit factory over their public address system:

> Force is not the only weapon in the desperate fight that [Hitler] is making to smash us and our freedom. He regards propaganda, the spreading of false news, intimidation and spying as weapons just as important in their place as tanks and aeroplanes. It is his policy to weaken an adversary before he tries to knock him down.
>
> *Berkshire Chronicle*, 14 June 1940

In addition to those who were ideologically opposed to the war, there were the defeatists, who, without necessarily any ideological prompting, thought Britain's cause was hopelessly lost. Given that an essential part of an Englishman's birth right is his freedom to grumble, that part of the Defence Regulations dealing with the spreading of alarm and despondency may have been one of the more difficult ones for parts of the public to accept. John O'Gorman of Cottisford found himself so charged, after being heard telling a group of young men that all the news in the papers was lies, half of London was down and that Spitfires were 'not a bit of use'. In summary, he said 'England is beat and we might as well pack in'. His grumbles earned him fourteen days behind bars. In similar vein, Ernest Chandler, a storekeeper at Reading Aerodrome who expressed the view to colleagues that Churchill, Morrison and Bevin should be put against a wall and shot, earned himself a fine.

Contrast these cases with that of Ivor Teague of Cowley, charged with 'injudicious talk' at work. He told his colleagues that London and England were as good as done for and that Hitler would land in London soon. His case was dismissed, on the curious grounds that a person should not be convicted if he had reasonable cause to believe that the report or statement was true. Whether any reasonable causes for belief were bouncing around inside the head of the next case was much more debatable:

> SURROUNDED BY A HOSTILE CROWD. GOVERNMENT CHARGED WITH A BREACH OF THE PEACE.
> Stated at Reading Borough Police Court on Saturday to have shouted 'You have not got much longer! England will soon fall and then you will see!' Nelson Noakes (53) of 11, Lydalls Road, Didcot was charged with using words which might have led to a breach of the peace. He pleaded guilty.
>
> Detective Constable A. Powell said Noakes was surrounded by a hostile crowd in St. Mary's Butts, Reading.
>
> Superintendent W. Osborne said that Noakes, a clerk in local government employ, was an eccentric who described himself as a faith healer. He called himself 'the Reverend Noakes'. He

frequently drank cheap wine and then became abusive. 'He was arrested principally for his own safety', he added.

Noakes, who said he had been drinking, was fined £1 or 14 days' imprisonment in default.

Berkshire Chronicle, 21 June 1940

Telephone installer Arthur Thearle chose the heart of the establishment to spread his message of doom. Whilst doing work at the residence of the Duke of Kent, he subjected the duke's butler (and a plainclothes policeman who happened to be within earshot) to a twenty-minute tirade, during the course of which he said that the Nazi flag would soon be flying from every principal building in England, that Hitler was cleverer than any man in this country, that Germany will have conquered France by the end of June 1940 and that Neville Chamberlain was a relative of Mussolini.

At the other end of the optimism spectrum were the relentlessly upbeat accounts of the progress of the war issued by official sources which, in the early stages in particular, bore scant resemblance to what was happening on the ground. During the Norway campaign of 1940, newspaper readers were treated to days of reports of how well the Allied forces were doing, only to be told of their subsequent ignominious withdrawal. The press were not happy, as this editorial comment from the *Oxford Mail* demonstrates:

The Service mind … tries to cover up things when they are going badly. It likes to feed the public on silly stories showing how much better are our soldiers and our airmen than those of the enemy. Then one day people are allowed to wake up to the truth and they are angry.

Oxford Mail, 7 May 1940

11

Divided by a Common Cause: Us and our Gallant Allies

Britain and Socialism: Red Peril to Uncle Joe

In the run-up to war, there was much pressure for the government to enter into some kind of alliance with Soviet Russia, as a means of bringing pressure on Hitler not to start hostilities. Britain was not the most obvious ally for the Russians, but the Germans were even less so, and the signing of a Russian-German non-aggression pact in August 1939 therefore came as a great shock:

> The Soviet-German non-aggression pact has so completely swept the ground from underneath the feet of our reds that they have been driven to write the utmost drivel.
>
> What are the facts? For many months we have been treated to a barrage of howls for alliance with Russia, all fostered by the Communist parties in every country on the instructions received from Moscow. Our Labour and Liberal parties have been thoroughly tricked.
>
> Letter to the *Slough Observer*, 1 September 1939

At the outbreak of war, Soviet Russia was widely seen in Britain as a force for evil virtually on a par with Nazi Germany, as this editorial from the first weeks of hostilities makes clear:

> It is now quite clear that Russia aims at keeping the war going as long as is necessary to tighten her hold on the Baltic and to spread Bolshevism into Europe ... The notion that Bolshevism has any sympathetic feelings towards the democratic nations can only be entertained by those unacquainted with its theory and practice. Moreover, those who have been holding up Communism as a super-religion or as a desirable social system must be in a state of bewilderment.
>
> *Berkshire Chronicle*, 13 October 1939

A letter to the *Spectator* summarised the view many British people had of Russia at that time:

> A society in which the state owns the land and capital and in which the state is owned by a despot and his satellites, who appropriate to themselves the profit from the labour of the worker and peasant alike. Russia under Stalin has more in common with Russia under Peter the Great or even Russia under Ivan the Terrible than with the 'bourgeois democracies'.
>
> Quoted in the *Berkshire Chronicle*, 3 November 1939

In January 1941, the British Government suppressed the communist newspaper the *Daily Worker* under the Defence Regulations, on the grounds that it repeatedly contained 'matter calculated to foment opposition to successful prosecution of the war'. Home Secretary Herbert Morrison explained his reasons:

> It is my firm conviction that freedom of the press should be maintained, even at the risk that it may sometimes be abused. There is, however, a wide distance between accepting such occasional risks and allowing the continuous publication of newspapers of which the deliberate purpose is to weaken the will of our people to achieve victory ...
>
> The Daily Worker has, by every device of distortion and misrepresentation, sought to make out that our people have

> nothing to gain by victory and that the hardships and sufferings of warfare are unnecessary and are imposed upon them by a callous government, carrying out a selfish contest in the interests of a privileged class …
>
> All other considerations are subordinated to the fantastic hope that the weakening of democratic institutions may provide an opportunity for the substitution of a Communist dictatorship.
>
> *Swindon Advertiser*, 22 January 1941

Within hours of the shutdown, a mimeographed pamphlet from the *Daily Worker* circulated, setting out the details of the suppression and calling for the British public to oppose it. How far did this appeal to the sacred proposition of free speech strike a chord with the British public, and in particular with their fellow journalists? Not very far, if this editorial from the *Portsmouth Evening News* was anything to go by:

> There is a tendency among our long-haired leftists to sound the tocsin of freedom over the suppression of the Daily Worker, the organ of the British Communist Party. Such a tendency should be eradicated.
>
> In the first place, the British Communist Party is not British, but merely the British branch of a foreign party whose policy is wholly of foreign dictation, framed in the interest of the dictators, and which the branch must follow without cavil or discretion, as witness the volte face of the British Communists over Poland. In a sentence the British Communists are not free agents, as are the members of our native parties, but must do as they have been told, and by the constitution of the party, the tellers of the doing are Stalin and the Russian Communists.
>
> In the second place, there is no difference in object between the Communists and Hitler, our declared enemy, with whom we are at war, in that the object of each is to subvert this country by arms if other means fail – in the case of

> Hitler by military conquest, in the case of the Communists by civil war …
>
> In the third place, the force used by the Communists against us is the Fifth Column and the Daily Worker has a place in this column only second in importance to the subversive work undertaken in our factories. Again, in a sentence, in tolerating the Daily Worker, we were acting no different from allowing Dr Goebbels to publish his own daily newspaper in London and Glasgow.
>
> *Portsmouth Evening News*, 28 January 1941

During 1940 and 1941, something called the People's Convention was promoted in Britain, and stimulated debate in the local press. It was backed by communist elements (though the party itself never officially adopted it) and many of its leading advocates were well-known and long-standing members of the Communist Party. It sought to persuade Labour supporters and trade unionists that the British coalition government was the tool of the rich, dominated by appeasers who bore much of the responsibility for a war from which they were profiteering, and who opposed the Soviet Union. According to the Convention's trade union opponents:

> The chief political objective is to turn out the present Government and replace it by a so-called 'People's Government'. Up to the present, nobody among the supporters of the Convention appears to know of whom the People's Cabinet will consist, except that it seems clear that none of the present leaders of the Labour Party will be among them.
>
> From a letter to the *Berkshire Chronicle*, 27 December 1940

One of the movement's champions, Mr D.N. Pritt MP, addressed the Oxford University Labour Club and told them:

> This war is the child of capitalism and it cannot do the working classes any good. It is said to be a war for freedom and

> democracy; it is a war for the freedom and democracy of the possessing classes and not for the freedom and democracy of the working classes … The manifesto of the People's Government Movement is based on a defence of the standard of living of the people, the preservation of civil liberties and trades union rights and privileges, the provision of proper air raid precautions and the establishing of a people's government which would end the war and give a true and lasting peace.
>
> *Oxford Times*, 6 December 1940

And how was it to do that? 'The only way to end wars is to get rid of the economic causes of war and this can only be achieved by the introduction of a socialist system.' The practicalities of achieving the peace were simple, in their view: 'The People's Government would go to the German working classes and offer them a peace with no annexations, no indemnities, equal economic opportunities and no exploitation. Such an offer would be accepted and would lead to the overthrow of the Hitler regime.' Should further assurance be needed: 'If this country had a People's Government, the Soviet Union would rally to the British cause and this would lead to a German collapse in about a week' (*Oxford Times*, 6 December 1940).

Predictably, this speech was like a red rag to the editorial bull of the *Oxford Times*:

> Oxford is rapidly gaining an unsavoury reputation as a centre of subversive propaganda. The speech of Mr D.N. Pritt M.P. to the University Labour Club on Friday was well calculated to strengthen that reputation. That anyone should be free to make such a speech with impunity in a country fighting for its life must astound other nations and provides in itself an unanswerable reply to Mr Pritt's preposterous suggestion that a Communist movement is needed to secure freedom in this country.
>
> *Oxford Times*, 6 December 1940

The Convention was resolutely opposed by the Labour Party and the trade unions, and Mr Pritt would go on to face expulsion from the party and calls from his constituency for him to stand down as their MP. The prospective Labour candidate for South Oxfordshire, the Hon. Logan Philipps, was also among those who found himself being expelled from the party for supporting the Convention. He was unrepentant, telling the local paper:

> Since the Labour Party has agreed to a truce with the largest capitalist party and I am determined to fight capitalism even in the war because I do not want a capitalist peace, I see that, from their point of view, the Labour Party leaders had no alternative but to expel me. I shall continue to work hard as a socialist and I am confident that, through the trend of events, I and my friends in Oxfordshire will soon be side by side again.
>
> *Berkshire Chronicle*, 9 May 1941

The People's Convention never really gained a foothold in mainstream public opinion, and in January 1942 was actively disowned even by the Communist Party of Great Britain.

The shifting position of Soviet Russia in the war years, from co-conspirator with Hitler in the dismemberment of Eastern Europe to victim of fascist invasion and main prosecutor of the war against Germany, tied everyone in ideological knots. Churchill, a committed anti-communist who had previously advocated military intervention to undermine the 1917 revolution, found himself having to ally with and arm the Russians. But he acknowledged that, if Hitler invaded hell, he would feel obliged to make at least a favourable reference to the devil in the Commons.

Most of all, it left the Communist Party of Great Britain doing political somersaults. Early in the war, they would no doubt have lobbied for a negotiated peace and possibly even

Hitler and Stalin become the playthings of the advertisers.

subscribed to the view that the Russian-German pact was no more than 'a defensive coming together of the two nations threatened by British encirclement' (which was the explanation Hitler gave when it was signed). In Manchester there were furious protests in October 1939 at plans by the Communist Party to stage an event, explaining that 'Russia fights for peace'. Their reasoning was that 'Stalin is mopping up the Baltic states, Poland and Romania in the interests of the higher morality'.

However, once Hitler launched Operation Barbarossa against the Russians in June 1941, the British Communist Party became one of the nation's most enthusiastic protagonists of the war, arguing for a second front and at the same time for egalitarian measures such as better air raid shelters for the working classes. Suddenly 'Uncle' Joe Stalin and his Red Army became Britain's gallant ally, bearing the brunt of the German onslaught, and

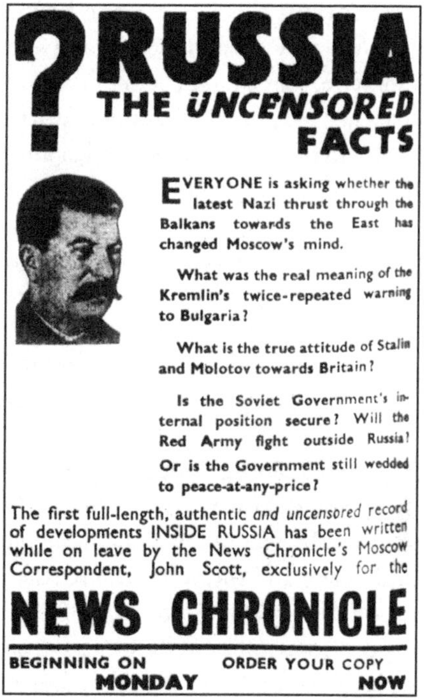

The press struggles to re-assess its attitude towards Russia at the start of Hitler's eastern campaign.

their system of government was suddenly (for many people) beyond reproach:

> The Red Army last week received generous tributes; never were tributes more justly earned.
>
> I suggest that the same high tribute should be extended to the Russian system of government, a system responsible for their success, spirit and endurance in war and peace.
>
> The moral strength arising from their system of government has provided the courage and inspiration which is the explanation of the Red Army's successes.
>
> Letter to the *Slough Observer*,
> 26 February 1943

Some curious alliances came to be forged by the necessities of war. A newly elected Conservative MP, Captain C.E. Mott-Radclyffe, sent a public letter of thanks to his local Communist Party in 1942, for their support during the election. His campaign vitriol had been directed against his opponent, who had stood as an independent:

> Independent candidates in these days are virtually, but perhaps unconsciously, Fifth Columnists. They have no policy, no loyalty. They merely stand for themselves and say what they like; and it is very easy to catch votes from innocent people.
>
> *Maidenhead Advertiser*, 17 June 1942

One consequence of this realignment was a good deal of rewriting of Soviet history. Anglo-Soviet friendship societies sprang up around the country and conducted energetic campaigns of fundraising and spreading the Russian party line. As one illustration, the Maidenhead Anglo-Soviet Committee was treated to a presentation on religion in Russia, which was reported in the local paper. From this, they learned that Soviet Russia was a veritable oasis of religious tolerance. It seems 'It was not until Germany attacked Russia that people began to learn the truth

Russia is by now firmly established as 'our gallant ally'.

about religion in the USSR'. But what of all those people said to be imprisoned for their religious beliefs? It turned out that their incarceration had nothing to do with their religion – they were simply enemies of the state.

Speakers elsewhere told their audiences that famine and illiteracy had been abolished in Russia, that the Russian army, unlike Britain's, was not dominated by the Old School Tie; and that officers were often elected by their fellow soldiers. At the same time, Stalin had been entirely justified in shooting most of his generals – 'it was a good thing that they were removed in time'. As for Stalin himself, he was 'definitely not a "world revolutionary" but working with the good of his own country as his object'. It had been Trotsky, 'being a Jew and therefore a man without a country, who was more inclined towards internationalism' and who had tried to undermine Russia's progress at every turn.

Another speaker told us that the Russian people were very much like us; facially, most Britons could pass for Russians, and they shared a sense of humour and a fondness for children and sport. In fact, the Russians were the 'happiest and most joyous people', if the Rotary Club speaker during Reading's Russia Week were to be believed. According to him, they enjoyed four to seven weeks' paid holiday a year, free medical and dental treatment, equal rights and wages for women, crèches for the children of working mothers and even freedom of expression – apparently, 'peasants and work people could be vociferous if they objected to anything'. Particularly vociferous, according to yet another Russian expert, were its womenfolk. He told his audience that a new type of woman had emerged in Russia:

> She may have lost many of the characteristics that we associated with woman, she was less modest and sensitive, but she was more confident and proud and had more character. Home life as we knew it had gone, the new home life based on affection, comradeship and equality had replaced it.
>
> *Berkshire Chronicle*, 10 July 1942

The BBC did not know which way to face. They ran a programme in which the national anthems of all the Allied countries were broadcast, but once the Russians joined the Allied side they could not bring themselves to broadcast their subversive anthem, the *Internationale*. Slough Labour Party registered a 'vigorous protest' against this decision and said that they:

> … repudiate completely the blind and ignorant opposition now being shown by sections of the ruling class of this country and it recognises and appreciates the splendid fighting resistance of the Russian forces in the common struggle against Fascism.
>
> *Slough Observer*, 11 July 1941

Despite the tune being a call to revolution, the *Observer*'s correspondent was in agreement with them:

> I fail to see what harm can be done by playing a tune on a brass band once a week, especially as it is quite a fine tune of its kind, with rather a Salvation Army style about it. It makes no difference to the Russians whether we play it or not – they will go on with the commendable process of slaughtering Germans to the last ounce of their strength.
>
> *Slough Observer*, 18 July 1941

At home, some were of the view that our own Labour Party, given free rein after the war, would turn Britain into some kind of anglicised communist state. Churchill – disastrously for his election prospects – tried to prey on precisely these fears during the 1945 General Election.

Given the huge degree of state control and the increased taxation that were made necessary by the war, it is not difficult to see where such fears might have stemmed from. But some, unlike Churchill, would not wait until after the war to voice their fears. In January 1941 the Maidenhead Chamber of Commerce raised its banner, vowing to fight any future government that tried to establish state ownership along the Soviet model in the country. The private trader had, they said, been taxed almost out of existence during the war years. Their only hope of fighting off this rising tide of socialism was to join the Maidenhead Chamber of Commerce. Their stirring rallying cry made front-page news, at least in Maidenhead.

The United States

> It is always impolite to criticize your hosts; it is militarily stupid to criticize your allies.
>
> *Instructions for American Servicemen in Britain*, p. 23

In 1942, the United States War Department issued instructions to its troops, who were about to depart for a posting in Britain, on how to co-exist with their hosts. In the introduction, it warned that 'the first and major duty Hitler has given his propaganda chiefs is to separate Britain and America and spread distrust between them. If he can do that, his chances of winning *might* return.' But there were times when we seemed to be doing rather well at falling out without any help from Goebbels and his colleagues. Many Americans were as shocked by British class divisions as the British were by some Americans' attitudes to racial differences. This latter was perhaps less to do with any liberalism on the part of the British, but more to do with the fact that black people were virtually unknown in most parts of Britain before the war, and seemed as exotic as creatures from another planet. In particular, the American authorities were alarmed at the ease with which British women fraternised with black GIs, and some of them conducted a public relations campaign to tell the British 'how to treat the blacks'. They warned that:

> They all carried knives and would certainly try to rape their daughters. Never invite them into your home and above all never … treat them as human beings, because they are not.
>
> Quoted in Nicholson, p. 197

The American population consisted of a great mix of immigrants from other nations, and there was a fear that those of, for example, German or Irish origin, would have at best mixed loyalties and, at worst, see it as an opportunity to fight old wars.

For many, the main problem with the influx of US service personnel was summed up in the saying that they were 'overpaid, over-sexed and over here'. The servicemen's guide warned the GIs that they were 'higher paid than the British "Tommy". Don't rub it in' and 'Don't show off or brag or bluster'. The GIs' affluence and their access to consumer luxuries largely unobtainable to the British nonetheless became a bone of contention between the Americans and at least some of their hosts:

> When pay day comes it would be sound practice to learn to spend your money according to British standards. They consider you highly paid. They won't think any better of you for throwing money around; they are more likely to feel that you haven't learned the common-sense virtues of thrift. The British 'Tommy' is apt to be especially touchy about the differences between his wages and yours.
>
> *Instructions for American Servicemen in Britain*, p. 6

This ill feeling was not helped by the fact that large numbers of GIs were concentrated in the United Kingdom, awaiting D-Day, whilst many of their British counterparts were serving overseas. Goebbels' propagandists actively sought to exploit feelings of jealousy and suspicions about what was going on back at home, behind their backs.

Not least, there were the problems that could arise from the temptation for each nation to criticise the other's conduct of

Britain and America were at least agreed on their choice of kitchen appliances.

the war. During Hitler's last desperate attempt at a counter-attack – the Battle of the Bulge – the *Manchester City News* took soundings of the state of relations between the two nations:

> Walking about Manchester during the recent days of the German breakthrough, I was shocked by the attitude of the average man and woman. They unanimously expressed relief that the Germans had broken through the American lines and not the British. Some were mildly savage and suggested that it would teach the Americans a lesson. Others said they felt that if it had been us instead of them their press would have given us a round drubbing and we should have been told that we were losing the war.
>
> ... The future peace of the world depends very greatly on the strength of the bond of friendship between America and Great Britain. Peace will come to earth first to men of goodwill, and if there is not goodwill between English-speaking nations, where can we expect to find it?
>
> Some of the American criticisms of Great Britain are not so much false as vicious. They should be killed, if necessary, with vigour. As The Economist put it 'To be told by anyone that the British people are slacking in their war effort would be insufferable enough to a people struggling through their sixth winter of a blackout, and bombs, and queues and rations and coldness – but when the criticism comes from a nation

that was practicing cash-and-carry during the Battle of Britain, whose consumption has risen during the war years, which is still without a National Service Act – then it is not to be borne'.

It is time Great Britain went her own way, with vigour, foresight and courage. We shall get nothing out of American goodwill if all we do to help it is appease it.

Manchester City News, 5 January 1945

In some respects the American enclaves in Britain were like a state within a state. They had complete jurisdiction over the behaviour of their troops, even for crimes committed outside the base, and in Bath (and no doubt elsewhere) the Snowdrops (American Military Police) even had their own dedicated cell in the city's police station, over which they again had complete control.

All of this was in marked contrast to Canadian troops based here, who were subject to British legal process and seemed to appear before it with almost depressing regularity, particularly in cases involving drunkenness and brawling. Norman Mackintosh, speaking to a Rotary Club meeting about Canada's war effort, offered the following explanation:

Speaking of the Canadian soldiers over here, allowance must be made for them, as the national drink of Canada is ice cream soda and they are not accustomed to the beer and whiskey they are getting here. They are now realising that, and are creating a good impression wherever they are stationed.

Slough Observer, 25 February 1944

An extreme example of American independence of action was to be seen in October 1944, when an argument broke out in a pub in the village of Kingsclere between some United States soldiers and their Military Police. This escalated into a shoot-out worthy of the wildest of Wild West saloons, which left the pub landlady and two of the soldiers dead. Despite it involving the murder of a British citizen, the British authorities were powerless to take any action against the surviving soldiers, who would face an American court martial. The coroner could not even conduct the landlady's inquest, pending the completion of the American proceedings (which led to nine soldiers being given life sentences for the three killings). The matter was considered serious enough in terms of Anglo-American relations for General Eisenhower to send a personal message, relayed through the local newspaper, expressing his sorrow and regret:

> … that this most unfortunate and regrettable affair, resulting in the death of a local resident, should have occurred and been caused by United States troops. He sincerely hoped that the effect of this occurrence would not tend to excite public opinion and tend to detract from the friendly good feeling and spirit of cooperation which existed between our two English-speaking nations.
>
> *Newbury Weekly News*, 26 October 1944

In another case, a GI slashed a policeman with a knife, leaving him with a wound requiring ten stitches. In reporting the subsequent trial, the local paper went out of its way to praise the American administration of justice, almost to the point of suggesting that any misbehaviour might be partly the fault of the British:

> How many of my readers noted the severe penalty inflicted on the American soldier by the American Army court martial, for the very un-English offence of slashing a policeman with a knife … Two years' hard labour, loss of all pay due and also all rights of American citizenship is a severe sentence and it indicates the determination of the American Army authorities that their forces over here shall suffer if they misbehave. Their determination places upon us all the obligation

> to see that nothing is done which in any way can cause resentment in the American forces or to provoke them into any hasty quarrels.
>
> *Slough Observer*, 3 March 1944

However, some members of the British public were keen on friendly good feeling between the two nations, and the United States military found it necessary to issue ground rules for US servicemen wishing to marry British women. The local press advised that they would require written permission from their commanding officer, and this would need to be applied for two months in advance. This gave the commanding officer time to establish that the marriage would not breach any American laws. This consent would have to be produced on the wedding day, to enable the marriage take place. The authorities were at pains to point out that the marriage did not confer American citizenship on the bride; it did no more than to facilitate her subsequent entry into the USA and any application she might make for citizenship thereafter. Any serviceman evading these regulations could find himself facing a court martial.

12

What Are We Fighting For? War Aims

VICTORY.

Winston Churchill

To give up buying is to surrender.

A businessman in *Portsmouth Evening News*, 29 September 1939

What were the British fighting for? An obvious question, but the answer was not so simple. The defence of Poland against German aggression was the immediate answer but, just a year before, Prime Minister Neville Chamberlain had said in the context of similar German threats against Czechoslovakian sovereignty that he could see no sense in going to war 'because of a quarrel in a far-away country between people of whom we know nothing'. How much less 'far-away' and how much better known to the general public was Poland? Not much, according to the *Slough Observer*. Their introduction to the subject began:

> At this time, the eyes of the world are centred on one point – Poland. Yet how many people know anything about

> this country? How many people could even describe the Polish flag?
>
> *Slough Observer*, 8 September 1939

The *Portsmouth Evening News* was not alone in the days leading up to the war in setting out war aims that were both pure and simple:

> Whatever happens, let us remember that our hands are clean, our conscience clear. We are not aggressors, we have no selfish ends to serve, no ambitions to gratify. Our aim is but to defend Freedom – the freedom of small peoples to live their own lives, the freedom of the world from tyranny backed by violence. In such a cause we fight with moral argument as well as material. Justice and right are with us, and we believe we cannot fail.
>
> *Portsmouth Evening News*, 1 September 1939

In the event, Polish resistance crumbled within four weeks, before the British and French Expeditionary Forces had a chance to make an effective intervention. Poland would not be 'liberated' from Nazi occupation until the Russians moved in, in 1944. So, with the original *raison d'être* for the state of war looking increasingly like a lost cause, as 1940 progressed and the British Expeditionary Force retreated back across the Channel, what was then the justification for it? Would victory mean something different and better in a post-war world, or just more of the same?

From the earliest days of the war, the lack of a definite statement of Britain's war aims was, to put it no higher, an embarrassment. As early as mid-September 1939 Goebbels decided to help out, by broadcasting Germany's understanding of our war aims, which included such things as the restoration of Austria under the Hapsburg Empire. The Ministry of Information

This advertisement makes an oblique reference to war aims, something which the Daily Herald encouraged people to discuss.

issued a denial, but had to admit that no British statement of war aims had yet been formulated. At home, *Picture Post* magazine also did the job for the government. Their 4 January 1941 edition, devoted to 'the Britain we hope to build when the war is over', drew a huge response from the public.

One problem with finding that message was that we had been far from a united nation as we entered the war. Desperately bad housing conditions, inadequate schools and health care, and the spectre of a poverty-stricken old age hung over a sizeable part of the population. It would not be enough to ask those people to buy into a perpetuation of the status quo.

In February 1940, the audience listening to a speech by Anthony Eden had thought they were going to get some answers to the war aims question when the following passage in his speech attracted tumultuous applause:

> Younger men would want to know why money was available in apparently unlimited quantity for re-armament, while for re-housing, road construction, education and for general social purposes it was rigidly and strictly limited.
>
> *Hampshire Chronicle*, 24 February 1940

However, having whetted their appetite, Eden immediately changed the subject. It was as if 'he either would not, or could not, give the reason for the existence of the state of affairs', the Winchester Rotary Club was told, by someone who had been a member of Eden's audience. At the local level, there were still those who saw it as being not strictly our war. This Buckinghamshire County Councillor was one such:

> The Jew, German, Czech, or any other refugee should be formed into a Legion of Honour and ... they themselves should go out into the front line and fight ... it is their battle ... If they are allowed to come into Aylesbury and Buckinghamshire and to take the jobs of those who are themselves going and fighting, then I think it would be a very undesirable thing and would have a very bad effect.
>
> *Bucks Herald*, 15 September 1939

In 1942, a government white paper with the unpromising title 'Report on Social Insurance and Allied Services' (better known as the Beveridge Report) was published. This laid down the foundations of the post-war welfare state and became (at least for the 86 per cent of the population that was said to support it) the nearest thing the nation had to a statement of war aims. For the sake of completeness, it should also be recorded that the *ITMA* man, comedian Tommy Handley, separately appointed his own advisor – 'His Fatuity the Minister of Social Hilarity' – who provided his own version of the report, 'Gone with the want'.

Looking Forward to Peace

As the immediate threat of invasion gradually receded, so speculation about the post-war world increased. It sounded as if the *Portsmouth Evening News* did not mind too much what the British post-war aims were (at least as far as the domestic agenda was concerned) so long as everyone was agreed on them and did not fall out. After the war (they said):

> … externally we want nothing out of the war except to restore their countries to those deprived of them and to see a Europe settled under conditions which will provide a better guarantee of peace and a chance of prosperity to the world as a whole …
>
> But what about post-war Britain herself and her future conditions? We have to envisage a country greatly impoverished compared with the end of the last war, and in especially marked degree compared with the vast surplus resources that were ours before that war … We cannot, once the war has been won, break our political unity and resume our party dog-fights, but must remain behind the Government until the peace also has been won and the country is advancing surely on its new path.
>
> *Portsmouth Evening News*,
> 24 January 1941

Implicitly, they seemed to be supporting the line promoted by Winston Churchill, of the country continuing with a Conservative-led government of national unity.

By February 1944, the local authorities were turning their minds towards the post-war world. Having operated for many years within a system in which local initiative was minutely controlled from the centre, they grew frustrated at the government's reluctance to make its intentions clear, prompting this from the *Manchester City News*:

> There is a considerable feeling among our Manchester City Councillors at the Government's slowness at announcing its future plans. Almost every aspect of post-war development is in abeyance, due to a general lack of information from Government circles. There has been so much centralisation during

> the last decade, that it is completely imperative for a local authority to declare that it will go ahead, taking for granted that it can manage without the Government.
>
> ... How much longer are we going to suffer these vague and unhappy predictions – the incompetence and timidity – which characterise responsible government departments?
>
> *Manchester City News*, 25 February 1944

Everyone with relevant expertise (and quite a few without it) had their own perspective on post-war priorities. Naturally enough, wish lists for a less austere way of life emerged. In a series of editorials, the *Manchester City News* tried to downplay some of the more ambitious ideas:

> There has been so much said about streamlined kitchens, post-war air travel and all the other luxury items of a new Arcadia that it is time we faced the hard facts. There is a danger that, in all this talk there will be such a false perspective that we shall find the luxury peddler getting through and the merchant of necessities held up by lack of materials.
>
> It is not refrigerators for the few that are wanted but reasonable standards for the many. We do not want gaily-painted hotels but happily painted homes. We may even have to put austerity before comfort, we are certainly going to put comfort before luxury ...
>
> Industrial re-equipment will have to come first, for our industrial machinery is worn out and in danger of large-scale breakdown. When this has been replaced, the next thing will be to equip hospitals and institutions and homes with the minimum of essential requirements. After this, we can begin to think about churches, colleges and schools. And then we may be able to turn our attention to theatres and hotels, refrigerators and air-conditioned rooms.
>
> In post-war days it will be our business to cut down the home market to the minimum, discouraging any form of

luxury and giving children, sick people and the aged first call on available goods. The next priority should be the people of Europe who are in the severest need. We refer not to the Germans, but to our allies. When these needs have been met and sufficient contributed to world requirements to establish our export trade, we can turn to the task of providing more for the home market.

Manchester City News, 9 March 1945

Planning the Post-war World

As early as 1944, construction equipment that had hitherto been used to build airfields was being redeployed to create housing sites, and thoughts turned to large-scale development proposals. A housing exhibition in Manchester carried out a survey of its visitors, apparently designed to establish the blindingly obvious. It found, for example, that people preferred detached or semi-detached houses to terraces, and that most people thought blocks of flats were only suitable for single people. A designer decreed that the fireplace would forever remain the focal point of the living room and that nothing – and certainly not those upstart televisions – was going to replace it.

Women's Institutes were keen that designers should hear the woman's point of view, and they canvassed their members on the most desirable features of a new home:

The requirements seem remarkably modest to modern eyes. The only features virtually everyone insisted on were electric light and an adequate water supply. Coal fires were the preferred form of heating and only a few decadent creatures wanted central heating. Refrigerators were also rarely mentioned but everyone wanted a north-facing larder with a cold slab. Other luxuries they aspired to were fitted cupboards, stainless steel sinks and what were referred to as 'rustless'

> steel windows ... Perhaps as a reaction to wartime conditions, there was not a lot of call for communal facilities like wash houses, though some at least wanted communal children's playgrounds provided and one individual wanted a community pigsty.
>
> Hylton (1996, 2011), p. 96

But others had bigger ambitions, as this editorial suggests:

> If all the things that are being planned for the post-war houses materialise, the average British housewife is in for a good time. Twice this week I have had first-hand information about American homes on which some of ours are likely to be planned. Among the amenities, they list a removable gadget at the bottom of the sink which grinds away refuse and washing machines – which do the family wash as if by magic – the washing-up machines, refrigerators, heating and cooking apparatus.
>
> *Liverpool Echo*, 14 April 1944

Correspondents to the *Newbury Weekly News* also volunteered their ideas, in response to a call for suggestions on how to plan their town of the future. One woman wanted the development of the town to be focused around the provision of a proper maternity hospital, while at least one military man had clearly developed a taste for communal living. His priority was:

> Firstly, the provision of a first-class hot and cold bath and shower house; I suggest fifty baths as a minimum. The provision of clean and up-to-date conveniences has long been wanted.
>
> *Newbury Weekly News*, 25 May 1944

Transport featured high in the list of planning considerations for a post-war world, but the *Maidenhead Advertiser* for one was sceptical of the ability of planners to arrive at a sensible conclusion. It pointed out that several planning acts had already been passed since 1909:

> ... each one more involved than its predecessor and the legal implications have become so complex as almost to baffle the expert. They alleged that not a few cranks had become active participants in the planning process which has not conduced to public confidence in the ability of self-styled planning experts. One urgent need, they decided, was for multi-track highways ... engineered on a modified railway principle – separate tracks for up and down traffic, easy gradients, big radius curves and very few connections with less important roads.
>
> *Maidenhead Advertiser*, 13 October 1943

Or, as we would call them, motorways. Others drew inspiration from the New York World Fair, with its vision of life in the distant future of 1960. This had seven-lane motorways, with traffic travelling at 50, 75 and 100 miles an hour:

> In traffic control towers experts advise drivers by radio control signals when and how they may safely move from one traffic lane to another.
>
> *Liverpool Echo*, 18 October 1940

One of the 'experts', but not one considered a crank, was Frederick Osborne of the Town and Country Planning Association, who also addressed a meeting in Maidenhead. Among his prescriptions for the nation's future transport needs was a Beeching-style review of rail services, leading to widespread track and station closures.

Fears were growing, particularly among the female workforce, about the likely shape of the post-war labour market. Highly paid work in munitions and other war-related industries was likely to come to a halt. Across a whole range of industries, men would return from military service, demanding their jobs back – jobs in which, in many cases, women workers had been employed for the duration of the conflict. In education, the National Association of Schoolmasters was opposed to any suggestion of a perpetuation of the wartime arrangements and, in particular, to the idea of equal pay for women teachers. This would, in their view, depress salaries below a point at which a male teacher could support a wife and family and would hand over the teaching of both boys and girls to women. This would be:

> … disastrous from the national point of view – a result already foreshadowed by the wave of juvenile delinquency, due, it is alleged, to the loosening of that firm and wise control which boys need and only men can provide.
>
> *Liverpool Echo*, 15 May 1944

As at the start of the war, there was no shortage of interest groups with their partial view of the brave new world. One thing not wanted from post-war development, according to Arnold Marsh, the General Secretary of the Smoke Abatement Society, was smoke:

> Unless we plan our fuel policy with wisdom, we shall be unable to bring to full fruition the plans for more pleasant and more noble towns, for better health, for amenities and for the destruction of the giant squalor.
>
> *Swindon Advertiser*, 2 July 1943

Another thing that wasn't wanted, the Building Trades Union told us, was prefabricated housing:

> Thrusting ersatz dwellings on the people is a tragic mistake – nothing short of a betrayal of the people's needs and hopes.

> We can abolish the slums. We can build to the highest standards all the houses required.
>
> *Liverpool Echo*, 18 May 1944

Perhaps understandably, given the welter of wartime regulation that was introduced, debates about post-war planning were not limited to the shape of our towns and countryside, but extended to include the extent to which the economy and people's lives as a whole should be centrally controlled. Ellen Wilkinson, a Labour Member of Parliament, expressed one view:

> It is of supreme importance that we should think about what the world is going to be like when the war is over. Men and women cannot be asked to make the supreme effort of body … and even of life itself without they have some sense of purpose … The main industries and arteries of the nation must no longer be allowed to remain the speculations of private capitalists.
>
> *Berkshire Chronicle*, 22 May 1942

Others viewed the idea of a socialist-style planned society with horror:

> It will be a highly collectivist society, somewhat along the lines of Nazi Germany with some of its more objectionable features eliminated, in which most human activities, including work, recreation, art, music and culture will be guided and directed by the State as an extension of the present social services.
>
> *Berkshire Chronicle*, 29 May 1942

> Many people feel that the blessed word 'planning' is being much over-worked. A writer in the *Economic Review* shrewdly comments 'two-thirds of what passes as planning is a straightforward attempt to establish monopoly and at least half of

> the remainder is downright nonsense. Every business enterprise must plan constantly, but planning has come to be almost synonymous with state direction of industry. The free market, private enterprise and business competition must be restored after the war.'
>
> *Berkshire Chronicle*, 30 January 1942

These fears were reinforced when Home Secretary Herbert Morrison opposed the setting up of a parliamentary scrutiny body:

> Mr Morrison, in earlier public speeches, conveyed the impression that he favoured veiled despotism, and there are other intellectuals on the Left who have made no secret of the line they would adopt if they got the masses in their power. It is obvious that if our lives and affairs are to be governed by orders and regulations framed behind our backs and administered by bureaucrats whose decisions cannot be challenged, and who are the instruments of an ambitious Minister, freedom would soon cease to exist. We have seen what has happened in totalitarian countries, and the New Despotism was rearing its head even before the war.
>
> *Liverpool Echo*, 18 May 1944

Others were worried less about the democratic implications of post-war planning than its cost:

> Are we living in a Fool's Paradise? It might be imagined so, considering the plethora of schemes which are being put forward in connection with post-war reconstruction. Most of them studiously avoid an estimate of what their proposals would entail and, which is more important still, how the taxpayer will be able to foot the bill. Any sense of reasonable finance seems to be fast disappearing.
>
> *Liverpool Echo*, 15 January 1943

Dan Tobey of the Liverpool Chamber of Commerce had a similar message for the planners. In his post-war world, every community would need to be financially self-supporting, but most of the planning blueprints he had seen would require substantial government subsidy:

> In order to have a beautiful city we must have the trade and industry that can afford to pay for it … Planners who put the cart before the horse cannot be accepted as guides to the new world … We cannot get a better world simply by wishing for it or planning it on paper.
>
> *Liverpool Echo*, 31 May 1944

The author of that editorial might have had in mind things like the post-war development wish list published by Chippenham Town Council, which included a new sewage works and water mains, a house-building programme with 100 units in year one, sites for churches, a maternity hospital, a clinic, a market, public conveniences, road widening and improvements, a civic, social and cultural centre, new open spaces, new riverside recreational facilities including new islands, new streets and shopping centres. One correspondent, the irascible Sweep of the *Slough Observer*, had had quite enough of planning:

> There is far too much of it … It is not beyond the bounds of possibility that they and their precious plans may be blasted to pieces before the war is over … No living person can yet foresee what will be the conditions of life when war ends and immediately following. At least that is the opinion of persons far higher up in the councils of state than most of us are ever likely to be, and yet, that does not prevent many of the smaller fry planning – planning – planning. If only they would give their energy at the moment to more vital things the war would be over quicker. I venture to

> suggest that many of the planners would do far more good if they would organise and go round the houses collecting such salvage as bones and rubber ... than what they do by getting huddled round a table talking about their plans for when peace comes.
>
> *Slough Observer*, 11 February 1944

The debate even entered into the consultation on a proposal to introduce family allowances – how far should the state take on the responsibilities of parenthood?

What Shall we do with the Germans?

Attitudes towards the Germans varied widely during the course of the war. Chamberlain's lukewarm prosecution of hostilities in the early days of the war made him hugely unpopular and led to his being forced from office. But even Chamberlain was a relentless warmonger in comparison to this correspondent to the *Portsmouth Evening News*, for whom even name-calling would have breached his own personal Geneva Convention:

> Will you allow me to thank you for the admirable restraint exercised by your paper. To the ordinary man, jokes about Goering's belly or Hitler's lovelock are distasteful. Let us leave ridicule and hate to the enemy ... Temperance, tolerance, good-temper, self-respect, serenity are weapons which common sense uses in overcoming insanity. This is a war of civilisation versus savagery – let us remain civilised.
>
> *Portsmouth Evening News*, 15 September 1939

Once the bombing of civilian targets began in earnest, it became more difficult to rely quite so much on serenity and good nature, but there were still those in the local newspaper correspondence columns who did not share the dictum of Arthur Harris, head of Bomber Command, that he who sows the wind shall reap the whirlwind:

> MORAL DECLINE OF THE MASSES
> One of the greatest condemnations of war is the gradual moral decline of the masses.
>
> This is evident today from the outcry from many quarters for retaliation against Germany. One hears of Civil Defence workers from some areas demanding that this nation should bomb towns in Germany in revenge for their bombing of ours, and this attitude appears to be growing among ordinary folk. Right-minded people know that GOOD can never be established by EVIL.
>
> Let them therefore beware, and use all the influence they have to stem this tide of hatred and bitterness, which, if allowed to develop, will surely lead to the disintegration of society, and so make impossible any hope of a better world.
>
> *Berkshire Chronicle*, 4 April 1941

As victory began to look increasingly certain, so the debate grew as to what should happen to the Germans after the war. As in the First World War, there were by this stage plenty of people in the 'make them pay' camp. Two women in a queue were overheard by a reporter, discussing the German civilians fleeing the Russian advance. 'Poor things,' said one of them, 'I can't help feeling sorry for them. After all, they are only human.' This prompted a fire-and-brimstone editorial in the local paper:

> How comforting for the Germans, who already boast about what they will do 'in the next war'. After ten years of pillaging, murder and destruction on a horrifying scale, these people who acquiesced in the whole beastly orgy are 'poor things' to two pleasant-faced women in an English queue. What promising material for the whines about

> 'sympathy' which will be their first move, as it was in 1918, to make the 'next time' possible ... Let us get it quite clear that misplaced sympathy for these bitter enemies is in the long run dangerous to peace.
>
> THESE PEOPLE MUST SOMEHOW BE TAUGHT HUMANITY. LET US NEVER ASSUME, UNTIL WE HAVE HAD LONG AND CONCRETE PROOF, THAT THEY HAVE LEARNT IT.
>
> *Manchester City News*, 2 February 1945

The *Slough Observer* carried an even more blood-curdling message:

> Wreak sufficient havoc upon them now, and we shan't have to bother our heads about the silly little handful of people in this country who have started talking about not being too hard on the Germans after the war. If the whole of Germany could be laid flat before the war finishes, there would be much less duty and justice for us to do them afterwards ... I would like to see Germany bombed until there aren't two bricks left standing on each other in the whole of Hunland.
>
> *Slough Observer*, 5 June 1942

And Finally ...

In lighter vein, one Manchester paper carried a comic column in which a group of sages, supposedly gathered in a public house, decided it was time to begin planning the fate of the German warmongers. Shooting, hanging and beheading were deemed to be too good for them, and they should instead be made a terrible example of, by suffering the same ghastly fate that was meted out to Napoleon – banishment to St Helens.

Or maybe you could just be like these two, and have no war aims at all?

'What are you going to do for a living, Harry, when the war's over?'

'Nothing, mate. I'm giving up work. Going to live by my wits, I am.'

'Lummy! Ain't you 'ad enough of rationing?'

Liverpool Echo, 16 June 1944

Select Bibliography

Bishop, Patrick, *Bomber Boys* (Harper, 2007)

Booker, Frank, *The Great Western Railway: A New History* (David and Charles, 1977)

British Railways Press Office, *Facts about British Railways in Wartime* (1943)

Brown, Mike, *Christmas on the Home Front* (Sutton, 2004)

Bryan, Tim, *Railways in Wartime* (Shire, 2011)

Charman, Terry, *Outbreak 1939: The World Goes to War* (Virgin Books, 2009)

Cheshire County Council, *Wartime Cheshire 1939–45* (undated)

Dendy Marshall, C.F. and Kidner, R.W., *History of the Southern Railway* (Ian Allan, 1968)

Doyle, Peter, *ARP and Civil Defence in the Second World War* (Shire, 2010)

Falconer, David and Jonathan, *Bath at War: The Home Front* (Sutton, 2001)

Ferneyhough, Frank, *The History of Railways in Britain* (Osprey, 1975)

Gardiner, Juliet, *Wartime: Britain 1939–45* (Headline, 2004)

———, *The 1940s House* (Channel 4 books, 2000)

Gillies, Midge, *Waiting for Hitler* (Hodder and Stoughton, 2006)

Goodall, Felicity, *Voices from the Home Front* (David and Charles, 2004)

Hardy, Clive, *Manchester at War* (First Edition, 2005)

Home Office, *Air Raid Precautions* (HMSO, 1938)

Hylton, Stuart, *Reading at War* (Sutton, 1996, The History Press, 2011)

———, *Kent and Sussex 1940: Britain's Front Line* (Pen and Sword, 2004)

———, *Their Darkest Hour* (Sutton 2001, 2003) reprinted as *Careless Talk* (The History Press, 2010)
———, *A History of Manchester* (Phillimore, 2010)
Inman, Ken and Helm, Michael H., *Bury and the Second World War* (self-published, 1995)
Lane, Andrew, *Austerity Motoring 1939–1950* (Shire, 1987)
Longmate, Norman, *How We Lived Then* (Hutchinson, 1971)
Maclaine, Ian, *Ministry of Morale* (George Allen and Unwin, 1979)
Ministry of Food, *Eating for Victory* (Michael O'Mara, 2007)
Morris, Colin, *History of the Hants and Dorset Motor Services Ltd* (David and Charles, 1973)
Nicholson, Virginia, *Millions Like Us: Women's Lives in War and Peace 1939–1949* (Viking, 2011)
Nock, O.S., *The History of the Great Western Railway* (vol. 3) (Ian Allan, 1967)
Overy, Richard, *The Morbid Age: Britain and the Crisis of Civilisation 1919–1939* (Allen Lane, 2009)
Pugh, Martin, *Hurrah for the Blackshirts!* (Jonathan Cape, 2005)
Robertson, Kevin, *Britain's Railways in Wartime* (Oxford Publishing Company, 2008)
Snape, Keith and Robinson, Helen, *When the Lights Come on Again* (Oldham Arts and Heritage Publications, 2005)
Vaughan, Adrian, *Railway Blunders* (Ian Allan, 2003)
War Department, *Instructions for American Servicemen in Britain* (US Government, 1942)
Wilson, A.E., *The Story of Pantomime* (Roman and Littlefield, republished 1974)
Wilson, A.N., *After the Victorians* (Hutchinson, 2005)

Newspapers

Berkshire Chronicle
Buckinghamshire Advertiser and Gazette
Buckinghamshire Herald
Dover Express
Hampshire Chronicle
Hants and Berks Gazette
Hastings Observer
Henley and South Oxfordshire Standard

Kent Messenger
Kent and Sussex Courier
Liverpool Daily Post
Liverpool Echo
Maidenhead Advertiser
Manchester City News
Manchester Evening News
Manchester Guardian
Newbury Weekly News
Oxford Mail
Oxford Times
Portsmouth Evening News
Slough Observer
Swindon Advertiser

Index